Documents of Medieval History 5

Advisory Editors

G.W.S. Barrow
Professor of Scottish History, University of Edinburgh
Edward Miller
Fellow, Fitzwilliam College, Cambridge

The Norman Conquest

R. Allen Brown

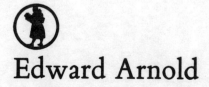

Edward Arnold

© R. Allen Brown 1984

First published in Great Britain 1984 by
Edward Arnold (Publishers) Ltd, 41 Bedford Square, London WC1B 3DQ

Edward Arnold (Australia) Pty Ltd, 80 Waverley Road, Caulfield East, Victoria 3145, Australia

Edward Arnold, 300 North Charles Street, Baltimore, Maryland 21201, U.S.A.

British Library Cataloguing in Publication Data

Brown, R. Allen
   The Norman conquest.——(Documents of medieval history)
   1. Great Britain——History——Norman period, 1066–1154——Sources
   I. Title   II. Series
   942.02'1   DA190

   ISBN 0-7131-6406-9

Text set in 10/12 pt Bembo Compugraphic
by Colset Private Ltd, Singapore
Printed and bound by Richard Clay (The Chaucer Press) Ltd, Bungay, Suffolk

Contents

To the former members of my Special Subject.

Preface

The Norman Conquest of England has been one of my particular interests for close on a quarter of a century. Formally, the relationship began with the invitation to write a book on the subject (subsequently *The Normans and the Norman Conquest*, now about to be republished in a second edition), continued with the teaching of a 'Special Subject' in the History School of the University of London, and is unlikely to end with the present volume. Less formally, an early engagement with castles led to military history which led to the Normans, not least because they dominate that period of compelling attraction and relevance which is the eleventh and twelfth centuries. The present volume of sources relating to the Conquest springs directly from my Special Subject and it is to the former members of that class that it is therefore dedicated.

My specific thanks must go to two ladies: my wife, who more or less cheerfully undertook the more than usually heavy load of typing, and my desk editor at Edward Arnold's who saw the outcome through the press. Those whose translations I have borrowed for certain of the sources are thanked by name with due acknowledgement in the appropriate parts of the text. I am no less grateful to those who have helped more personally with my own translations and other problems, but I do not name them here lest it might seem that I were wrapping myself in a cloak of respectability. The truth is that any and all mistakes are mine.

R. Allen Brown
Thelnetham, Suffolk
11 April 1984.

Acknowledgements

The author and publishers would like to thank the following for permission to include copyright material:

Cambridge University Press for A.J. Robertson, *The Laws of the Kings of England from Edmund to Henry I* and *Anglo-Saxon Charters*; Christopher Erlington for *Berkshire* (1906) and *Suffolk* (1911) from *Victoria County Histories*; Manchester University Press for F.E. Harmer, *Anglo-Saxon Writs*; Methuen & Co. Ltd for D. Whitelock, *The Song of the Battle of Maldon*, *The Laws of Knut*, *Letter of Pope John XV*, *Hemming's Cartulary* from *English Historical Documents*, i, and *The Anglo-Saxon Chronicle*; Oxford University Press for F. Barlow, *Life of King Edward the Confessor*.

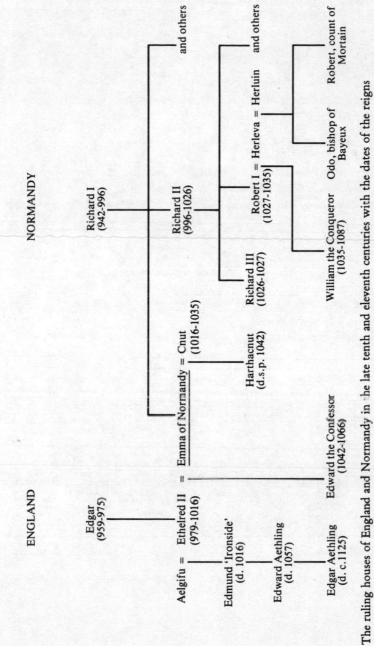

ENGLAND   NORMANDY

The ruling houses of England and Normandy in the late tenth and eleventh centuries with the dates of the reigns

xi

England and Wales in 1066

Areas of Scandinavian Settlement

0   Miles   50

Newcastle upon Tyne
Carlisle
Durham
Richmond
York
Stamford Bridge
Tadcaster
Gate Fulford
Riccall
Pontefract
Blyth
Lincoln
Rhuddlan
Chester
Caernarvon
Derby
Nottingham
Belvoir
Stafford
Tutbury
Shrewsbury
Lichfield
Leicester
Peterborough
Norwich
Montgomery
Tamworth
Ramsey
Dudley
Rockingham
Ely
Richard's Castle
Warwick
Coventry
Huntingdon
Eye
Leominster
Worcester
Northampton
Aldreth
Bury St Edmunds
Hope-under-Dinmore
Bedford
Cambridge
Ipswich
Hereford
Evesham
Chipping
Buckingham
Clavering
Colchester
Ewyas Harold
Winchcombe
Norton
Hertford
Monmouth
Great Berkhamsted
St. Albans
Waltham
Maldon
Gloucester
Oxford
Dorchester
Holy
Cross
Rayleigh
Chepstow
Abingdon
Little Berkhamsted
Barking
Malmesbury
Wallingford
Southwark
Canterbury
Bristol
Bath
Lacock
Windsor
Guildford
Rochester
Sandwich
Wells
Wherwell
Tonbridge
Dover
Glastonbury
Old Sarum
Battle
Romney
Montacute
Clarendon
Winchester
Arundel
Hastings
Crediton
Exeter
Bosham
Chichester
Bramber
Lewes
Pevensey
Selsey
Totnes
Isle of Wight
St-Valery-sur-Somme
Fécamp
Rouen
Bayeux
Dives-sur-Mer
Caen

xii

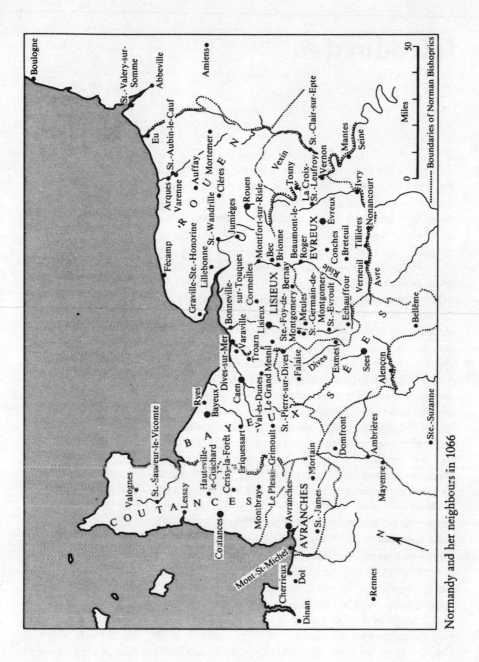

Normandy and her neighbours in 1066

Introduction

This necessarily short Introduction is obviously not the place for a full history of the Norman Conquest of England. That would need another and a different sort of book, while a compressed history would be of little use to anyone. Further, to attempt either would be to go against the purpose of this volume and the series of which it forms a part, which is to present as much as possible of the evidence relating to the subject for the reader to discover the truth for himself, or at least to consult and investigate while studying the Conquest in one or more of the several good books available. Suggestions for such reading are made in the Bibliography.

Nevertheless, certain guidelines to the study of the Norman Conquest are called for. The first is that the subject is controversial, and always has been. It was controversial, obviously, in 1066 (and before). William of Malmesbury, writing in *c.*1125, makes it clear that the rights and wrongs of the case were controversial in his day (**146**). In our own day, however absurd it may seem, the English-speaking world even of professional historians still tends to be divided into English and Normans. To take sides may be fun, but the reader should be warned at once against the instinctive but unhistorical identification of the Anglo-Saxons (or were they Anglo-Scandinavians?) as 'us' and the Normans as 'them'. The question 'Who were the English in 1066?' is no less telling than the more fashionable question 'Who were the Normans?'. But the modern controversy is not merely the age-old hot debate of the justice of the Norman cause, but also very much one about the results of the Conquest, continuity or change. How important was the Norman Conquest in the history of England? Was it or was it not a cataclysmic event? This debate is waged right across the board, from, let us say, the effects of 1066 upon learning and scholarship to those upon the Church itself, from its effects upon art and architecture to those upon society and the State. And since one is dealing in these matters with the fundamental question of inheritance – of who, English or Norman, contributed what to the generally accepted excellence of post-Conquest England – there is unfortunately opportunity here also for the taking of sides on grounds of misplaced national prejudice and insularity. Insularity, it may be suggested, has especially bedevilled the modern study of the Conquest by English historians. It is a fatal flaw because the Norman Conquest of England only comes into focus if set in the context of far-flung and ever widening Norman enterprise in the eleventh century, in France itself, in Italy and Sicily, and in Antioch on the First Crusade. The evidence presented in this volume for eleventh-century Normandy and England is as full and comprehensive as is possible, yet the volume would be even better than it tries to be if it could be doubled in size to include Norman activities in all other places.

Another guideline must be that there is much more to the proper study of the Norman Conquest than the famous date, 1066. On the one hand, though Hastings rightly ranks as one of the decisive battles of the western world, even the military conquest of England was scarcely complete before 1070, to say nothing of the Norman settlement which follows, while the results of it all only begin to be apparent when the dust has settled, and take decades and centuries to be worked out. On the other hand, and less obviously perhaps, there are what it is inadequate to call the antecedents of the conquest. Edward Augustus Freeman[1] many years ago saw the beginning of the Norman Conquest in 1002 with the marriage of king Ethelred II of England (979–1016) to Emma of Normandy, daughter of the Norman duke Richard I (942–96). Very recently John Le Patourel made the most pertinent of remarks touching the history of the Normans: 'Norman expansion began as it went on; its origins were the origins of Normandy itself.'[2] Though Norman expansion was most certainly backed up by an increasingly formidable military expertise which often seems irresistible, its no less characteristic means, whether directed by the ducal court as with England and Maine, or by private enterprise as in southern Italy or Antioch, were those of marriage, aristocratic penetration, piecemeal settlement and the imposition of lordship. The affair of England only seems different from the others, and more an outright military conquest, because the unforeseen drama of Hastings obscures the more long-term reality. In the broad view, it may be suggested, Hastings was not meant to happen. Certainly by 1066 increasingly close bonds between England and Normandy, and the infiltration of Norman lords and Norman influence through the households and connections, first of queen Emma, and then of the Norman-minded Edward the Confessor (who had spent most of his first 40 years as an exile at the Norman court), had brought it about that William the Conqueror could claim to be the legitimate successor to the English throne. The childless Edward the Confessor's nomination of duke William as his heir, upon which the Norman sources unanimously insist, assuredly caused the opposition of the Godwin faction as early as 1051, but in the event it was only the resistance of Harold Godwinson, and his perjury in Norman eyes, which occasioned the Battle of Hastings in 1066. Even so, the Normans were able to see their victory as the Judgement of God.

There is another dimension also to the closening relations between England and Normandy in the eleventh century. This is the Scandinavian element in both, which, though it may not help directly to explain the eventual conquest of the one by the other, is certainly relevant to the understanding of both societies. The origins of historic Normandy are as a Viking settlement in northern France, recognized and legitimized at the so-called Treaty of St Clair-sur-Epte in 911, whereby Charles the Simple, king of the West Franks, granted territories about the lower Seine and Rouen to the Viking leader Rollo. These origins matter, even though by the mid-eleventh century one of the most remarkable features of the Normans is the degree to which they had cast off their Viking ancestry to become more Frankish than the Franks. In England, however, the case is different. Here, to the Danes of Alfred's day, settled in or dominating that half of the land to

---

[1] *The Norman Conquest*, i (1970), pp. 301–2.
[2] *The Norman Empire*, Oxford, 1976, p. 12.

north and east which is the Danelaw, must be added the outright conquest of the whole kingdom by Swein Forkbeard and Cnut the Dane in 1014 and 1016, their succession by the latter's two sons Harold Harefoot and Harthacnut (respectively 1035–40 and 1040–2), and the establishment as the result of these events of an aristocracy and ruling class at least part Anglo-Scandinavian. The Scandinavian element in pre-Conquest England requires, it seems, more emphasis than it receives, and for some quarter of a century this country was an integral part of the late Viking and Scandinavian world. In 1066 invasion came not only from Normandy but also from Norway, and Harold Hardrada, as another claimant to the English throne, marched through the blood of Gate Fulford into York in the evident expectation of that support which he received there. As for the Norman invasion which swiftly followed, in no way can it be seen as yet another Viking incursion upon England, but, rather, the roles are reversed: Anglo-Scandinavian tactics and housecarls and battle-axes put up a very stiff resistance to Norman and Frankish chivalry throughout the day at Hastings, and William of Poitiers, at least, thought that Harold of England fought there with Danish reinforcements (**48**).

Another guideline for the proper study of the Norman Conquest is the necessity to know at least as much about Normandy as England. The vice of insularity has already been mentioned in this Introduction, and one cannot but feel that some of the things said about the Conquest in the past could never have been said if those historians concerned, however eminent, had been as familiar with their Norman history as their English. At the least we are dealing not merely with the negative fact of defeat but with the positive fact of victory, with the remarkable conquest of the far larger, rich and potentially powerful kingdom of England by a single, small, feudal province of emergent France. The positive reasons for that triumph must lie in Normandy, and in the hearts and minds of that ebullient society spurred on by the *élan* of a conscious *élite*. If, as they did, the Normans excelled in contemporary warfare – in France (but not yet in the Old World of Anglo-Scandinavian England) increasingly based upon knights and castles – it is to be realized that military tactics and organization are only the tip of the iceberg, one aspect of the totality which is a society or state. In truth, Norman achievement in this age was comprehensive, almost total, so that the study of Norman religion, Norman monasticism and the Norman Church, is no less relevant to an understanding of the Norman Conquest, and its results, than a study of their chivalry and their cavalry and their castles. Their great churches, imperial in scale and concept, still rising over Normandy and England (where they are larger yet), are no less evidence of their wealth, enterprise, aspirations and self-confidence, than their amazing territorial expansion, which is itself the result amongst other things of economic growth, an expanding population, the export of younger sons and surplus knights. By the end of the eleventh century there was a kind of Norman commonwealth of states and settlements, of which England was one item only, stretching from the marches of Wales to Antioch; and the Normans were coming to regard themselves as a Chosen People holding victory as a fief from God.[3] The sum of all this, and the secret, is 'Normanitas', the spirit and the ethos of the Normans, which is the ultimate explanation

[3] Le Patourel, *Norman Empire*, pp. 353–4.

of their deeds. Against it, Harold's half-reluctant kingdom in 1066 could not prevail, and to understand that negative fact requires, no less, a close study of pre-Conquest England and its history, of the several peoples who formed its society, and of the institutions which bound them together or failed to do so. The difference between England and Normandy will then become apparent. In thus weighing the balance, it will be best to put aside any misplaced and insular national prejudice, and to reflect that an overemphasis upon Old English achievement, however admirable in many fields that may have been, is not likely to explain the Old English ultimate defeat at Hastings and thereafter.

Clearly, then, the following pages must contain more than a piecemeal collection of relatively short extracts from the written sources, more or less directly recording the political and military facts of 1066 and subsequent campaigns. Our purpose is the study in as much depth as possible of two societies, their preceding histories, the causes both long-term and short-term of their confrontation in 1066, and its results. The method adopted is to be as generous as space and cost will allow. The selections and extracts are drawn from as wide a range of written sources as possible, including all those most important and directly relevant as well as many others more peripheral. So far as the literary sources are concerned – contemporary or near-contemporary histories, chronicles and biographies – while there are inevitably some short extracts from minor works recording statements or comments not to be found elsewhere, from the major works numerous and long extracts are given, so that the reader may come closer to that world we have lost on both sides of the Channel, its institutions, leaders and peoples, attitudes and assumptions. In the selection of documents, and extracts therefrom, generosity has also been the principle applied, for the evidence gained from this kind of written source about great events and great matters tends to be cumulative, here a little, there a little, showing through, so to speak, the immediate business of the compiler recording a grant of property, or defining a law or custom, or whatever. Yet documents, too, reflect the society which produced them if read in sufficient quantity and with perception. It is hoped that enough have been selected to show, first, the principal types of document then in use (though wills are absent) – charters, leases, writs and letters, laws and surveys – and thus the degree to which society, both in England and Normandy, was moving in this period from a primitive dependance upon the spoken word and oral testimony towards a sophisticated reliance upon written record and government by writing. By such means also the level of literacy may be estimated, while laws and land tenure, for example, point more directly to the nature of society, as letters may to individuals and their concerns. Nevertheless there are snags, and generosity has to be limited by its cost. There can be very few plates or other illustrations in this volume, and therefore the Bayeux Tapestry, a unique pictorial narrative source, is seriously under-represented by only five scenes (**198–202**), and though we have also the seals of Edward the Confessor and William the Conqueror as kings of England (**197**), that whole category of direct evidence of the past comprised by surviving artefacts, *i.e.* architectural, artistic and archaeological evidence, is otherwise wanting.

Another problem of selection has been chronological, where in time to start and finish. While there could obviously be a case for illustrating the whole history of pre-Conquest

Normandy and (a larger task) pre-Conquest England, in practice, with only a few exceptions, the starting point chosen has been 1002. The end is much more difficult to decide and can only be arbitrary. The more cataclysmic the Norman Conquest is regarded, the more long-term will be its results, some of which in some sense are with us still. The only reasonable yet practical date seemed to be 1087 with the death of William the Conqueror, by which time the new régime is established and the changes which it brought about made manifest.

All the extracts and documents in this volume are, of course, printed in translation. It is no good pretending that this is not a disadvantage, symptomatic of our declining educational standards. In the history of the West an ignorance of Latin especially cuts us off from our medieval past, and if the importance of the past to the present is accepted then it must be accepted also that the so-called medieval periods are at least as important as those more modern – as witness our present subject of the Norman Conquest with all its effects upon the history of England and of Europe. There is no perfect substitute for reading anything in the language in which it was written, and the best use that could be made of the translations here offered would be as an aid to working through the original texts. Failing that, one can only make the best of a bad job. On my side, I have sought to make the translations as harmless a substitute as possible. Where there is any doubt or, as is more often the case, where the translation is crucial because of the implications arising, I have put the original word or words in parenthesis. Many of the translations, *faute de mieux*, are my own, but where a good and established translation already exists in print – as, notably, in the case of Dorothy Whitelock's edition of the Anglo-Saxon Chronicle, or the translations printed opposite the Latin in the series of Oxford (formerly Nelson's) Medieval Texts – this has been gratefully and with acknowledgement used for obvious convenience. In such cases very occasional minor alterations have been made, usually only of a word or the spelling of a proper name, in the light of recent research or in the interest of consistency. The original language of all the sources printed is Latin except where otherwise stated, and in practice the only alternative is the vernacular Anglo-Saxon of most of the Old English texts.

One other problem, or potential problem, remains. In a volume of selected extracts and documents there is, as in any anthology, a residual subjective element. The user, one step away from reality by reading translations, is then another by reading only someone else's selection of what is most important. The remedy here must again be generosity, plus that professional principle of any historian composing any work of history, which is to make a judicious and unslanted selection from all the evidence available. Further, there is by design no interpretation in the pages that follow. The introductory notes to each section or item merely present and explain the sources and the documents, and any other notes are confined to a minimal textual commentary, the identification of persons and the supplying of dates. The object of the exercise is that the reader or student should study the subject through the original sources, and to that end the sources should be left so far as possible to speak for themselves.

Abbreviations

Battle	*Proceedings of the Battle Conference on Anglo-Norman Studies*, now *Anglo-Norman Studies: Proceedings of the Battle Conference*
DB	*Domesday Book*, 2 vols., 1783
EHR	*English Historical Review*
FW	Florence of Worcester: *Florentii Wigornensis Monachi Chronicon ex Chronicis*, ed. B. Thorpe. 2 vols., London, 1848–9
RHS	Royal Historical Society
TRHS	*Transactions of the Royal Historical Society*
VCH	Victoria County History

I Literary and narrative sources

The chronicles, histories and biographies concerning the Norman Conquest of England drawn upon here are arranged in three sections, namely Norman, Old English and Anglo-Norman. These divisions are inevitably a little arbitrary in some cases, but the first two sections may be regarded as roughly contemporary with the events they relate or as written by contemporaries, and the third more obviously as retrospective. Such divisions are also useful in allowing us to make more conveniently the necessary allowances for at least potential bias in the sources thus grouped together, and to compare and assess the relative value and quality of those from the Norman and Old English sides.

Norman

The works extracted in this section are those of William of Jumièges and William of Poitiers, the two principal Norman sources for the history of the Conquest, together with Gilbert Crispin's *Life of Herluin* and the tract on the death of William the Conqueror. The *Carmen de Hastingae Proelio*, or *The Song of the Battle of Hastings*, has been omitted. Though at one time generally regarded as probably written by Guy, bishop of Amiens, before 1068, and thus both very early and of automatic importance, this work has recently and convincingly been dismissed as a mere literary exercise of much later date and no historical value.[1] In such a case its inclusion seemed more likely to confuse than enlighten, and the necessary arguments for and against its authenticity to be inappropriate to the purpose of this present volume. Notes on the date, authorship, provenance and value of the sources used are given at the head of each extract.

William of Jumièges

The *Gesta Normannorum Ducum* (*The Deeds of the Dukes of the Normans*) is almost certainly the earliest of the Norman literary sources relating to the conquest of England, written, it is generally agreed, in *c.*1070–1. Its author, the monk William, referred to by Orderic

---

[1] 'As a source for the history of the Norman Conquest it is simply ridiculous', R.H.C. Davis, 'The *Carmen de Hastingae Proelio*', *EHR*, xciii, 1978 (p. 261). For the contrary view, see the Introduction and notes of the recent critical edition by C. Morton and Hope Munz, *The Carmen de Hastingae Proelio of Guy bishop of Amiens*, Oxford Medieval Texts, 1972. For a discussion of the problem, see, *Battle*, ii, 1979.

Vitalis as William 'Calculus', was a member of the important and well informed abbey of Jumièges, which was a prestigious ducal foundation (or refoundation, by William Longsword, *c.*935–42) in Upper Normandy, in the Seine valley, not far from Rouen. The abbey had also close connections with England through abbot Robert (sometimes surnamed 'Champart'), *i.e.* that Robert of Jumièges who was appointed by Edward the Confessor first bishop of London (1046) and then archbishop of Canterbury (1051). The new church of Edward's own foundation of Westminster Abbey (consecrated at Christmas 1065) was modelled upon the great abbey church of St Mary at Jumièges, begun by abbot Robert *c.*1040 and dedicated in the presence of the king-duke, William the Conqueror, himself on 1 July 1067. (27) In consequence, among the most important features of William of Jumièges' *Gesta Normannorum Ducum* are the notices of English history he inserted into his work and, more especially, the illustrative emphasis he placed upon the pre-Conquest connections between England and Normandy and their respective princely houses.

In his work William of Jumièges was himself the continuator of Dudo of St Quentin; that is to say, for the earlier period he abbreviated Dudo's history,[1] itself written between *c.*996 and *c.*1015, commissioned by dukes Richard I and Richard II, and covering the reigns of Rollo, the first duke (911–31), William Longsword (931–42) and Richard I (942–96). For that period William of Jumièges also used, to a much lesser extent, certain other sources such as the *Miracula Sancti Benedicti*, the *Historia Francorum Senonensis* and the *Vita sancti Aichadri*. Thereafter, however, he based his account upon his own knowledge and observation (1, 9) with the assistance of the *Historia Francorum Senonensis* and probably the charters of his abbey. His Books V–VII, from which all save two of the extracts printed below are taken, cover respectively the reigns of dukes Richard II (996–1026), Richard III and Robert I (1026–1035) and William the Conqueror down to the final pacification of England in 1070. The *Gesta Normannorum Ducum* was undoubtedly popular in its day and thereafter, some 40 copies of various versions being known to have existed in the libraries of England and France in the eleventh and twelfth centuries. In that period it went through many editions; *i.e.* it was widely copied, often with alterations, insertions and continuations. The most important enlarged editions, in each case continuing the history down to the writer's own day, are those of Orderic Vitalis (after 1113) and Robert of Torigny (*c.*1139).

William of Jumièges' *Gesta* begins with a dedicatory letter to William the Conqueror (1) and was written with the particular purpose of legitimizing the duke's succession to the English throne. This, however, is no more than to say that he has a case to argue, and, while the undoubted bias of his narrative may easily be seen and allowed for, it would be an unwise historian (though there are some about) who would reject out of hand on that account any statement of fact he may make. Finally, seldom giving dates, he can be vague or faulty in the sequence of events, and he can occasionally make outright mistakes, as when he says that Harold fell at the beginning, instead of at the end, of the battle of Hastings (25).

---

[1] *De Moribus et Actis primorum Normanniae Ducum* (ed. J. Lair, Caen, 1865). Cf. No. 1 below.

The only acceptable edition at present is that of Marx, cited below. Over and above Marx's own introduction, the best commentary in English upon the work is that of Elizabeth van Houts, 'The *Gesta Normannorum Ducum*: a history without an end', in *Proceedings of the Battle Conference in Anglo-Norman Studies*, iii, 1980, and to which this note is much indebted. Dr van Houts is herself preparing a new and necessary edition of the work. For Dudo of St Quentin see also Gerda C. Huismen in *Battle*, vi, 1984; Eleanor Searle in *Viator*, 15, 1984.

Source: *Guillaume de Jumièges, Gesta Normannorum Ducum*, ed. J. Marx, Société de l'histoire de Normandie, Rouen-Paris, 1914.

1 The dedicatory letter prefacing the volume

Pp. 1–3 Letter of William monk of Jumièges to William king of the English

To William, by the will of the Supreme King pious, victorious and orthodox king of the English, William, the monk of Jumièges though the most unworthy of all monks, sends the strength of Samson to overcome his enemies and the wisdom of Solomon to determine justice.

This presumptuous work concerning the deeds of the dukes of Normandy, O most prudent and serene king, I have put together so far as I was able from divers books and, dedicating it to your Highness, I have determined to add to the number of our histories by relating again the best and most devout deeds of those of our ancestors who have held the highest secular office in former times. I have sought to do this not by embellishing my work with the dignified elegance of the rhetoricians, nor yet with the venal grace and wit of polished language, but in plain and intelligible style to reach the understanding of the average reader. Your Majesty is surrounded by outstanding men of letters steeped equally in practical experience, who with drawn swords patrol the city, confounding the treacheries of malefactors and busily guarding with unceasing vigilance the couch of the Solomon of divine law. Many have shown in many ways how the vigour of that rare genius bestowed upon you as a gift by the Heavenly Steward prevails with wondrous effectiveness, whether by leadership in war or in all those matters which you propose to undertake or accomplish. Graciously receive, therefore, this small gift of my trivial labour, for in these pages you will find the most noble and memorable deeds, both of yours and of times past.

I have drawn the earlier part of my narrative, down to Richard II, from the history of the expert Dudo, who himself diligently obtained the information which he wrote down for posterity from count Ralph,[1] the brother of Richard I. The rest is my own, derived partly from the true relation of many men, given credence equally by their years and their experience of affairs, and partly by the certain witness of my own eyes. The origin of Rollo, born of pagan princes and much of his life passed in paganism until reborn in holy infancy by the life-renewing font, I have cut out from my account, as also the story of his dream and many other matters of that kind, for I consider them pure flattery and neither

[1] Of Ivry.

honest nor edifying in the telling. If anyone wishes to accuse a man vowed to sacred learning of presumption or any other fault in undertaking such a study, let him know that the motive of this little work is in my opinion not unworthy, for the surpassing merits of outstanding men both in secular and divine affairs, of lasting merit in the eyes of God, should be commemorated also amongst the living. Assuredly it is not fitting for one willingly and with devout heart straitly enclosed by claustral walls for the greater glory of the heavenly Jerusalem, and by the honour of the monastic habit and the profession of his life cut off from the world, to take pleasure in the refreshing breeze of popular approval which in fact is pernicious flattery, or to be involved in wordly blandishments. Here you will find, O most wise conqueror of kingdoms, both your peace and your wars, together with those of your most illustrious and devout father duke Robert, and of your eminent ancestors, who, as famous princes of terrestial chivalry, with perfect faith, joyful hope and fervent love striving for heaven, passed their lives as valiant knights of Christ and His devoted followers. May the Emperor who rules over the Eternal Empire, trusting in whom you emerged victoriously from the gravest perils and triumphed miraculously over all opposition, may He the most powerful of all guardians watch over you in all your undertakings, and be ever the fount of that wisdom in ruling which He has given you, so that when at length the fortunate course of your earthly reign is ended, O pious, victorious and orthodox king, adorned with the ring and tunic of eternal glory, you may be received into that royal court which is the place of true and everlasting felicity.

Bk IV (concerning the reign of duke Richard I, 942–96)

2 *c. xviii, pp. 68–9* At that time Emma his [Richard I's] wife, the daughter of Hugh the Great, died without children. He, however, soon afterwards married in the Christian manner a most beautiful maiden called Gunnor born of the most noble Danish stock, and from her begat sons, namely Richard[1] and Robert[2] and Mauger[3] and two others,[4] together with three daughters. One of whom, called Emma, married Ethelred king of the English, which king begat through her king Edward, and also Alfred who was long afterwards slain by the wiles of earl Godwin. . . .

Bk V (concerning the reign of duke Richard II, 996–1026)

3 *c. iv, pp. 76–7* About this time,[1] Ethelred [II], king of the English, although he was married to Emma the sister of duke Richard [II], nevertheless fell out with the duke on a

---

[1] The future Richard II.
[2] Archbishop of Rouen 989–1037.
[3] Later count of Corbeil.
[4] One of whom was Geoffrey, count of Rouen.

---

[1] The following incident, for which William of Jumièges is the sole source, is dated by Marx to *c.*1000. A. Campbell also suggested a date before rather than after Ethelred's marriage to Emma in 1002 (*Encomium Emmae Reginae*, Royal Historical Society, Camden 3rd Series lxxii, London, 1949, p. xliii).

number of matters and was eager to bring harm and shame upon him. He therefore ordered a great fleet to be raised and that a force from the whole kingdom should meet it on a named day, properly furnished with hauberks (*loricas*) and helmets. The English gladly obeyed his commands and with one accord assembled by the ships. The king therefore, having seen that the force was strong and excellently equipped, called the leaders to him and explained his plan, strictly commanding them in royal fashion to put all Normandy to fire and sword, save only Mt St Michel because a place of such sanctity and religion should not be burnt. Duke Richard, his duchy subdued, his hands tied behind him, they were to bring captive but alive before the king himself. With this he ordered them swiftly on their way. The ships were launched upon the high seas and, ploughing the waves with a favourable wind, crossed to make a landing on the banks of the Saire.[2] There, erupting from the ships, the English fired the whole of the neighbouring coastal region. But when this was reported to Nigel[3] he summoned the knights (*milites*) of the Cotentin together with a multitude of lesser folk and attacked them unexpectedly, wreaking such carnage upon them that almost none survived to carry home the news of the disaster. One of their number, however, saw it from afar, having dropped behind through exhaustion from the long march. So terrified as to forget the weariness of his body, he ran as fast as he could back to the ships and related to those who were guarding them the fate of the others. Whereupon they all with one accord took to three of their stoutest vessels and rowed in fear of their lives to a bay of the sea, where they raised their sails aloft and with a following wind set the fastest course to their king. He at once demanded duke Richard from them. To this they replied, 'We, O sublime king, have seen nothing of the duke, but we have fought to our ruin with the ferocious people of a single county, where not only are the men the fiercest fighters but the women also fight, using the yokes used for carrying pitchers to brain the most formidable of their adversaries. In consequence all your warriors (*milites*) are slain.' When he heard this the king, realizing his folly, was full of shame and sorrow.

4   *cc. vi–vii, pp. 78–81* contain an account of Ethelred's St Brice's Day massacre of the Danes in England (13 November 1002), king Swein of Denmark's invasion in revenge, his alliance with duke Richard II of Normandy, and his eventual capture of London in 1013. Whereupon:

c. vii, p. 81 . . . Then king Ethelred, at Winchester, seeing himself completely abandoned by the English, carried off his treasure and went with his wife and his sons, Edward and Alfred, to duke Richard in Normandy. He was honourably received by the duke, given magnificent hospitality, and spent all his time with him at Rouen.

5   *c. viii* On the death of king Swein in England (3 February 1014) his son Cnut prepared a great expedition against that country:

p. 82 . . . While these things were happening, king Ethelred, hearing of the death of

[2] Near Val-de-Saire according to Marx, *i.e.* on the north-east corner of the Cherbourg peninsula, south of Barfleur.
[3] *Vicomte* of the Cotentin.

Swein, prepared a fleet and returned joyfully to his kingdom with his wife, leaving, however, his sons Edward and Alfred with their uncle [duke Richard II]. . . .

6 Ethelred died in London (23 April 1016) beseiged by Cnut.

c. ix, pp. 82–3 . . . King Cnut thus, when he heard of the death of the king, with the counsel of his retainers (*fideles*) and looking to the future, had queen Emma brought from the city, and after a few days married her according to the Christian rite, giving for her, before the whole army, her weight in gold and silver. In the fulness of time he had by her a son, called Harthacnut, afterwards king of the Danes, and a daughter, called Gunnhild, who married Henry[III] emperor of the Germans. The Londoners, despairing of relief and long suffering from famine, opened the gates of the city and submitted themselves with all they had to the king. After which all the strength of the English kingdom fell under the power of king Cnut. We have inserted these matters into the narrative of our work so that the origins of king Edward may be shown to those who do not know them. Now, however, our pen must be directed back to our proper subject from which we have somewhat digressed.

7 *cc. x–xi, pp. 83–6* relate the wars between duke Richard II and count Odo of Chartres over the castle of Dreux (1013 or 1014), during which duke Richard built the castle of Tillières-sur-Avres against count Odo and obtained military aid from the kings of Norway and Sweden, whose forces invaded Brittany.

c. xii, pp. 86–7 Then Robert king of the French, hearing of the atrocities which the pagans[4] had perpetrated in Brittany, and that duke Richard had invited them to repress the contumacy of count Odo, and fearing that they would destroy Frankia, summoned the magnates of his kingdom and commanded both the disputants to come before him at Coudres.[5] There, when he had heard from each of them the cause of their dispute, he assuaged their anger and made peace between them on the following terms, namely that Odo should keep the castle of Dreux and the duke reciprocally recover the land which had been taken from him, while the castle of Tillières should remain forever as it then was, *i.e.* in the power of the duke and his heirs. . .

8 *c. xvii, pp. 96–7* The same duke [Richard II], though renowned far and wide for the manifest excellence of his achievements, was yet pre-eminent as the untiring champion of Christ, so that he was rightly known as the pious father of monks and clerks and the guardian of the poor. While esteemed for these and other comparable virtues, he was stricken by a serious illness. Having summoned archbishop Robert with all the magnates of Normandy at Fécamp, he told them that his life was now ending. At once a great sorrow fell upon everyone in all the apartments of the palace. Monks and clerks bitterly lamented such a bereavement of a beloved father; the faces of the warrior heroes were suffused with tears for the loss of an invincible leader; the crowds of poor and needy at the

---

[4] Vikings.
[5] Marx put this assembly not later than 1014 (p. 87, n. 1).

crossroads of the town bewailed the deprivation of their comforter and protector. Finally, with the recognition and approval of the magnates, the duke set his son Richard to rule over his duchy, and his brother Robert in authority over the county of the Hiémois in such a way that he would render the service due from it to Richard. Then, having readily disposed of all those things which pertain to the honour of God, in the year 1026 of the Incarnation of Our Lord he died [23 August], going the way of all flesh, Our Lord Jesus Christ reigning in the deity of the Father and of the Holy Spirit for ever and ever. Amen.

Bk VI (concerning the reigns of dukes Richard III, 1026–7, and Robert I the Magnificent, 1027–35)

9 *c. i, pp. 97–8* The author, having reached the period of the dukes of his own time, shows himself to be an independent source:

. . . Their deeds we know partly from our own observation and partly from the relation of truthful informants, and have resolved to make known to a wider public so far as our meagre talent has allowed. . .

10 *c. ii* In this single chapter devoted to the brief reign of Richard III (which includes an account of his quarrel with his brother Robert, and the siege of the latter's castle of Falaise before their reconciliation and the duke's subsequent death, by poison 'as many say'), some later redactions have the following notice concerning Nicholas, the duke's son (d. 1092)[1]:

p. 99 This duke Richard had a son called Nicholas who, having professed as a monk at Fécamp, subsequently became abbot of the monastery of St Peter and St Ouen at Rouen and enriched that place with many honours and gifts at his own expense. Furthermore, having demolished the old monastery, he undertook the building on a grand and wondrous scale of a new one, which was in large part finished when he died in Christ at a great age. He lies buried, as is fitting, before the high altar of his new church. . .

11 *c. viii, pp. 105–6* This chapter contains the following notice concerning duke Robert the Magnificent's relations with Brittany:

Alan count of the Bretons, carried away by reckless effrontery, stubbornly sought to withdraw himself from the service of duke Robert. The duke led a great army against him, and not far from the river Couesnon planted a castle called Chérrueix to fortify the frontier of Normandy and to humble the arrogance of his puffed-up adversary. Thence he invaded Brittany and fired the whole county of Dol. That having been gloriously accomplished, he returned to Normandy with a huge booty. Whereupon Alan, burning to avenge the insult inflicted upon him, immediately followed him with a large force with the intention of destroying the county of Avranches. Then Nigel [II, lord of St-Sauveur-le-Vicomte] and Alfred the Giant, custodians of the aforesaid castle, came upon them and, engaging them in battle, wrecked such havoc amongst the Bretons that they could be seen

---

[1] See Elizabeth van Houts, *Battle*, iii, 1980, pp. 108–9.

strewn all over the flat fields and river banks like sheep. Count Alan, thus, withdrawing into his own country, came in sorrow and dishonour to Rennes.

12 *c. ix, pp. 109–10* Not long after Ethelred king of the English was driven from his kingdom by Swein king of Denmark and sought refuge in Normandy, as related above, he himself returned to England, leaving his two sons, Edward and Alfred, to be cared for by Richard [II] their uncle. Brought up in the hall of the Norman dukes, they were treated with such honour by duke Robert, after the death of his father *i.e.* duke Richard, that bound to them by the closest ties of affection he adopted them as brothers. Moved by their long exile,[2] he sent envoys to king Cnut demanding that, their banishment now being surely more than sufficient, he should be merciful to them and for love of him, albeit too late, restore to them their own. Cnut, however, rejected these salutary admonitions and sent the envoys back empty-handed. Whereupon the duke, enraged, took counsel with the magnates of his duchy and commanded a great fleet at once to be constructed. This fleet, brought together from all the maritime regions of Normandy, and rapidly but carefully supplied with anchors, arms and hand-picked men, he caused to be stationed on the shore at Fécamp. Thence having got under way at a given signal, they were driven by a gale until after great peril they were at length brought to the island which is called Jersey. This happened, I believe, by the will of God for the sake of king Edward, whose reign He wished to bring about without bloodshed. At Jersey the fleet was long held up as the contrary winds continued to blow, so that the duke was in despair and overwhelmed by bitter frustration. At length, seeing that he could in no way cross [to England], he sailed his ships in another direction and landed as soon as possible at Mont St Michel.

13 *c. xi, pp. 111–12* These things having been firmly settled [*c. x, p. 110*, count Alan of Brittany, under threat of further attack by land and sea, and through the mediation of Robert archbishop of Rouen, made peace with duke Robert and returned to his service with an oath of fealty], behold! envoys arrive sent by king Cnut to the duke, announcing that the king was ready to restore half the English kingdom to the sons of Ethelred, and establish peace for his lifetime, because he was gravely ill.[3] Therefore the duke, having already postponed his naval expedition, broke off that enterprise until he should have first returned from Jerusalem which he had long had a burning desire to visit. . . . He summoned Robert archbishop of Rouen, his uncle, and the magnates of his duchy, and made known to them his intention of undertaking the Jerusalem pilgrimage. All were astounded at his words, fearing every kind of disorder into which the country would be thrown as the result of his absence. He, however, presented to them William his only son, then just seven years old and whom he sought to make his heir, earnestly requiring them to accept him as their lord in his place and render their military service to him. In spite of the tender years of the boy all in the city rejoiced at this proposal, and according to the duke's decree forthwith acclaimed him their prince and lord with ready unanimity,

---

[2] What follows in this chapter is unique to William of Jumièges among contemporary sources, though William of Malmesbury was later to refer to it (*Gesta Regum*, ii, 300).

[3] For this William of Jumièges is again the sole authority.

pledging their fealty to him with inviolable oaths. These matters thus settled according to the duke's desires, he put his young son in the care of tutors and guardians who would wisely look after him until he reached his majority, and, having made all dispositions necessary for the good government of the country, and having taken a devout farewell of all, he set off with the noblest retinue on that most holy journey[4]. . . .

Bk VII (concerning the reign of duke William the Conqueror, 1035–87)

14 *c. i, pp. 115–16* . . . He [William] thus deprived of a father in the years of his youth, was brought up by the shrewd foresight of his guardians in such a way as to develop his naturally noble attributes. During his minority many of the Normans, renouncing their fealty to him, raised earthworks (*aggeres*[1]) in many places and constructed for themselves the strongest castles (*munitiones*). When they felt themselves thus sufficiently secure, a number of them immediately rebelled, stirred up sedition, and inflicted cruel destruction upon the country. In such a fury of civil discord, indeed, while Mars the god of war rampaged, whole troops of warriors lost their lives in vain, as when Hugh de Montfort and Walkelin [de Ferrières] met in battle and both were killed. Soon after that, as the madness waxed, the very guardian of the boy-duke, Gilbert count of Eu, was slain.[2] So, at various times, were Turold the young prince's tutor[3] (*pedagogus*) and Osbern his steward[4]. . . .

15 *c. iv, pp. 119–20* At this time Robert archbishop of Rouen died and was succeeded by Mauger, the brother of duke Robert [the Magnificent] and thus the uncle of duke William. For duke Richard II, after the death of [the countess] Judith, took another wife called Papia by whom he had two sons, *viz* Mauger the archbishop and William of Arques. This William obtained from the young duke [William], then flourishing in his adolescence, the county of Talou, supposedly as a fief (*beneficium*) in return for which he would serve him as a vassal (*fidelis*). However, puffed up by pride of noble birth, he raised the castle (*castrum*) of Arques upon the summit of its hill and, assuming arbitrary power and secure in royal support,[5] he dared to revolt against the duke. The duke, seeking to turn him from this madness, summoned him by envoys to come and submit. But he, treating such an embassy with contempt, armed and fortified himself to rebel with overweening confidence. The duke therefore gathered the Norman forces and at once went against him to break his arrogance and dug earthworks (*aggeres*) to establish a siege-castle

---

[4] Duke Robert died at Nicea in 1035 on his way back from Jerusalem.

[1] The word *agger* could legitimately be translated 'mound' *i.e.* 'motte'.
[2] Count Gilbert of Brionne, d. *c.* 1136. See Marx, n. 2, to p. 116.
[3] Presumably Thurkill of Neufmarché. See Marx n. 3 to p. 116 and Orderic Vitalis, *Ecclesiastical History*, ed. Chibnall, iv, 82.
[4] Osbern, son of Herfast, father of William fitz Osbern.
[5] *I.e.* that of Henry I, king of the French.

(*castrum*) at the foot of the hill. He himself then withdrew, having placed within it ample provisions and handpicked warriors to render it impregnable. [The French king Henry then advanced with a strong force to relieve the castle and encamped at St Aubin.] When the duke's knights (*milites*) learnt of this they sent some of their number to attempt to draw off from the royal army some of the enemy who could then be ambushed and taken by surprise. This they succeeded in doing, drawing off a considerable number and by [feigned] flight leading them into the trap. For suddenly those who seemed to be fleeing wheeled round and set about their pursuers, with the result that Enguerran count of Abbeville[6] was run through and slain with many others and Hugh Bardulf with many more was captured. [King Henry provisioned Arques but then withdrew, and soon afterwards William of Arques yielded up the castle and went into exile[7]]

16   *c. v, pp. 120–1*   At this time Cnut king of the English died, to be succeeded by Harold [Harefoot] his son by his concubine Aelgifu. When he heard of this long-awaited death, king Edward, who was still at the court of the duke, set sail as soon as possible with 40 ships filled with armed men and crossed the sea to land at Southampton where he met a great host of English gathered against him. He at once engaged them and slew a large number. Although the victor, he withdrew to the ships with his men, for he saw that he could not obtain the English kingdom without a larger force, and putting the fleet about he returned to Normandy with rich booty.

17   *c. vi, pp. 121–2*   Meanwhile his brother Alfred with a considerable force went to the port of Wissant and thence crossed the sea to Dover. From there advancing into the interior of the kingdom he came up against earl Godwin. The earl took him into his protection, but that same night played the role of Judas by betraying his trust. For although he had given him the kiss of peace and eaten with him, in the dead of night he had him bound and sent with many of his followers to king Harold in London. The rest of Alfred's knights (*milites*) he either dispersed about the kingdom or shamefully slew. When Harold saw the aethling he at once ordered his companions to be beheaded and the prince to be taken to Ely and there have his eyes put out. And thus the most noble prince Alfred was done to death without justice. Not long afterwards Harold died and was succeeded by his [half-] brother Harthacnut, returned from Denmark and the son of Emma, the mother of Edward. Harthacnut soon established himself as king and summoned Edward, his brother, from Normandy to be with him at his court. He himself, however, died less than two years later, leaving Edward as heir of the whole kingdom . . .

18   *c. vii, pp. 122–4*   . . . While the duke [William] thus daily grew in stature, it came about that he had to contend with a certain hard-hearted former companion of their boyhood together, Guy, son of Reginald count of the Burgundians, to whom he had formerly given the castle (*castrum*) of Brionne more firmly to bind his fealty. But he,

---

[6] *I.e.* Enguerran II, count of Ponthieu.
[7] The date of the siege of Arques is probably 1052–3.

carried away by the arrogance of pride, like Absalom, began to draw many magnates from their allegiance to the duke and into the abyss of his perfidy, to the extent that he engaged Nigel *vicomte* (*presidem*) of the Cotentin in this conspiracy and completely detached him and many others from their sworn service to the choicest of princes. That most prudent duke, seeing how utterly deserted he was by his own men, and how determinedly and continuously they fortified themselves with the defences of their castles (*municipiorum*), fearing that he might be cast down from the throne of his duchy and some rival claimant raised up in his place, out of necessity sought the aid of Henry king of the French. Whereupon the king, mindful of the help he had himself formerly received from the duke's father, at once assembled a French force, entered the county of the Hiémois, and came to Val-eÌ-Dunes, where he met an army of picked and bellicose warriors with drawn swords eager to give him battle.[8] The king and the duke, undaunted by their violent attacks, went into action with a counter-charge of knights (*militum*) and inflicted such slaughter upon them that those not cut down by the sword were drowned as panic-stricken fugitives in the river Orne. A happy victory indeed, which in a single day brought about the fall of so many castles (*castella*) and dens (*domicilia*) of evil deeds. Guy, however, escaped from the battle, shut himself up behind the barred gates of Brionne [castle], and held out for some time, hoping to be relieved. While the king returned to France, the duke straightway followed the rebel and completely invested the castle (*castellum*), raising siege-castles (*munitiones*) on either side of the river Risle.[9] Seeing that in no way could he escape and threatened by starvation, Guy was compelled by his friends to seek the duke's mercy as supplicant and penitent. The duke, having consulted with his advisers, took pity on his wretchedness and treated him generously, ordering him to be confined to the ducal household. Then all those magnates who had renounced their fealty to the duke saw that he had either blocked or destroyed every way of escape, and so gave hostages and bent their stiff necks to him as their lord. Thus, with castles (*castella*) everywhere destroyed, none dared henceforward show a rebellious heart against him.

19 *c. viii, pp. 124–7* Geoffrey surnamed Martel, count of the Angevins, a man of great cunning, frequently harassed his neighbours with injuries and intolerable afflictions. One of whom, count Theobald [III, of Blois], he captured by trickery and long held imprisoned until he extorted from him by violence the town of Tours with many castles (*castellis*). Next, on the pretext of various disputes, he began to attack the duke, destroying Normandy by violent pillage and gaining control of the castle (*castrum*) of Domfront.[10] The duke came up, ready for war, to reconnoitre Domfront, and saw it encircled with steep and lofty crags and inaccessible to assault. Without delay he summoned his Norman forces and constructed strong siege-castles (*castella*) about it to block all access and egress. While he was for some time delayed in these preparations, lo! scouts arrive and report that the castle (*castrum*) of Alençon can be taken without loss. At once the duke set off, leaving

---

[8] The date is 1047.

[9] The castle at this date was on an island in the river.

[10] Evidently by winning over the garrison? – *intra Danfrontis castrum seditiosis custodibus immissis.* The date is either *c.*1048 or, more probably, 1051.

a force to man the (siege-)castles (*castrum*), and rode through the night with his army to reach Alençon at dawn. There he found, in a certain castle (*municipium*) on the other side of the river, those who mocked him with insults.[11] Whereupon, having roused the ardour of his troops, he took the castle, put it to the flames and burnt it. At his command the mockers had their hands and feet cut off under the eyes of the populace of Alençon.

They, dismayed at such severity, fearful lest similar penalties should be inflicted upon them, threw open their gates and surrendered the town (*castellum*) to him, preferring to yield it than endure the danger of such mutilation to themselves. These things achieved, and a garrison left behind, the duke quickly returned to Domfront. But the men of Domfront, when they heard how the duke and his warriors waged war, and despairing of any help or relief, gave hostages and submitted themselves and their fortress[12] (*castellum*) to his lordship. Then the duke, leaving a garrison behind, rode out and, anxious to check count Geoffrey, came to Ambrières,[13] where at the mouth of the river he raised a castle and put knights (*milites*) and provisions in it. Matters thus advantageously settled, he re-entered Normandy and returned to Rouen.

20   *c. ix, pp. 127–8*   Now that the duke had emerged from adolescence and was flourishing in the vigour of his youth, his magnates began to discuss seriously with him the question of marriage and succession. Hearing that Baldwin of Flanders had a certain daughter descended from royal stock called Mathilda, fair in person and noble in disposition, he, having first taken counsel, sent envoys to ask her father for her hand. Count Baldwin rejoiced at the proposal, and not only decided to grant the request but also brought the princess, together with immense gifts, as far as the castle (*castrum*) of Eu.[14] Thither the duke came, accompanied by a retinue of knights (*milites*), and betrothed himself to her in lawful marriage, and led her with great celebration and honour into the walled city of Rouen . . .

21   *c. x, pp. 129–30*   At this time Mauger archbishop of Rouen began to indulge in folly, and drawn by folly resigned his archbishopric to the duke.[15] The duke afterwards bestowed it with the authority of an ecclesiastical synod upon Maurilius, a distinguished monk of Fécamp and a man of many virtues.

Ever since the Normans had first occupied the lands of Neustria the French had been envious of them, urging their kings to go against them, and declaring that the lands they occupied they had taken by violence from the royal forbears. King Henry, roused by these calumnies, by the evil promptings of the envious, and provoked by the duke's activities, entered Normandy with two armies: one, made up of chosen nobles and proven warriors,

[11] The nature of the insult is said by Orderic Vitalis to have been (in his interpolations to William of Jumièges, ed. Marx, p. 171) that the defenders of the castle on the left bank of the Sarthe beat hides before him and shouted 'Tanner' in allusion to the lowly occupation of his mother's parents.
[12] Presumably both castle and fortified town.
[13] On the borders of Normandy and Maine.
[14] Near the northern border of Normandy.
[15] He was deposed at the council of Lisieux in June 1055.

he placed under the command of his brother Odo and directed to subdue the Pays de Caux, while the other he himself commanded, with Geoffrey count of the Angevins, and with the objective of devastating the county of Evreux. When therefore the duke saw himself and his people thus oppressed he was moved by a deep and noble sorrow, but forthwith picked a force of knights (*milites*) and sent them with all speed to check the pillagers of the Pays de Caux. He himself, with a large force, shadowed the king and inflicted punishment on anyone he was able to capture from the royal army. Meanwhile the other Norman force came up with the French at Mortemer,[16] engaged in arson and immorality with women. Battle was joined immediately at daybreak and was maintained by both sides with continuous slaughter until noon. At length, however, the French were overcome and fled, including their leader, Odo the king's brother. Without doubt in that battle the greater part of the most eminent French nobility was cut down; the remainder were held in captivity throughout Normandy. When the king learnt of their misfortune, saddened by his losses, he withdrew as soon as possible and rapidly from the Norman attrition.

22 *c. xi, pp. 130–1* gives a compressed and chronologically inaccurate account of the Norman conquest of the neighbouring county of Maine which in reality resulted from two campaigns respectively in *c*.1054 and *c*.1063.

c. xii, pp. 131–2 King Henry, therefore, burning to avenge the injury which the duke had done him, summoned Geoffrey count of the Angevins and with a large army led a second expedition into Normandy. Crossing the county of Exmes, he penetrated the Bessin until at length, on his way back, he came to the ford of the Dives.[17] When the king had reached the other side, the centre of his army halted because the tide had come in and they could not cross the flooded river. The duke came up swiftly and at once attacked them under the very eyes of the king, and so cut them up that those who were not slain by the sword were thrown into captivity throughout the length and breadth of Normandy. The king therefore, seeing the destruction of his army, withdrew from the Normans as fast as he could and vowed never to attack them again. Soon after, he died,[18] leaving his son Philip as the heir to his kingdom of the French.

23*c. xiii, pp. 132–3* Edward, too, king of the English, by Divine disposition lacking an heir, had formerly sent Robert [of Jumièges] archbishop of Canterbury to the duke to nominate him as the heir to the kingdom which God had given him. Furthermore he afterward sent to the duke Harold, the greatest of all the earls of his dominions in riches, honour and power, that he should swear fealty (*fidelitatem faceret*) to him concerning Edward's crown and confirm it with Christian oaths. Harold, hastening to fulfil this mission, crossed the narrow seas and landed in Ponthieu, where he fell into the hands of Guy, count of Abbeville,[19] who at once took him and his companions prisoner. When the duke heard of this he sent envoys and angrily caused them to be released. Harold remained

---

[16] The battle of Mortemer was fought in February 1054.
[17] Near Varaville. The action was fought in 1057.
[18] Henry I died on 4 August 1060.
[19] Or of Ponthieu, of which Abbeville was the chief town.

with the duke for some time, and swore fealty concerning the kingdom with many oaths, before being sent back to the king laden with gifts.

At length king Edward, having completed the term of his fortunate life, departed this world in the year of Our Lord 1065. Whereupon Harold immediately usurped his kingdom, perjured in the fealty which he had sworn to the duke. The duke at once sent envoys to him, exhorting him to withdraw from this madness and keep the faith which he had sworn. But he not only would not listen but caused the whole English people also to be faithless to the duke. Then there appeared in the heavens a comet which, with three long rays, lit up a great part of the southern hemisphere for 15 nights together, foretelling, as many said, a change in a kingdom.

24 *c. xiv, p. 134* Duke William therefore, who himself by right should have been crowned with the royal diadem, seeing Harold daily grow in strength, quickly caused a fleet of 3,000 vessels to be built and anchored at St Valery (sur-Somme) in Ponthieu, loaded both with splendid horses and the finest warriors, with hauberks and with helmets. Thence with a following wind, sails spread aloft, he crossed the sea and landed at Pevensey, where he at once raised a strongly entrenched castle (*firmissimo vallo castrum condidit*). Leaving a force of knights (*milites*) in that, he hastened on to Hastings where he quickly raised another. Harold, hastening to take him by surprise, raised an immense army of English and, riding through the night, appeared at the place of battle in the morning.

25 *c. xv, pp. 135* The duke however, in case of night attack, ordered his army to stand to arms from dusk to dawn. At daybreak he marshalled the squadrons of his knights (*legiones militum*) in three divisions and fearlessly advanced against the dread foe. He engaged the enemy at the third hour (9 a.m.) and the carnage continued until nightfall. Harold himself fell in the first shock of battle,[20] pierced with lethal wounds. The English, learning that their king had met his death, despairing of their lives, with night approaching, turned about and sought safety in flight.

26 *c. xvi, pp. 135–6* The victorious duke returned to the battlefield from the pursuit and slaughter of his enemies in the middle of the night. Early next morning, the loot having been collected up from the fallen foe and the corpses of his own cherished men buried, he began his march towards London. It is said that in this battle many thousands of English lost their lives, Christ in them exacting retribution for the violent and unlawful death meted out to Alfred, brother of king Edward. At length the fortunate war-leader who was no less protected by good counsel, leaving the high-road, turned away from the city at Wallingford, where he crossed the river and ordered camp to be pitched. Moving on from there he came to London, where an advance-party of knights (*milites*) on entering the city found a large force of rebels determined to make a vigorous resistance. At once engaging them, the knights inflicted much sorrow upon London by the death of many of

---

[20] William of Jumièges here disagrees with the other contemporary sources which state that Harold fell at the end of the battle – as, indeed, its pattern confirms.

her sons and citizens. At length the Londoners, seeing that they could resist no longer, gave hostages and submitted themselves and all they had to their noble conqueror and hereditary lord. And thus his triumph duly completed in spite of so many perils, our illustrious duke, to whom our inadequate words do not begin to do justice, on Christmas Day, was chosen king by all the magnates both Norman and English, anointed with holy oil by the bishops of the kingdom and crowned with the royal diadem, in the year of Our Lord 1066.

27 *c. xvii, p. 137* Soon afterwards he returned to Normandy,[21] and there he ordered the dedication of the abbey church of St Mary at Jumièges. Throughout the holy mystery, reverently celebrated with the utmost religious rejoicing, the duke was present, an eager worshipper with devout heart at these nuptials of the bride of Christ. The dedication was celebrated with spiritual joy on 1 July 1067 by the following bishops: Maurilius, *i.e.* the archbishop of Rouen, John of Avranches, Geoffrey of Coutances, Hugh of Lisieux and Baldwin of Evreux . . .

28 William of Jumièges ends his narrative of events with the following sentences, evidently relating to 1070 and the end of the Conqueror's devastating campaign in the north of England during the preceding winter. From it is evidently derived Orderic Vitalis' better known passage on castles in England, there attached to the northern campaign of 1068.[22]

c. xxi, p. 142 . . . The king, however, governed by that prudence which he always followed in all things, carefully surveyed the lack of fortification of his kingdom and caused strong castles to be raised in suitable places, manned by a picked force of knights (*militum*) and large numbers of stipendiaries (*stipendiorum*). At length the storm of wars and rebellions dying out, he now both clemently rules and even more prosperously and powerfully reigns in glory over the whole English kingdom.

Epilogue, pp. 142–4. The *Gesta Normannorum Ducum* ends with the longer of the two 'Epilogues' printed by Marx, eulogizing King William and his eldest son and heir, duke Robert.

William of Poitiers

The *History of William the Conqueror (Gesta Guillelmi ducis Normannorum et regis Anglorum)* is arguably the most important of our sources relating to the Norman Conquest, and certainly the most important for the invasion and campaign of 1066. It was written by a well informed, well connected and very well educated contemporary in the 1070s, certainly not before 1071,[1] a little later than the *Gesta Normannorum Ducum* of William of Jumièges

---

[21] In the spring of 1067.
[22] *Ecclesiastical History*, ii, 218. No. **127** below.

[1] The date of the latest event known to have been recorded in the work.

(*c*.1070–1) which it uses, probably in *c*.1073–4,[2] and before the death in July 1077 of the author's bishop, Hugh of Lisieux, to whom he refers as living. Almost all we knew about William of Poitiers is derived from Orderic Vitalis who is conscientiously, and conveniently, informative about the sources he himself used. Orderic (137) says that William was born at Préaux in Normandy, where his sister became the superior of the nunnery of St Léger; that in his youth he had served the duke (William) as a knight; that he then gave up the career of arms and went to the schools at Poitiers (hence his name), returning to Normandy as a clerk to become, first, the duke's chaplain, and subsequently archdeacon of Lisieux under bishops Hugh and Gilbert. In this outline of a career there are only two datable points: on his own testimony William was at Poitiers at the time of the siege of Mouliherne (32), *c*.1048 or 51, and he must have been archdeacon of Lisieux on either side of 1077, *i.e.* the date of the death of bishop Hugh.

No original manuscripts of the work are known to survive, modern editions being based upon André Duchesne's edition of 1619. Further, the now lost manuscript which Duchesne himself used lacked both the beginning and the end, and thus we have William of Poitier's text only in that truncated state. It begins in mid-sentence with an account of English affairs on the death of Cnut (1035), and has nothing, for example, on William's parentage, birth or accession: it ends, also in mid-sentence, in the course of 1067–8, though we know on the authority of Orderic Vitalis that it originally continued to *c*.1071.[3] To a certain degree what is missing from the beginning may be estimated from the use made of it by William of Malmesbury in his *Deeds of the kings of the English* (*Gesta Regum*), and from the end from Orderic's *Ecclesiastical History*.[4] Orderic also states that it had been the author's intention to continue his work down to the death of William the Conqueror but that he was 'prevented by unfavourable circumstances.'[5] If those unfavourable circumstances were a loss of favour at court (caused perhaps by a too close association with Odo bishop of Bayeux) they might also explain what seems to have been the comparative lack of success of the book in its day, implied by the absence of known surviving manuscripts[6] (cf. the 40 or more of William of Jumièges, which are certainly a measure of his success). That evident failure to be widely circulated, however, should not be overstressed. William of Poitiers' work was certainly used, and with approval, by Orderic Vitalis and by William of Malmesbury, as it was also by the compiler of the *Liber Eliensis* and, later in the twelfth century, by Ralph of Diceto.

[2] I cannot see that the reference to the dedication of the Abbaye aux Hommes at Caen to St Stephen (No. 39 below) means that the actual ceremony of dedication or consecration (13 September 1077) had already taken place when William of Poitiers wrote. For the date of that consecration ceremony, see L. Musset, *Actes de Guillaume le Conquérant et de la reine Mathilde pour les abbayes Caennaises* (Mém. Soc. Ant. Norm. xxxvii), 1967, pp. 14–15.

[3] Ed. Chibnall, ii, 258. No. 137 below.

[4] See R.H.C. Davis, 'William of Poitiers and his History of William the Conqueror' (cited at the end of this introduction) pp. 99–100. For both William of Malmesbury and Orderic Vitalis, see pp. 98, 114 below.

[5] Ed. Chibnall, ii, 184. No. 137 below.

[6] Cf. R.H.C. Davis, *op. cit.*, pp. 91–3.

The *History of William the Conqueror* is very much a planned literary work, a biography no less, steeped in the classics which the author had studied at Poitiers (Caesar, Cicero, Sallust, Lucan, Statius, Virgil . . .), with a marked interest also in jurisprudence, written in a polished and self-conscious Latin, and with a theme. That theme, even more than in the work of William of Jumièges, is the deliberate justification of William the Conqueror, in all his acts and policies, especially the conquest of England. But as with the *Gesta Normannorum Ducum* (and the Bayeux Tapestry), so here: the bias must not be allowed to detract overmuch from the historical value of the work. The Norman Conquest of England was a remarkable achievement by any standards, and came at a time when Norman arms were carrying all before them in far-off Italy and Sicily: 'it merited not just a history but a panegyric'.[7] A panegyric from the pen of William of Poitiers it most certainly received. And why not? Yet the pride and the prejudice, and the flattery of William the duke and king, this Fortune's favourite and God's favourite who can do no wrong,[8] are transparently obvious. In this as in all other ways the book is what its most recent editor has called it, 'l'echo direct de la cour anglo-normande'.[9] Within the panegyric there is a wealth of facts and details, some judiciously selected from other sources, not least William of Jumièges, but most derived from personal knowledge and personal contacts, compiled and intelligently put together by a man uniquely qualified as both clerk and knight, closely connected with the court and, indeed, for years part of it. One may add that William of Poitiers must have known his hero from their joint youth up, and stress that as both former knight and former chaplain of the duke he is able to bring us closer to the heart of Normandy in the mid-eleventh century than any other writer of that age or later. Amongst the many other riches of this often mistakenly maligned work we find a heady mixture of something a good deal more than conventional piety and an ex-soldier's delight in feats of arms. It is no wonder that, as one example, William of Poitier's account of Hastings is incomparably the fullest and the best we have.

The most recent and important discussion of William of Poitiers and his *History*, in addition to Raymonde Foreville's introduction to her standard edition of the work, is R.H.C. Davis, 'William of Poitiers and his History of William the Conqueror', in *The Writing of History in the Middle Ages: Essays presented to Richard William Southern*, ed. R.H.C. Davis and J.M. Wallace-Hadrill, Oxford 1981.

Source: *Guillaume de Poitiers, Histoire de Guillaume le Conquérant*, ed. and trans. Raymonde Foreville (Classiques de l'histoire de France), Paris, 1962. To Professor Foreville's (French) translation of her Latin text the following translations are much indebted.

The beginning of William of Poitiers' book is missing and the existing text begins as follows

29 *(1) pp. 2−4*[1] [When Cnut died] he lost with his life the kingdom of England, which

---

[7] *Ibid.*, p. 72.
[8] Cf. Pierre Bouet, 'La *felicitas* de Guillaume le Conquérant dans . . . Guillaume de Poitiers', *Battle*, iv, 1981.
[9] Raymonde Foreville, p. xxi.

---

[1] Raymonde Foreville in her edition of William of Poitiers slightly altered Duchesne's division of the work into two Parts, and subdivided each part into numbered sections, Part 1 comprising 59 and Part II 49. For ease of reference, Foreville's section numbers are given here in parenthesis beside the page numbers which also, of course, refer to her edition.

he owed only to conquest by his father and himself and to nothing else. That crown with the throne were then obtained by his son Harold [Harefoot, 1035–40], who because of his love of tyranny was scarcely worthy of him. Meanwhile Edward and Alfred were still exiles at the court of their kinsman, prince William, having formerly fled as boys to their uncles in Normandy to save their lives. Their mother was Emma, daughter of Richard I, and their father Ethelred, king of the English. But, in truth, on the genealogy of these two brothers and the Danish conquest of their inheritance others have written enough.[2]

There follow (pp. 4–12, paragraphs 2–5) an account of the respective expeditions of Edward and Alfred to England with the death of the latter, very close to the account given by William of Jumièges (**16, 17**); an apostrophe to earl Godwin accusing him of responsibility for Alfred's death and swearing that William 'the most glorious duke' will avenge his perfidy upon his son Harold; and a notice of the death of Harthacnut (1042) who succeeded Harold Harefoot as king of the English.

30 *(6) pp. 12–14* Now at last the most joyful and longed-for gladness dawned for those especially who desired peace and justice. Our duke, already adult in sagacity and bodily strength if not in years, took up the arms of knighthood (*arma militaria sumit*); whereat a tremor ran through all France. Armed and mounted he had no equal in all Gaul. It was a sight at once both delightful and terrible to see him managing his horse, girt with sword, his shield gleaming, his helmet and his lance alike menacing. For as he looked magnificent in princely apparel or the habiliment of peace, so to be in his war-gear especially became him. Henceforth in him courage and virtue shone forth with surpassing splendour. Now he began with the utmost eagerness to defend the churches of God, to protect the weak, to impose laws which should not be burdensome, to do justice which should in no way depart from equity and moderation, and above all to prevent murder, arson and robbery. For unrestrained lawlessness then prevailed everywhere, as we have shown above.[3] Finally he began to remove entirely from his houschold those whom he knew to be incapable or dishonest, to take counsel of the wisest and the best, to resist manfully the attacks of external enemies, and to exact vigorously the service due from his own men.

31 The following account of the siege of Brionne follows an account of the rebellion of 1047 and the battle of Val-ès-Dunes. Both are derived mainly from William of Jumièges (pp. 3–7 above), but add some useful details. Thus William of Poitiers names Ralph of Briquessart, vicomte of Bayeux, and Hamo 'aux Dents', lord of Torigny, amongst the conspirators.

(9, 10) pp. 18–20 Having most shamefully fled [*i.e.* from Val-ès-Dunes], Guy [of Burgundy] hastened with a large mounted force to Brionne. That castle (*oppidum*) seemed impregnable by the combination of its natural site and its construction, for over and above those other fortifications which the necessities of war make normal, it had a stone hall which served as a keep (*arx*) for its defenders and was itself surrounded by the unfordable waters of the river Risle. The victor [*i.e.* duke William], quickly following up, closely besieged the fortress, raising siege-castles (*castella*) on either bank of the river which

---

[2] A reference, no doubt, to, amongst others, William of Jumièges.
[3] Presumably a reference to the lost early part of the work.

flowed round it, and from them daily launched intimidating assaults, entirely denying any possibility of egress. At length,[4] beset also by shortage of food, the Burgundian sent envoys to ask for mercy. The duke, moved by the kinship, submission and wretchedness of the vanquished, did not inflict a severer punishment but allowed him to remain at his court. . . .

The Normans, once vanquished, all submitted to their lord and many gave hostages. Then at his command they immediately and completely demolished the castles (*munitiones*) which they had constructed in their seditious zeal. . . .

32 *(11, 12) pp. 22–6* After these events he [duke William] rendered the most zealous fealty to the king [of the French], as when requested to give aid against certain powerful enemies. For king Henry, angered by the insults of Geoffrey Martel,[5] led an army against him and besieged and took his castle of Mouliherne[6] in the *pagus* of Anjou.

The Norman contingent on that expedition excelled those led by the other counts and even that led by the king, and their renown reaches the author then studying in Poitiers. The king himself is obliged to reprimand the young duke for his reckless bravery; which is then illustrated as follows:

. . . Wishing to give the slip to his contingent, he withdrew from the army for a while, taking with him 300 knights (*equites*). Subsequently he detached himself from these again and rode off with only four. Whereupon there appeared from the enemy's side 15 splendidly armed and mounted knights. At once he attacked the boldest of them with couched lance,[7] taking care not to run him through. His hip, however, was broken by the force with which he hit the ground. Then the duke pursued the others for a distance of four miles. Meanwhile the 300 whom he had left behind, riding in search of their lord (for they feared the consequences of his bravery), suddenly saw count Theobald[8] with 500 knights (*equites*). They were filled with sadness, for they supposed they saw an enemy force and that their lord was held captive among them. Each encouraged the other by his determination to undertake the hazardous enterprise of freeing him. Then, identifying Theobald's force as allies, they rode on further and came upon that knight of the 15 whom the duke had met, still lying on the ground and incapacitated by his broken hip. A little further on they met their lord, in high spirits and leading seven knights (*milites*) whom he had captured.

33 *(14) pp. 28–32* It was also by his [duke William's] aid and counsel that Edward [the Confessor] at length, after the death of Harthacnut,[9] sat crowned upon the paternal

---

[4] According to Orderic Vitalis, the siege occupied three years (*Ecclesiastical History*, iv, 210). For the site, see above p. 11 n. 9.

[5] Count of Anjou, 1040–60.

[6] 1048 or 1051.

[7] The words used, *lanceam projicit*, could in themselves equally mean 'threw his lance' (*i.e.* like a spear), but the whole context of the Latin, not least the unhorsing, seems to prevent this – *Continuo incurrens lanceam projicit, audacissimum cavens perfodere. Coxa autem dirupta est alliso terrae.*

[8] Theobald III, count of Blois and Chartres.

[9] 8 June 1042.

throne, made worthy of that majesty as much by his wisdom and the singular distinction of his conduct as by the antiquity of his house. The English, indeed, in their deliberations determined upon the most advantageous course, agreeing to accede to the just demands of Norman envoys rather than to contend with Norman power. They eagerly arranged Edward's return to them with only a small Norman escort to avoid Norman conquest if the Norman count should come himself, for they well knew his reputation in war.[10] Edward, on the other hand, gratefully remembering with what generous munificence, what singular honour, what affectionate intimacy, prince William had treated him in Normandy, by all of which he was even more closely bound to the duke than by ties of kinship; nay more, remembering also with what zeal the duke had helped to restore him from exile to his kingdom, determined as a matter of honour to repay him in equal measure – and as an appropriate gift resolved to make him the heir of the crown obtained by his efforts. To this end, with the assent of his magnates, and by the agency of Robert archbishop of Canterbury[11] as his ambassador in this matter, he sent him, as hostages of the most powerful family in the kingdom, the son and the grandson[12] of earl Godwin.

34   The preceding section relates the expansionist policies of Geoffrey Martel, count of Anjou, and his seizure of Alençon in *c*.1048–9 or 1051.

(16–19) pp. 34–44   William, who could be relied upon to defend, even to extend, the right of his father and of his ancestors, advanced with an army against the Angevin territories in order to retaliate by taking from Geoffrey first Domfront and then Alençon. Whereupon the treachery of one of his knights (*miles*) almost caused the death of him who had no fear of the wide territory of his enemy.

On the approach to Domfront he turned aside with 50 knights (*equites*) willing to ride with him for extra pay. But one of the Norman magnates perfidiously revealed the plan to the defenders (*castellanis*), informing them of his position and intention, and of his preference for death rather than flight. As soon as possible 300 knights (*equites*) and 700 foot (*pedites*) were sent out and attacked him from the rear. He, however, intrepidly wheeled about and threw to the ground the first who dared to come against him. The rest at once lost heart and fled back to the fortress (*munitio*),[13] gaining a lead because they knew the way. The duke nevertheless did not abandon the pursuit until the gates were closed upon them, and took one prisoner with his own hands.

More determined than ever after these events to besiege the place, the duke raised four siege-castles (*castella*) about it. The site of the town (*oppidum*) denied its rapid capture either by force or art, for the rugged rock of the escarpment kept even foot-soldiers at bay unless they approached by two narrow and difficult ways. Count Geoffrey had sent

[10] Duke William could scarcely have had any personal military reputation in 1042.
[11] Abbot of Jumièges, 1037; bishop of London, 1044; archbishop, 1051.
[12] Respectively Wulfnoth and Hakon.
[13] Domfront comprises both castle and fortified town.

hand-picked men to aid and direct the defence. The Normans, however, harassed them with continuous and ferocious attacks. The duke himself was the first among those who inspired terror in the defenders. Sometimes he was for long periods on the look-out, riding through the night or hidden under cover, to see if attacks could be launched against those attempting to bring in supplies, or against those carrying messages, or those seeking to ambush his foragers. At other times, that the reader may appreciate just how confident he was in enemy territory, he went hunting. It is a region full of forests abounding in wild beasts. Often he diverted himself with the flight of falcons and more often with that of hawks. Not the difficulty of the place, the harshness of winter, nor any other adversity could bend his iron will to break off the siege.

The besieged were awaiting relief from [Geoffrey] Martel to whom they had sent for help. They had no wish to give up a lord under whom they could freely amass wealth by brigandage, just as the inhabitants of the town had been seduced by the same attraction. They knew all too well how brigands and robbers were hated in Normandy and rightly handed over to justice, to be rarely if ever acquitted. They feared the same application of law to their own crimes.

Geoffrey brought up huge forces of horse and foot to relieve Domfront. When this was reported to him, William entrusted the continuation of the siege to experienced knights (*milites*) and hastened to meet him. He sent ahead as scouts Roger of Montgomery and William fitz Osbern, both young and vigorous, who discovered in full the presumptuous intention of the enemy from his own mouth. He announced to them that he would be at Domfront the next morning to arouse William's watch with his trumpets. He gave notice of the horse he would ride into battle, his shield and his armour. To this they replied that he had no need to wear himself out by advancing further, for he whom he sought would straightway appear before him, and in their turn they described the horse, the arms and the armour of their lord.

This news when reported back served only to increase the eagerness of the Norman advance, and the duke, most ardent of all, urged on those who were already making haste. No doubt this most dutiful young prince sought the overthrow of a tyrant, which the senates of both Rome and Athens held to be the finest of all noble deeds.[14] But Geoffrey, overcome with sudden fear, sought safety in flight with his whole army before he had even seen his advancing adversary.

Thus the Norman duke was presented with the chance of an unopposed invasion to lay waste the lands and possessions of his enemy, and so to bring eternal shame upon his name. But he understood the wisdom of restraint in victory and that he who cannot refrain from vengeance is not truly great. He was content therefore to turn aside from the path of victory.

Behold! he came next quickly to Alençon[15] and took it with scarcely a blow, for the town (*oppidum*), in spite of the strength of its site, defences and garrison, fell so rapidly into his hand that he, too, might have uttered those proud words, 'I came, I saw, I

[14] The author here quotes some of the words of Cicero, *De officiis*, III, 4–19.
[15] William of Jumièges (19) gives more details of the taking of Alençon.

conquered'.[16] The dread news very soon reached Domfront. Despairing of anyone's ability to relieve them after the flight of so famous a warrior as Geoffrey Martel, they also capitulated as soon as they could when they saw the prince of the Normans had come back once again to attack them. Men with a knowledge of the past assert that both those castles (*castra*) were founded[17] with the licence (*concessu*) of count Richard [II], one after the other, on the borders of Normandy, and that they were and should be in the lordship of him and his successors. The victor returned home, bringing new pride and celebration to the entire country and spreading ever more widely abroad the love and the fear of his name.

There follow (pp. 45–83) William of Poitiers' accounts of the marriage of William to Mathilda of Flanders, the rebellion of William count of Arques and the siege of the castle of Arques, the battles of Mortemer and Varaville, and the planting of the castle of Ambrières on the borders of Normandy and Maine. (15 and 19–22) The deaths of the French king, Henry I, and of Geoffrey Martel, count of Anjou, are then noted.

35 *(36) pp. 84–6* It is well known that the utterances of men are more prone to cite evil than good, most often because of envy or occasionally as the result of some other depravity. The noblest deeds are represented by unjust perversity. Thus it sometimes happens that the good actions of kings, princes and other magnates, not having been truthfully reported, are condemned by men of good will in future ages, while misdeeds which should in no wise be imitated are taken as exemplars for usurpation or other evils. Wherefore we hold it our bounden duty to record as truthfully as possible how this William (whom we commemorate in writing and whom we wish both in present and future times to be pleasing to all and displeasing to none) was to take possession of the principality of Maine, as of the kingdom of England, not simply by force but also by the laws of justice.

There then follows (pp. 86–100) a long account and justification of the acquisition of the county of Maine, accomplished by 1064.

36 *(41–2) pp. 100–6* About the same time, Edward king of the English, who had already established William as his heir and whom he loved as a brother or a son, gave a guarantee more important than anything hitherto. He resolved to forestall the inevitability of death, for whose approaching hour this holy man, seeking heaven, made ready. To confirm his former promise by a further oath he sent to him [William] Harold, of all his subjects the greatest in riches, honour and power, whose brother and nephew had previously been accepted as hostages for the duke's succession.[18] This was a most prudent move, for his power and authority might be expected to contain the dissent of the entire English people if in their faithless inconstancy they were moved in any way to rebel.

Harold, hastening to carry out this mission, escaped from the perils of a Channel

---

[16] *Veni, vidi, vici*, words written by Julius Caesar in a letter to his friend Amintius.
[17] By William of Bellême.
[18] Respectively Wulfnoth and Hakon. Cf. **33**.

crossing by coming ashore in Ponthieu, where he fell into the hands of count Guy.[19] He and his companions were imprisoned, a misfortune which for so great a man was even worse than staying at sea in the storm. For cunning born of greed has brought about amongst certain peoples of Gaul an appalling practice, barbarous and far removed from all Christian justice. They seize the powerful and the rich, throw them into prison and inflict violence and torture upon them. Then, weakened by every sort of ill-treatment and close to death, they are released, most often for a large ransom.

Duke William, as soon as he heard what had happened to Harold who had been sent to him, dispatched envoys to secure his release by both prayers and threats, and set off to meet him with due honour. Guy, in the event, brought Harold of his own volition to the castle (*castrum*) of Eu and presented him to the duke, though he might have tortured or killed or ransomed him, for which the duke in consequence gave him appropriate thanks, wide and rich lands, and great sums of money in addition. The duke then brought Harold with all honour into Rouen, the chief city (*caput*) of his principality, where the courtesy of generous hospitality and celebration made good the hardships of the journey. He rejoiced, no doubt, to have such a guest, the envoy of his most dearly beloved kinsman and friend, and he hoped that Harold would be a faithful mediator between himself and the English amongst whom he stood second only to the king (*a rege secundus*).

At a council convened at Bonneville [sur-Touques][20] Harold publicly swore fealty to him by the sacred rite of Christians. And according to the entirely truthful relation of certain most notable men of utter integrity who were present at the time, at the end of the oath he freely added the following clauses: that he would be the agent (*vicarius*) of duke William at the court of his lord king Edward as long as the latter lived; that he would strive with all his influence and power to bring about the succession of the English kingdom to William after Edward's death; that he would meanwhile hand over to the custody of William's knights (*milites*) Dover castle (*castrum*), fortified by him (Harold) at his own expense, and also that he would place in the keeping of the duke's castellans (*custodes*) other castles (*castra*), abundantly supplied, in various parts of the kingdom where the duke should require them to be raised (*firmari*). The duke, having accepted Harold as his vassal by homage (*jam satelliti suo accepto per manus*[21]), at Harold's request, before the oath, enfeoffed him with all his lands and powers (*terras ejus cunctumque potentum dedit petenti*). Indeed it was not expected that Edward, already ill, would live much longer. Then, because he knew him to be warlike, courageous and eager for renown, the duke supplied him and his followers with arms and splendid horses, and took them with him on a campaign into Brittany: treating him thus, guest and ambassador, as a companion in

[19] In this passage there are echoes of William of Jumièges, which, of course, are less clear in translation. Cf. 23.

[20] A favourite residence of duke William, not far from Lisieux where William of Poitiers was archdeacon. Harold's 'Oath', which is here, in the only detailed account we have, represented as the full feudal ceremony of commendation – homage, fealty and investiture – whereby a man becomes the vassal of a lord, is placed at Bayeux by the Tapestry (199)and the Rouen by Orderic Vitalis writing, of course, much later. William of Jumièges names no place (23).

[21] The reference is to homage by the *immixtio manuum*.

arms, the duke also bound him more closely in fealty and obligation by such an honour. Brittany at this time was presumptuously at war with Normandy.

37 William of Poitiers next (pp. 106–12) gives an account (and justification) of the expedition into Brittany on which Harold accompanied William and which is illustrated on the Bayeux Tapestry. There is no reference, however, to the knighting of Harold at the end of the campaign as shown on the Tapestry.

(46) p. 114 On their return (from Brittany) the duke kept his favoured guest with him a little longer before letting him go, laden with gifts which were worthy both of him [Edward] by whose command he had come and of him [William] whose honour he had come to augment. In addition, his nephew, [22] one of the two hostages, was released for his sake to return with him. Therefore we address these few words to you, Harold. How, after these things, do you dare to rob William of his inheritance and wage war upon him whom by sacred oath you have recognized as of your race, and to whom you have committed yourself by hand and mouth? You should have suppressed [the opposition] which you perniciously incited. Accursed were the favourable winds which filled your ill-omened sails on your return! Wicked was the unruffled sea which could endure to bear you, basest of men, to the shore! Doomed was the peaceful port which received you who were bringing so great a calamity to your country!

'Part I' of the work in Raymonde Foreville's edition ends with a long section (pp. 114–46) on duke William's virtues as a ruler and his good government – his piety and generous patronage of the Church, not least the monasteries, his love of justice in peace and war, his maintenance of the peace, etc. – from which the following extracts are taken:

38 *(51) p. 125* In his princely office, albeit a layman, he gave acute advice to abbots and bishops in matters of ecclesiastical discipline, constantly exhorting, severely castigating. Whenever, at his command and insistence, the prelates met in synod, the metropolitan[23] with his suffragans, to deal with the state of religion, of clerks, monks and laity, he tried always to be there to preside, so that he might add his zeal to their zeal, his foresight to theirs; for he did not want to be dependent upon anyone else's report as to what had been done in matters all of which he ardently desired to be treated carefully, properly and reverently.

If perchance he heard of some serious offence with which the bishop or archdeacon had dealt too leniently, he ordered the alleged perpetrator of this breach of divine majesty to be imprisoned until the cause of the Lord should be decided with strict equity, while he accused the bishop or archdeacon concerned of being themselves offenders against divine justice to be brought to judgement and severely punished.

39 *(52) pp. 126–8* He loved to converse with those clerks or monks whose lives he knew were in conformity with their profession, and based his conduct upon their advice. On the other hand he withheld his favour from anyone of ill-repute. He cherished as his

---

[22] Hakon. Cf. Nos **33, 36** above.
[23] *I.e.* the archbishop of Rouen.

closest intimate a certain Lanfranc, concerning whom it was an open question whether he should be more respected for his unparalleled knowledge of both secular and sacred literature or for his unparalleled observance of the monastic rule. He venerated him as a father, revered him as a master, and loved him as a brother or a son. He entrusted to him the direction of his soul, and placed him on a lofty eminence wherefrom he could watch over the clergy throughout all Normandy. For the vigilant care of such a man, upon whom an equal wisdom and sanctity conferred an unique authority, was able to provide security in any adversity.

It was by a kind of pious force that the duke made him abbot of the monastery of Caen,[24] for he resisted the appointment as much by fear of high rank as love of humility. Thereafter William endowed with wide possessions, and with silver, gold and ornaments of every kind, the abbey which he raised from the foundations at his own great expense, on a vast and splendid scale and in a beautiful style, well worthy of the protomartyr Stephen whose relics it was to magnify and in whose honour it was to be dedicated[25] (*dedicandum erat*). No one could put a greater value than he did upon the office of prayers rendered to heaven. He repeatedly sought and paid for the prayers of the servants of Christ, especially when war or some other crisis threatened. . . .

40 Unlike many, duke William was not guilty of nepotism or indulgence to those of his own family, as witness the deposition of his uncle, Mauger archbishop of Rouen:

(53–4) pp. 128–32 He, the son of [duke] Richard II, abused his sacred office, behaving as though it belonged to him by right of birth. Moreover, he had never received the pallium, the principal symbol and vestment of archiepiscopal authority, the Roman pontif who normally sends it having withheld it on account of his unworthiness. . . . [His lack of discipline, his impoverishment of his church to support his luxurious living, his lack of obedience to the Papacy and repeated refusals to attend councils at Rome]. The prince, therefore, seeing that admonitions were no longer enough in a matter of such gravity, and fearing that further tolerance would bring down upon him the wrath of the Supreme Judge, deposed his uncle in the public assembly of a holy synod, the apostolic vicar and all the Norman bishops concurring with the sentence as canon law requires.[26]

The duke provided Maurille [Maurilius] to the vacant see, brought back from Italy where he stood out above all other abbots, supremely worthy of the high office of archbishop by reason of his birth, his character and his doctrine.

41 *(56–7) pp. 134–6* This same prince exalted many churches, giving careful consideration to the appointment of prelates, not least those of Lisieux, Bayeux and Avranches. For

[24] *I.e.* St Stephen's or the Abbaye aux Hommes (as opposed to Mathilda's foundation of Holy Trinity or the Abbaye aux Dames). Lanfranc was appointed in 1063.
[25] The church was dedicated in 1077 – not 1073 as often stated. See Orderic Vitalis, *Ecclesiastical History*, ed. Chibnall, ii, 148 n. 3; L. Musset, *Actes de Guillaume le Conquérant et de la reine Mathilde pour les abbayes Caeŋnaises*, Caen, 1967, pp. 14–15.
[26] At Lisieux, 1055, in the presence of the papal legate Erminfrid of Sion.

he appointed there supremely capable bishops, Hugh to Lisieux, his own brother, Odo, to Bayeux, and John to Avranches. In their election his judgement was based upon their worth, not the elevation of their birth by which they were his kinsmen. . . .

Odo[27] from his boyhood up has been the object of unanimous acclaim. His renown has spread from Normandy to distant regions, but the zeal and goodness of this man of great liberality and humility merits even greater fame.

42 *(1–2) pp. 146–52*[28] And now unexpectedly there came a true report, the land of England was bereft of her king Edward, and his crown was worn by Harold.[29] Not for this insane Englishman the decision of a public choice, but, on that sorrowful day when the best of kings was buried and the whole nation mourned his passing, he seized the royal throne with the plaudits of certain iniquitous supporters and thereby perjured himself. He was made king by the unholy consecration of Stigand, who had been deprived of his ministry by the justified fervour of papal anathema.[30]

Duke William took counsel with his vassals (*cum suis*) and determined to avenge the wrong by arms and in arms to claim his inheritance, although many magnates argued persuasively against the enterprise as too hazardous and far beyond the resources of Normandy. In addition to her bishops and abbots, Normandy had at this time in her councils outstanding lay lords who shone as luminaries and ornaments in any assembly: Robert count of Mortain;[31] Robert count of Eu, brother of Hugh bishop of Lisieux of whose life we have written above; Richard count of Evreux, son of archbishop Robert;[32] Roger de Beaumont; Roger of Montgomery; William fitz Osbern; Hugh the *vicomte*.[33] By their sagacity and zeal the safety of the duchy might be assured. . . . Yet we learn that in all deliberations everyone gave way to the wisdom of the prince, as if he knew in advance by divine inspiration what should and should not be done. 'To those who act with piety God has given wisdom' says one well versed in divinity',[34] and the duke had lived with piety from his youth. Whatever he was pleased to command, all obeyed unless prevented by some overwhelming necessity.

There is not space to relate in detail how he carefully organized the building of ships and their fitting out with arms and men, provisions and all other necessities of war, and how the enthusiasm of all Normandy was kindled. Nor did he take less care over the government and security of Normandy in his absence. A large force (*miles*) of volunteers also assembled from other lands, partly attracted by the well known liberality of the duke but all confident in the justice of his cause.

All looting was forbidden and 50,000 men (*milites*) were fed at his own expense while

[27] Odo de Conteville, half-brother to the Conqueror, appointed bishop of Bayeux in 1049.
[28] In Raymonde Foreville's edition 'Part II' of the work begins here.
[29] Edward died on 4/5 January, 1066, and Harold was crowned on 6 January, the day of the funeral.
[30] Stigand had been intruded upon Canterbury after the uncanonical expulsion of archbishop Robert of Jumièges in 1052.
[31] Like Odo of Conteville above, half-brother to the Conqueror.
[32] *I.e.* Robert, son of Richard I and archbishop of Rouen 987–1037.
[33] Presumably vicomte of Avranches.
[34] St Augustine.

contrary winds delayed them for a month at the mouth of the Dives. Such was his moderation and prudence: he made generous provision both for his own knights (*milites*) and those from other parts, and would not allow anyone to pillage anything. The sheep and cattle of the neighbouring peasantry were safely pastured either in the meadow or in the open country. The crops awaited untouched the sickle of the harvester and were neither arrogantly ridden down by horsemen (*equites*) nor cut by foragers. Weak or unarmed, any man might ride where he would, singing on his horse, without trembling at the sight of soldiers.

43 *(3) pp. 152–4* At this time there sat upon St Peter's chair at Rome Pope Alexander [II], a man full worthy to be obeyed and consulted by the entire Church, for he gave good advice and just decisions. . . . The duke begged the support of this pontiff, informing him of his undertaking, and received of his benevolence a standard as a sign of the approval of St Peter, behind which he might advance more confidently and securely against his enemy. And with Henry [IV] the Roman emperor, son of the emperor Henry [III] and grandson of the emperor Conrad, he had recently made a pact of friendship by the terms of which Germany (*Germania*) would come to his aid against any enemy at his request. Swein king of the Danes[35] pledged his faith through envoys, but showed himself rather the faithful supporter of his [*i.e.* William's] enemies, as the reader will learn in what follows concerning his defeat.[36]

44 *(4–5) pp. 154–8* Meanwhile Harold was ready to give battle whether by land or sea, covering most of the shore with an immense army, and cunningly sent over spies. To one of these, who was captured and tried to conceal the reason for his presence in accordance with his orders, the duke showed the greatness of his spirit in these words: 'Harold has no need', he said, 'to waste his gold and silver buying the service and skills of you and those like you who came to spy upon us. He will learn from me and in my presence more surely and sooner than he wishes our aims and intentions. Take him this message from me, that he need fear nothing from us, but pass the rest of his days in peace, if in the space of one year he does not find me in whatever place he thinks to be most secure.'

The Norman magnates were amazed at so grandiose a promise, and many did not hide their alarm. In the ensuing discussion despair made them exaggerate Harold's strength and diminish their own. He abounded in riches whereby powerful kings and princes were brought into his alliance; he had a numberless fleet with expert crews long experienced in maritime dangers and battles; the wealth and therefore military resources of his country far exceeded those of our land. Who could hope to have a ship completed within a year as required[37] or find crews for those that were thus completed? Who would not be afraid

[35] Swein II Estrithson.

[36] A reference to the invasion fleet sent by Swein to the north of England in the winter of 1069–70. No account of this is to be found now in the truncated text of William of Poitiers which has come down to us (see p. 16 above).

[37] Perhaps a reference to specific agreements with the Norman magnates each to provide ships as well as men. See Foreville p. 150 n. 2.

that this new expedition would reduce the prosperous condition of Normandy to penury? Who would not affirm that even the power of a Roman emperor would be insufficient for so hazardous an undertaking?

The duke, however, strengthened the resolve of the alarmists with the following speech: 'We all know', he said, 'the cleverness of Harold: he may inspire fear, but he also raises our hopes. He dispenses his wealth to no effect, wasting his gold without strengthening his position. He does not dare to promise the least part of that which belongs to me. I, however, shall promise and give away as I please those possessions which are now said to be his equally with those which are mine at present. Without doubt he will overcome who is prepared to bestow not only his own property but that of his foe. The lack of a fleet shall be no hindrance to us for we shall soon rejoice in sufficient ships . . . wars are won by the courage rather than the number of soldiers (*milites*). Furthermore, Harold will fight not to lose what he has unjustly seized; we seek what has been given to us, which we have gained in return for the services we have rendered. . . .

Truly it was known to this wise and orthodox prince that the omnipotence of God, which avoids all injustice, would not allow a just cause to fail, especially as his intention was not the increase of his own wealth and glory but the reform of Christian practice in that land.

45 *(6–8) pp. 158–68*[38] Now the entire fleet, equipped with the utmost foresight, and which had long lain in the mouth of the Dives and the neighbouring harbours awaiting a south wind to take them to England, was blown by westerlies into the roadstead of St Valery [sur-Somme]. There too by prayers and offerings and vows the duke committed himself with utter confidence to the will of heaven, this prince whose spirit could not be broken by delay or contrary winds, by the terrors of the deep or by the timorous desertion of those who had pledged their service. Rather, he met adversities with prudence, concealing the loss of those who were drowned as far as he could by burying them in secret, and increasing the rations every day in order to mitigate their scarcity. Thus by encouragement of all kinds he was able to restrain those who were afraid and put heart into the dismayed. He strove by prayer to obtain a favourable instead of a contrary wind, and brought out from the church in solemn procession the body of St Valery, confessor beloved of God, in which demonstration of humility all those who were to go with him on the expedition took part.

When at last the longed-for wind blew, thanks were rendered to Heaven with hands and voice, and a tumult arose as each shouted encouragement to the other. As quickly as possible the land was deserted and the uncertain voyage eagerly begun. So compelling was their haste that if, here, one called for his esquire (*armigerum*) and, there, another called for his companion, most were in so great a hurry that they were heedless of attendants (*clientes*), companions, and even needs, fearing only that they might be left behind. The duke himself, burning with impatience, urged and chided on board anyone whom he thought to linger.

[38] In the passage describing the Norman crossing which follows there are conscious echoes of the Aeneid of Vergil.

Fearing lest they reach the opposite shore before daybreak and so incur danger in a hostile and unknown roadstead, the duke issued verbal orders that as soon as they gained the high sea the ships were to lie at anchor close to him for part of the night, until they should see a lantern lit at his masthead, and then at the sound of a trumpet at once set course.

A passage of classical allusions follows in which the number of ships is put at over a thousand − p. 162

During the night the ships got under way after their wait, the vessel bearing the duke[39] leaving the others behind, as if by its own equal speed it would answer the will of him who was hastening ardently to victory. At dawn an oarsman, ordered to the masthead to see if any following ships were coming up, reported that nothing was in sight save sea and sky. Anchor was cast at once, and to prevent any fear or alarm among his companions the intrepid duke cheerfully ate a hearty breakfast washed down with spiced wine as though he were in his solar at home (*in coenaculo domestico*), asserting that the rest of the fleet would soon appear, guided by God to whose care he had committed them . . . [classical allusions] . . . Asked a second time, the look-out shouted that four ships approached; the third time, that there were so many that they looked like a forest of trees bearing sails. How the duke's hope was then transformed into rejoicing, and how from his innermost heart he magnified the divine mercy, we leave to each reader to imagine.

They were borne by a favourable wind to Pevensey where they made an unopposed landing. For Harold had gone to Yorkshire to give battle to his brother [Tostig] and Harold [Hardrada] king of the Norwegians. Nor is it to be wondered at that his brother, driven by the injuries done him and striving to regain his lost honour, brought alien arms against Harold [Godwineson], whom his own sister [Edith], so different from him in character, opposed with her prayers and counsel albeit unable to resist him with arms − this man defiled by luxury, this cruel murderer insolent in stolen riches, the enemy of justice and good. For Edith, a lady endowed with the sagacity of a man, and understanding moral rectitude which she honoured by her life, wanted the English to be ruled over by William whom king Edward her husband had adopted as a son and established as his heir, wise, just and strong.

46 *(9−10) pp. 168−70*[40] Joyfully the Normans, having gained the shore, occupied first Pevensey, where they raised a castle (*munitio*), and then Hastings, where they raised another, each to serve as a defence both for themselves and for their ships . . . [more classical allusions, to Marius and Pompey the Great with particular reference to their caution in enemy territory]. William, however, without hesitation and with an escort of only 25 knights (*milites*), himself made a reconnaissance of the area and its inhabitants. Returning thence, on foot because of the difficulty of the way, he bore on his shoulder the hauberk (*lorica*) of one of his vassals (*suae satellitis*) as well as his own − and though this was done

[39] This was the *Mora*, given by the duchess Mathilda herself according to the list of ships and men printed by J.A. Giles, *Scriptores Rerum Gestarum Willelmi Conquestoris*, London, 1845, pp. 21−2.
[40] At this point Duchesne began his Part II of the work, with the heading, 'War between duke William and Harold king of the English'.

with a laugh, and the reader may also laugh, it is really a matter for serious praise since he thus relieved of the iron bundle no less a man than William fitz Osbern, renowned for his strength both of body and spirit.

A certain rich inhabitant of those parts, a Norman by race, called Robert, son of the noble lady Guimora,[41] sent to Hastings, to the duke who was both his lord and kinsman, a message in these words: 'King Harold has fought with his own brother and with the king of the Norwegians, the doughtiest warrior under Heaven, and in one battle has slain both and destroyed their huge armies. Elated with victory he is now moving swiftly against you at the head of a great force: against whom your men can no more prevail in my opinion than a pack of as many dogs. You have a reputation for prudence and have so far acted prudently both in peace and war. Exercise now caution and self-control lest by your temerity you fall headlong into a danger from which you will not be able to escape. I recommend that you stay within your defences for the time being and do not give battle.' To the messenger the duke replied as follows: 'For the recommendation wherein your lord enjoins caution, though it would have been more seemly to advise without insult, take back my thanks to him with this rejoinder. I shall not seek the shelter of fosse or walls but do battle with Harold as soon as possible; nor would I doubt my ability to destroy him and his had I but 10,000 men of the same bravery as the 60,000 that in fact I lead.'[42]

47 Duke William receives a monk-ambassador who had arrived the previous day:

(11–13) pp. 172–80 . . . On the morrow, seated in the midst of his magnates (*primates*), he summoned the monk and said to him, 'I am William, by the grace of God prince of the Normans.[43] That which you related to me yesterday, now repeat before these present.' And so the legate spoke as follows: 'Thus king Harold commands you. You have invaded his land with an arrogant temerity beyond comprehension. He certainly remembers that king Edward long ago decided that you would be his heir, and that he himself in Normandy gave surety to you concerning that succession. Nevertheless, he knows that this kingdom is his by right, as granted to him by gift of that same king his lord upon his deathbed. For since the time when the blessed Augustine came into England it has been the common custom of this nation that a gift made at the point of death is held as valid.[44] Wherefore he requires you to withdraw from his land with your forces. Otherwise he will break the friendship and all agreements made with you in Normandy and place all responsibility for it upon you.'

Having heard Harold's injunction, the duke asked the monk if he would safely conduct an envoy to his lord. The monk promised he would have as much care for such a envoy's safety as for his own. At once the duke entrusted a certain monk of Fécamp with the

[41] Sometimes, but doubtfully, this Robert has been identified as Robert fitz Wimarch of Rayleigh in Essex. See Foreville, p. 170, n. 1.

[42] These numbers are of course exaggerations. Six to seven thousand on each side is the usual modern estimate of the forces engaged at Hastings.

[43] The previous day, on first meeting the monk, the duke had pretended to be his own steward.

[44] *I.e.* overrides any previous bequest except a formal *post obitum* grant. See Ann Williams, *Battle*, i, 1978, pp. 165–6.

following message to bear swiftly to Harold. 'Not with temerity nor unjustly, but with resolutions and by the dictates of equity, have I crossed into this land, of which my lord and kinsman made me the heir, as Harold himself acknowledges, on account of the great honours and services which I and my forbears conferred upon him, his brother[45] and their followers; and as he believed me the most worthy of all his race so also he held me the most able both to support him while he lived and to govern the kingdom after his death. Assuredly this was not done without the consent of his magnates, but with the counsel of archbishop Stigand and of earl Godwin, earl Leofric[46] and earl Siward,[47] all of whom confirmed by oath and pledge of hands (*jurejurando suis manibus confirmaverunt*) that after Edward's death they would receive me as lord, nor during his lifetime would they seek in any way whatever to prevent my succession to this country. He [Edward] gave me as hostages the son and the grandson of Godwin. Finally, he sent Harold himself to Normandy, that he might there swear in my presence what his father and the other aforesaid magnates had sworn in my absence. On his way to me he fell into the peril of captivity, from which I delivered him by the exercise of both prudence and *force majeure*. He did homage to me[48] and gave me pledge of hand concerning the English kingdom (*sua manu securitatem mihi de regno Anglico firmavit*). I am ready to submit my cause against him to legal judgement, whether by the law of the Normans or of the English, whichever he prefers. If then either the Normans or the English decide according to the truth of equity that he ought by right to possess this kingdom, then let him hold it in peace. If, however, they decide it is in justice to be rendered to me, then let him give it up. But if he rejects this proposal, I do not think it right that my men or his should fall in battle when the dispute between us is no fault of theirs. Be it known, therefore, that I am ready to wage my life against his that the English kingdom by right falls to me rather than to him.'

William of Poitiers informs us that Harold receiving this message on the march, turned pale and was silent for a long time, giving orders only that the advance should continue. Eventually, the monk-messenger again requesting an answer to duke William's challenge to single combat, *i.e.* the judicial combat, *duellum*, to avoid the slaughter of armies −

Harold lifted up his face to heaven and said: 'May God this day judge the right between me and William'.

48 *(14−24) pp. 180−204* Meanwhile a troop of chosen knights (*equites*) sent out on reconnaissance soon reported the enemy's approach. For the enraged king hastened his march still more when he heard of the devastation of the lands about the Norman camp. He planned to fall upon them unawares by a sudden or a night attack. And so that they should find no refuge in withdrawal he had sent a fleet of 700 warships to cut them off at sea. The duke at once ordered all those who could be found in the camp to arm (for the

---

[45] *I.e.* Alfred.
[46] Earl of Mercia, d. 1057.
[47] Earl of Northumbria, d. 1055.
[48] *Se mihi per manus suas dedit*, lit. 'gave himself to me by his hands', *i.e.* did homage by the *immixtio manuum*.

greater part of his army was out foraging on that day[49]). He himself attended with devotion the mystery of the Mass and fortified his body and soul by partaking of the Body and Blood of the Lord. He humbly hung about his neck the relics whose protection Harold forfeited by breaking the sacred oath which he had sworn upon them. There were present in his household (*comitatus*) two bishops from Normandy, Odo of Bayeux and Geoffrey of Coutances, together with many clergy and a number of monks. The clergy led prayers before the battle. The military were horrified when they saw the duke donning his hauberk reversed to the left. But he only laughed and feared it not at all as an ill-omen.

The author (who admits he was not present) next gives a version of the speech made by William to his men before the battle. He reminded them of their invariable former victories under his command. They must fight now in accordance with their renown and the reputation of their country. There was no alternative, with the enemy in front and the sea behind. Victory would bring honour and riches. Their military superiority would overcome the greater numbers of the oft-defeated English. Their cause was just and therefore God was with them.

This is the good order in which he [duke William] advanced, with the banner which the Pope had sent in the van. He placed infantry in front armed with bows and crossbows,[50] and behind them other infantry more heavily armed with mail tunics (*loricatos*); in the rear the contingents of mounted knights (*turmas equitum*), himself in the centre thereof with an élite force, so that he could direct everything with hand and voice. If any author of antiquity had written of the army of Harold he would have told how at his passage the rivers were drained and the forests levelled.[51] For vast forces of English had come in from all regions. Some were drawn by love for Harold, all by love for their country, which they, albeit misguidedly, wished to defend against aliens. The land of the Danes, their kith and kin, had sent them abundant help. Yet not daring to fight on equal terms with William whom they feared more than the king of Norway,[52] they took up position on higher ground,[53] on a hill by the forest through which they had just come. At once abandoning the aid of horses, they drew themselves up in very close order. The duke and his army, nothing daunted by the hard going, slowly advanced up the steep slope.

The terrible sound of trumpets on both sides announced the opening of the battle.[54] The eager courage of the Normans gave them the first strike, just as when contenders meet in a trial for theft the prosecution speaks first. So the Norman foot, coming in close, challenged the English, raining wounds and death upon them with their missiles. They, on the other hand, valiantly resisted, each according to his ability. They threw spears and weapons of every kind, murderous axes and stones tied to sticks. By these means you

---

[49] *I.e.* Friday 13 October.
[50] The Latin is somewhat ambiguous – *Pedites . . . sagittis armatos et balistis. Sagittae* means 'arrows' (or 'bolts'); *ballista*, in classical Latin a large siege-engine, certainly comes to mean also hand-crossbow in the twelfth century. There is little or no other known evidence for the use of crossbows as early as 1066 and only bowmen appear on the Tapestry. On the other hand William of Poitiers, as a former knight, was very well informed in military matters.
[51] There are echoes in this section of Juvenal and Lucan.
[52] *I.e.* Harold Hardrada whom he had recently defeated at Stamford Bridge.
[53] Hereabouts are echoes of Sallust.
[54] Echoes of Sallust again.

would have thought to see our men overwhelmed as though by a deadly mass. And so the knights (*equites*) came up in support, and those who were last became first. Spurning to fight at long range, they challenged the event with their swords. Even the war-cries of the Normans on the one side and the barbarians on the other were drowned by the clash of arms and the groans of the dying. Thus for some time the fight was waged with the utmost vigour on both sides. The English were greatly helped by the advantage of the high ground which they, in the closest array, could hold on the defensive; also by their great number and massed strength; and, further, by their weapons[55] which could easily find a way through shields and other defences. Thus they vigorously resisted or repulsed those who bravely attacked them at close quarters with the sword. They even wounded those who hurled javelins at them from a distance. Terrified by this ferocity, behold! the footsoldiers and also the Breton knights (*equites*), together with all the auxiliaries on the left wing, are driven back. Almost the whole ducal army falls away – though this may be said without disparagement of the invincible Norman race. The army of imperial Rome, containing the cohorts of kings, accustomed to victory by land and sea, fled at times when it knew or thought its leader to be slain. The Normans now believed their duke and leader had fallen. Their retreat was not thus an occasion of shameful flight but of grief, for he was their whole support.

The duke therefore, seeing a large part of the enemy line launching itself forward in pursuit of his retreating troops, galloped up in front of them, shouting and brandishing his lance. Removing his helmet to bare his head, he cried: 'Look at me. I am alive, and, by God's help, I shall win. What madness puts you to flight? Where do you think you can go? Those you could slaughter like cattle are driving and killing you. You are deserting victory and everlasting honour; you are running away to destruction and everlasting shame. And by flight not one of you will avoid death. 'At this they recovered their morale. He himself was the first to charge forward, sword flashing, cutting down the foe who deserved death as rebels to him, their king. The Normans, enflamed, surrounded some thousands of those who had pursued them and annihilated them in an instant, not one of them surviving.

Thus encouraged they renewed their attack upon the vast army which in spite of heavy losses seemed no less. The English, full of confidence, fought with all their might, determined above all to prevent any breach from being opened in their ranks. They were so densely massed that the dead could scarcely fall. However, breaches were cut in several places by the swords of the most redoubtable knights (*milites*). They were closely followed up by the men of Maine and Aquitaine, the French, the Bretons, but above all by the Normans with a courage beyond compare. A certain Norman esquire (*tiro*[56]), Robert, son of Roger de Beaumont and nephew and heir, through Adeline his mother, of Hugh count of Meulan, having that day his first experience of battle, bore himself in a way worthy of eternal praise, with great courage victoriously attacking at the head of the troop (*legio*) which he commanded on the right wing. But we have not the ability, nor is it our

[55] Presumably the great two-handed battle-axe is particularly meant here.
[56] A young man serving the apprenticeship of knighthood.

purpose, to relate as they deserve the feats of arms of individuals. The most accomplished and prolific writer, who had been an eye-witness of that battle, would find difficulty in describing each and every one. For our part we must now make haste so that, having reached the culmination of the fame of count William, we may write of the glory of king William.

The Normans and their allied forces, realizing that they could not overcome an enemy so numerous and standing so firm without great loss to themselves, retreated, deliberately feigning flight (*terga dederunt, fugam ex industria simulantes*). They remembered how, a little while before, flight had been the occasion of success. The barbarians exulted with the hope of victory. Exhorting each other with triumphant shouts, they poured scorn upon our men and boasted that they would all be destroyed then and there. As before, some thousands of them were bold enough to launch themselves as if on wings after those they thought to be fleeing. The Normans, suddenly wheeling their horses about, cut them off, surrounded them, and slew them on all sides, leaving not one alive.

Twice they used the same strategem to the same effect, and then attacked more furiously than ever the remaining enemy, still a formidable force and extremely difficult to surround. It was now a strange kind of battle, one side attacking with all mobility, the other enduring, as though rooted to the soil. The English began to weaken, and as if confessing their guilt by their submission, suffered the punishment. The Normans shot, smote and pierced: it seemed as if more movement was caused by the falling dead than by the living. Those who were only wounded could not withdraw, but died in the press of their companions. Thus Fortune (*felicitas*) sped to accomplish William's triumph.

There were present at this engagement Eustace count of Boulogne; William, son of count Richard of Evreux; Geoffrey, son of Rotrou count of Mortagne; William fitz Osbern; Aimeri vicomte de Thouars; Walter Giffard; Hugh de Montfort; Ralph de Tosny; Hugh de Grandmesnil; William of Warenne; and many others famed in knightly renown (*militaris praestantiae fama*) whose names should be recorded in the annals of history amongst the most celebrated warriors. William however, their leader, so much excelled them all in bravery as in military skill that he may be held the equal or superior of those ancient leaders of the Greeks and Romans so much praised in books. He was a noble general, turning back the retreat, inspiring courage, sharing danger, more often commanding men to follow than urging them on from the rear. It is very clear that his own surpassing courage and daring set the example to his followers. Not a few of the enemy, though unwounded, lost heart at the mere sight of this marvellous and terrible knight (*eques*). Three horses were killed under him. Three times he leapt to his feet undaunted and swiftly avenged the death of his steed. Then one could see his agility, his strength of body and spirit. Shields, helmets, hauberks (*loricas*) were riven by his furious and flashing blade, while yet other assailants were clouted by his own shield. His knights (*milites*) were astonished to see him a foot-soldier (*peditem*), and many, stricken with wounds, were given new heart. Not a few, from whom strength was ebbing with their blood, leant upon their shields to fight manfully on, while others who could do no more, with hands and voice urged on their companions to follow the duke without fear, and not let victory slip from their grasp. He himself was the help and saviour of many.

There follows a paragraph (pp. 198–200) in which William is compared to his advantage with various classical heroes, and the author, unequal to his task, resolves quickly to end his true relation of a battle won by strength and justice.

Now as the day declined the English army realized beyond doubt that they could no longer stand against the Normans. They knew that they were reduced by heavy losses; that the king himself, with his brothers and many magnates of the realm, had fallen; that those who still stood were almost drained of strength; that they could expect no help. They saw the Normans, not much diminished by casualties, threatening them more keenly than in the beginning, as if they had found new strength in the fight; they saw that fury of the duke who spared no one who resisted him; they saw that courage which could only find rest in victory. They therefore turned to flight and made off as soon as they got the chance, some on looted horses, many on foot; some along the roads, many across country. Those who struggled but on rising lacked the strength to flee lay in their own blood. The sheer will to survive gave strength to others. Many left their corpses in the depths of forests, many collapsed in the path of their pursuers along the way. The Normans, though not knowing the terrain, pursued them keenly, slaughtering the guilty fugitives and bringing matters to a fitting end, while the hooves of the horses exacted punishment from the dead as they were ridden over.

Courage,[57] however, returned to the fleeing English, who in a steep rampart and a labyrinth of ditches found a perfect opportunity to renew the fight. For this nation, being descended from the ancient Saxons, the most ferocious of men, are always eager for combat. They would not withdraw unless compelled by an overwhelming force. They had recently defeated with ease the Norse king with his great army. The duke, coming up at the head of his victorious banners, was surprised to see these troops making a stand, but, although he assumed them to be newly arrived reinforcements, neither halted nor turned aside. More formidable with only the stump of a broken lance than those fully armed, with a great shout he halted the withdrawal of count Eustace who with 50 knights (*milites*) had already turned back and was about to give the signal for retreat. He in turn privily urged retreat upon the duke, predicting speedy death for him if he went on. Even as he spoke Eustace was struck a resounding blow between the shoulders, the gravity of which was immediately shown by blood spurting from his ears and mouth, and he was borne off by his companions more dead than alive. The duke, scorning fear as shame and dishonour, attacked and rode down the enemy. In this engagement a number of the noblest Normans lost their lives, their valour nullified by the impossible terrain.

49 *(25) pp. 204–8* His victory thus won, the duke returned to the field of battle, to be met with a scene of carnage which he could not regard without pity in spite of the

---

[57] In the following paragraph we evidently find the origin of one version of the well known story of the Malfosse, though it will be noted that the dramatic incident of Norman knights riding into a concealed ravine with heavy casualties is not present in it. For that we have to wait until the twelfth century. For a full discussion see R. Allen Brown, 'The Battle of Hastings', *Battle*, iii, 1980, pp. 18–21.

wickedness of the victims and although to slay a tyrant is honourable, glorious and praise-worthy. Far and wide the ground was covered with the flower of English nobility and youth, soiled by their own blood. The king's two brothers[58] were found lying beside him. He himself, all dignity lost, was recognized not by his face but by certain indications and was carried to the ducal camp, where the duke entrusted his burial to William surnamed Malet, and not to his mother,[59] who offered for her beloved son his weight in gold. He knew very well that to take gold in such a matter was not fitting, and he held Harold to be unworthy of burial as his mother wished, when his greed was the cause of so many others lying unburied. It was said in mockery to be appropriate to leave him as the keeper of the shore and sea which he had so recently sought to defend in his insanity.

There follows an apostrophe to the dead Harold, accusing him of fratricide and usurpation, laying upon him the responsibility for the calamity of Hastings, and ending:

Your last hours show with what right you were elevated to the kingship by the grant of Edward on his death-bed. The comet, the dread of kings, which blazed in the heavens after your enthronement foretold your doom.

50 *(26–7) pp. 208–12* With classical allusions the author extols the moderation and clemency of William after his great victory whereby he had subdued all England in a single day between the third hour and the evening.

Having buried his dead, and left a force at Hastings under an energetic commander, he advanced to Romney which he punished at his pleasure for the damage they had inflicted upon some of his men, who had come there by mistake and been set upon by the savage populace in an action involving heavy losses on both sides. Thence he moved to Dover where he had been informed a large multitude was gathered. The place seemed impregnable. At his approach the English took fright and lost all confidence both in their natural and man-made defences and in their numerical strength. That fortress (*castellum*) is sited on a cliff whose natural steepness has been everywhere artificially scarped, rising like a wall sheer out of the sea as high as an arrow can be shot. Just as the defenders, however, were about to yield the place, some of our men-at-arms (*armigeri*), lusting for loot, fired it . . . The duke, not wishing those to suffer who had begun negotiations with him to surrender, paid for the rebuilding of the houses and made good the other losses . . . Having taken the fortress he spent eight days adding those fortifications (*firmamenta*) which it lacked[60] . . .

51 *(28–9) pp. 212–20* Notwithstanding dysentry in his army, the duke left a garrison at Dover and moved on, received the submission of Canterbury, and himself fell ill at a place called 'the Broken Tower' –

. . . Meanwhile Stigand archbishop of Canterbury, who was a most influential personage

---

[58] Gyrth and Leofwin.
[59] Gytha.
[60] Usually taken as referring to the raising of a castle within the enclosure of the Old English borough on the cliff top.

amongst the English because of his great wealth and eminence, threatened to continue hostilities with the support of the sons of Aelfgar[61] and other magnates. They had nominated as king Edgar aethling, a young boy of the royal race of Edward, and they were determined to have as king no one but a compatriot. . .

The Normans burn the suburbs of London south of the Thames and the duke makes a circuitous march about the city.

. . . The duke then continued his march without meeting any resistance, crossed the Thames by ford and bridge, and came to the town (*oppidum*) of Wallingford. There came to him Stigand, the metropolitan bishop, who did homage to him and confirmed it with an oath of fealty (*manibus ei sese dedit, fidem sacramento confirmavit*), renouncing the aethling whom he had irresponsibly elected. Thence proceeding, as soon as he came within sight of London the leading citizens came out to him and placed themselves and their city in his obedience, as the men of Canterbury had done before them, and gave all the hostages he named and required. After this, both the bishops and other magnates prayed him to take the crown, pleading that they were accustomed to serve a king and wished only for a king to be their lord.

William hesitates to take the throne at this stage and would prefer his wife to be crowned with him. He takes counsel and is persuaded by his knights and their spokesman Aimeri, vicomte of Thouars.

. . . Therefore, while he himself stayed nearby, he sent a party ahead into London to raise a castle (*munitionem*) in the city[62] and to make all necessary preparations for his royal splendour . . .

52   (*30) pp. 220–2*   On the day ordained for the coronation, the archbishop of York,[63] a lover of justice, a man of sober years, wise, good and eloquent, addressed the English in fitting style and asked them if they would have their lord [William] crowned. All gave their joyful assent without hesitation, as though heaven had given them one mind and one voice. The Normans readily accepted the will of the English, the bishop of Coutances[64] having addressed them and sought their decision. But the armed and mounted guards outside who had been set about the monastery, hearing the great shout in a foreign tongue, took it for some treachery and fired the neighbouring houses. Thus an archbishop loved equally for his holy life and his unblemished reputation consecrated the elected king, placed the royal diadem upon his head, and set him upon the regal throne, in the assenting presence of many bishops and abbots, in the church of St Peter the Apostle which rejoiced to hold the tomb of king Edward, on the holy feast of the Nativity in the year of the Incarnation 1066. He had refused to be consecrated by Stigand, whom he knew to be rightly condemned by papal anathema. The insignia of regality became him no less than

[61] Edwin earl of Mercia, and Morcar earl of Northumbria.
[62] This is presumably the foundation of the royal castle which subsequently becomes the Tower of London.
[63] Ealdred. The place is the new church of Westminster Abbey.
[64] Geoffrey de Montbray.

his virtues qualified him to rule. His sons and his grandsons will reign over the English land of which he has taken possession by hereditary right confirmed by the oaths of the English as well as by right of war. He is crowned by the consent of the English and not least by the will of their magnates. And if anyone wishes to know the blood relationship, it is to be noted what close links there are between king Edward and the son of duke Robert, whose aunt was Emma, sister of Richard II, daughter of Richard I, and mother of Edward . . .

53 *(31–2) pp. 222–30* Two long sections relate the wealth of England and the rich gifts which the Conqueror made therefrom to his followers but more to poor monasteries in many regions. To the church of St Peter and the Pope he sent great quantities of gold and silver and –

ornaments which Byzantium herself would have held as precious. Also the famous banner of Harold, worked with the image of a fighting man in pure gold, rendering by this booty a *quid pro quo* for the gift which the apostolic beneficence had sent to him[65] . . . In a thousand churches of France, Aquitaine, Burgundy, the Auvergne and other regions the memory of king William will be perpetually celebrated.

The finest gifts, however, were sent to his beloved Normandy, where the whole duchy rejoiced at the elevation of their prince to the kingship. Even England will come to love this prince whose warrior race has triumphed in Apulia and Sicily, and against Constantinople and Babylon. William had not sought the death of Harold but had wished to increase his power and had betrothed his daughter to him.[66] In the event he had released England from a tyrant.

54 *(33) pp. 230–6* The author praises William's rule after his coronation, his clemency, the good laws he issued, the justice he dispensed, above all the peace he maintained, including the discipline exacted from the occupying forces, his knights being prohibited illicit relationships with native ladies and even from drinking much in taverns. His taxes were carefully regulated.

p. 234 . . . He utterly disapproved of the pontificate of Stigand, which he knew to be uncanonical; but he thought it better to await a formal papal sentence than to depose him too hastily. There were other reasons also why he temporized and treated honourably one whose authority among the English was great. . . .

55 *(34–5) pp. 236–8* He left London[67] and stayed for some days in a nearby place called Barking while certain fortifications were completed in the city[68] to contain the restlessness of its vast and savage population. For he saw it was of the first importance to hold down the Londoners. It was there that Edwin and Morcar, highest in degree perhaps of all the

[65] *I.e.* the papal banner.

[66] *I.e.* in 1064. This is perhaps a reference to Agatha, said to have been betrothed successively to Harold of England and Alphonse of Leon, See D.C. Douglas, *William the Conqueror*, London, 1964, pp. 393–5; M. Chibnall, *Ecclesiastical History of Orderic Vitalis*, ii, 136, n. 1.

[67] *I.e.* soon after his coronation. The season is still the winter of 1066–7.

[68] *I.e.* the future Tower of London (cf. above) and doubtless the other two early Norman castles in London, Montfichet and Baynard's Castle.

English by their birth and power, sons of the renowned Aelfgar, came in to submit to him. They besought his pardon for anything they might have done against him, and placed themselves and all their possessions in his mercy. Many other nobles and magnates did the same, amongst them earl Copsi[69] . . . The king graciously accepted the oaths which they offered him, generously bestowed his favour upon them, restored to them all their possessions, and held them in great honour.

Proceeding thence, he came to divers parts of the kingdom, arranging everything to his convenience and that of the inhabitants. Wherever he went all laid down their arms. There was no resistance, but everywhere men submitted to him or sought his peace . . . The aethling [Edgar] himself, whom after the fall of Harold the English had thought to make king, he endowed with wide lands and took into the closest circle of his affection because he was of the race of king Edward, and also so that the boy in his youth should not too bitterly regret the loss of the honour to which he had once been chosen. Many English received by his liberal gift more than they had ever received from their fathers or their former lords. He placed capable castellans (*custodes*) with ample forces of horse and foot in his castles (*castella*), men brought over from France in whose loyalty no less than competence he could trust. He gave them rich fiefs (*opulenta beneficia*) in return for which they willingly endured hardship and danger. But to no Frenchman was anything given unjustly taken from an Englishman.

56 *(36–7) pp. 238–42* At *Guenta* (Norwich *or* Winchester[70]) the Conqueror raised a castle (*munitio*) and put it in the custody of William fitz Osbern – 'whom of all his friends he had loved the most since their boyhood together and had raised up high in Normandy' – with a commission to govern all England towards the north in his absence. Dover castle (*castrum*) he committed to his brother Odo, with command of the adjacent south coast –

This Odo, bishop of Bayeux, was known to excel in affairs both ecclesiastical and secular. In the first place, his goodness and prudence is witnessed by the church of Bayeux which with great zeal he set in excellent order and embellished, for though yet young in years he was more mature in capacity than older men.[71] Next, he served all Normandy and added distinction to it. In synods concerned with the affairs of Christ, in councils where secular matters were discussed, he was outstanding both for his discernment and his eloquence. All were agreed that in munificence he had no equal in all France. His love of justice merited no less praise. He never took up arms, nor ever wished to; yet he struck fear in the hearts of warriors. For truly he supported war with invaluable counsel as necessity required, so far as his religion would allow. To the king, whose uterine brother he was and whom he embraced with so great a love that he would not be separated from him even in battle, from whom he both received and expected great honours, he was uniquely and immovably loyal. Normans and Bretons alike willingly served him as an ideal lord. Nor were the English such barbarians that they could not see well enough that this prelate, this governor, was to be feared but also to be revered and esteemed.

[69] Earl of Northumbria.
[70] See Brown, *Normans and Norman Conquest*, p. 186, especially n. 221.
[71] Odo was very young when appointed to the see of Bayeux.

57 *(38) pp. 242–6* The king, thus having arranged for the government of his kingdom, returned to Pevensey – a place whose name is worthy of record since in that part he had first landed. The ships lay ready for the crossing in every particular and, as was entirely fitting, equipped with white sails after the manner of the ancients. . . .

There assembled at Pevensey also a mounted company of English. For he had decided to take with him those of them of whose loyalty or power he was suspicious, archbishop Stigand, the aethling as the kinsman of king Edward, three earls, namely Edwin, Morcar and Waltheof, together with many others of the high nobility. . . . As for those knights (*milites*) who were returning to their own country after serving him faithfully in so great an expedition, he rewarded them liberally at the same port so that they all might rejoice to have shared with him the rich fruits of victory. . . . [Thus] in the month of March [1067] he returned to his native land after a success even greater than our pen can relate.

58 *(39–40) pp. 246–54* In a long passage comparing William the Conqueror to his advantage with Julius Caesar, the author asserts again (p. 250) that William delivered England from the tyranny of Harold, and adds that by taking the throne himself 'one ruler held sway over all those regions which were formerly under as many kings'. He observes further that whereas Caesar limited himself to commanding his troops, rarely himself fighting –

It seemed dishonourable to William, and of little use, in those campaigns in which he destroyed the English, to fulfil the role of a commander if he did not also fulfil the role of a knight (*militis*), as he had been accustomed to do in his other wars.

59 *(41–5) pp. 254–62* This section continues the relation of king William's triumphal visit to Normandy in 1067, begun in **57** above. Though it was still winter and the penitential season of Lent, the whole duchy celebrated as though it were a major festival and the sun shone as though it were summer. William's rich gifts (from his English tribute) to churches are again emphasized –

(42) pp. 256–8 . . . To his abbey at Caen,[72] built at his own expense from the foundations on a vast and splendid scale in honour of the blessed Stephen protomartyr, as noted above, **(39)** he now brought many gifts so precious in material and workmanship as to be cherished to the end of time . . . The women of the English race excel in embroidery and cloth of gold; the men in all kinds of craftsmanship. For this reason the Germans, who are expert in similar arts, are accustomed to dwell among them. The merchants also who voyage to distant lands bring in works of art. . . .

(43) p. 258–60 . . . He found Normandy in good order – For it had been governed excellently by our lady Mathilda, now called queen by all though not yet crowned. Her prudence had been supported by the counsel of experienced men, of whom the most eminent was Roger de Beaumont, son of the illustrious Humphrey, because of his advanced years more able to attend to domestic affairs; military matters he now left to his young son [Robert], of whose bravery in the battle against Harold we have said something above. **(48)** But, truly, if no neighbours dared to invade a land which they knew to

[72] *I.e.* St Stephen's, *alias* the 'Abbaye aux Hommes', consecrated in 1077.

be almost devoid of warriors (*milites*), we may be sure it was primarily due to the king himself whose return they feared.

(44–5) pp. 260–2   He celebrated Easter[73] at the abbey of the Holy Trinity at Fécamp, reverently honouring the Redeemer in the feast of His Resurrection, in the presence of venerable bishops and abbots. He stood humbly in the choir with the religious, and compelled the crowds of knights (*milites*) and people to interrupt their diversions to attend holy office. The powerful count Ralph, stepfather of the French king and many other nobles of France were present at this court.[74] They like the Normans looked with curiosity at the long-haired English. . . . When they saw the apparel of the king and his vassals (*satellites*) woven and worked with gold, they thought anything they had seen before vile. They wondered also at the gold and silver cups whose number and beauty passed all belief. . . .

He spent all that summer and autumn and part of the winter on this side of the sea, devoting all that time to his beloved country.[75]

60   *(46) pp. 262–4*   Meanwhile Odo bishop of Bayeux and William fitz Osbern laudably performed their respective stewardships in the kingdom; sometimes they acted singly and sometimes together. . . . Also the local governors, each placed in a castle (*munitio*), zealously administered their districts. . . . But neither fear nor favour could so subdue the English as to prefer peace and tranquility to rebellions and disorders. . . . They repeatedly sent envoys to the Danes or to anyone else from whom they could hope for help. Moreover, those others who fled into exile either thought they were free of Norman power or plotted to return with foreign aid.

61   *(47–9) pp. 264–70*   The last two complete sections of the work (47–8) contain accounts respectively of the abortive attack upon Dover castle by count Eustace of Boulogne at the invitation of the local English in 1067, and the murder of earl Copsi in the same year. It now ends with an incomplete sentence beginning another section –

(49) p. 270   Some [English] bishops were anxious to serve the king, especially Ealdred archbishop of York. . .

Gilbert Crispin, Vita domini Herluini abbatis Beccensis: The Life of Herluin abbot of Bec

The *Vita Herluini* is one of the most rewarding minor works of the time and place. Indeed, it is minor only in its brevity and in the sense that it is not ostensibly the history of a country, like the Anglo-Saxon Chronicle, nor did its author set out to write the history and deeds of princes, like William of Jumièges or William of Poitiers. It is the biography of Herluin, founder of Bec (now Le Bec Hellouin). It thus becomes the early and earliest

[73] April 8.
[74] Fécamp was a ducal palace as well as an abbey.
[75] William returned to England on 6 December 1067.

history of Bec itself, from its foundation in *c*.1034, through its dramatic and unforeseen expansion, to the days of its greatest prestige in the later eleventh century. It is also, incidentally, the earliest life of Lanfranc, the source, in fact, for much of the later *Vita Lanfranci* (*c*.1140–56) attributed to Miles Crispin. And through Lanfranc and through Bec, both of whom played so large a part therein, we are led to the heart of the Norman ecclesiastical revival of the mid-eleventh century and the Norman reformation of the English Church after 1066. Yet this is not all. Though great matters are there, explicit and implicit, in the *Vita Herluini*, it remains essentially a local history, that is, the history of one man and his foundation, and thus we are brought very close to the grass roots of Normandy in its most formative epoch. Those who know it may almost see again the valley of the Risle in these pages, or imagine the monastic buildings rising to grace it – for alas! all those of Herluin and Lanfranc are gone. There is an immediacy, a sense of direct contact with the past (such as is found elsewhere, perhaps, only in the pages of Orderic Vitalis), as, for example, in the prolonged and precious glimpse of the nature of knighthood and service in the household of a great Norman magnate of the age (count Gilbert of Brionne, ancestor of the Clare – **62**), or the exuberant and lavish celebration of the dedication of one of the great contemporary Norman Romanesque churches, the church of St Mary at Bec, in 1077 (**64**. The same year saw the dedication also of St Stephen's at Caen and bishop Odo's cathedral at Bayeux). Of course there are snags. There is the almost inevitable element of hagiography, though this in fact is devoted more to Bec than to either of the heroes of the work, Herluin and Lanfranc. For the *Vita Herluini* 'was a memorial to the community as much as to the founder, a *liber memorialis* from which those who followed could learn the ethos of Bec in the earliest days'.[1]

Herluin died in 1078, soon after the dedication by the then archbishop Lanfranc. His *Life* was written after 1093 by Gilbert Crispin, at that time abbot of Westminster and a man supremely qualified for the task. The scion of one of the new Norman noble houses (he was Gilbert III), well connected, not least with the lords of Brionne, he had himself been placed at Bec as a young oblate in *c*.1055. He was oblate and monk there for 25 years, thus serving God not only under Herluin but also under Lanfranc and Anselm successively as priors, until the former summoned him (like so many of the Bec *alumni*) to England and to Canterbury in 1080. He was appointed abbot of Westminster in 1085 and died in 1117–18.

Other dates to help frame the Life in its context are, 1034 as the date of Herluin's release by count Gilbert and his first humble foundation; *c*.1042 for the arrival of Lanfranc, who was made prior within three years; 1060 for the foundation of the third and final church, completed in 1073 and dedicated in 1077. Lanfranc was removed to be made abbot of St Stephen's, Caen, in 1063, and was appointed archbishop of Canterbury in 1070. In *c*.1059, Anselm arrived at Bec.

The standard work on Gilbert Crispin remains *Gilbert Crispin Abbot of Westminster*, Cambridge, 1911, by J. Armitage Robinson, who printed the only modern edition of the

---

[1] C. Harper-Bill in *Studies in Church History*, xv, p. 19. Cf. M. Gibson, *Lanfranc of Bec*, pp. 23–5. Both works are cited in full below.

Vita Herluini as an appendix to that book. The standard work on Bec-Hellouin is, of course, the labour of love of le Chanoine André Porée, now happily reprinted, *Histoire de l'Abbaye du Bec*, 2 vols., Evreux, 1901; Brussels, 1980. The most recent discussion of the *Vita Herluini* is by Christopher Harper-Bill, 'Herluin, abbot of Bec, and his biographer', *Studies in Church History*, xv, 1978. Much relevant information will also be found in Margaret Gibson, *Lanfranc of Bec*, Oxford, 1978.

Source: J. Armitage Robinson, *Gilbert Crispin Abbot of Westminster (ut supra)*, pp. 88–110. For the translations which follow I am much indebted to Dr Christopher Harper-Bill and Mrs Diana Webb.

62 *pp. 87–91* His [Herluin's] father was descended from the Danes who had first occupied Normandy; his mother was closely related to the dukes of Flanders; he was called Ansgot, she Heloise. Gilbert count of Brionne, a grandson of Richard I, duke of Normandy, through his son count Godfrey, had charge of his upbringing, and treated him with the utmost favour among all the nobles (*primates*) of his court. He had great aptitude for the pursuit of arms and devoted himself to it with no less enthusiasm. All the chief families of Normandy held him in high esteem, and extolled his knightly prowess and physical accomplishments. He disregarded anything dishonourable, but concentrated all his efforts upon those honourable affairs which are highly valued at courts. He was eager to be outstanding among his fellow knights both in the household and in the field, and thus he had not only won singular favour with his lord, but had acquired a reputation and a ready welcome with Robert, duke of the whole country,[2] and with the lords of other regions. . . .

Herluin, thus happily placed, was more than 37 years old when at long last his mind began to be inflamed by the divine love, so that his love of the world grew lukewarm and with the passing days gradually cooled, as he turned the eyes of his heart from eternal things on to himself. He went frequently to church, prayed with devotion and often prostrated himself in tears. Forgetful of all trivialities, he was seen less frequently in court. He was held there only by his efforts to obtain his lands as well as himself for God, and this he finally achieved, extracting them from his lord by dint of great perseverance. Often he would spend the night praying in churches and in the morning be the first to arrive at his lord's table. As he did not want to practice abstinence amongst his companions, he absented himself on various contrived pretexts, often passing the whole day in fasting. He did not devote himself as before to arms or physical pursuits, in itself sufficient indication of the conflict in his mind, which he had hitherto been careful to conceal. To relinquish knighthood (*militia*) and all other worldly affairs was the sum of his desire. . . . Thus renouncing arms, dressed in cheap clothing, his beard and hair uncut, Herluin long remained among the other members of the household with that one intention of which we have spoken – he was the Israelite about to flee from Egypt. . . . Still he sat gladly beside his lord at table and, surrounded by all kinds of dishes and his roistering companions, he ate coarse bread and drank water. They all laughed at him and thought that all he did was madness. His lord and his followers could do nothing by threats, slights or promises, in all

[2] *I.e.* duke Robert I 'the Magnificent', 1027–35.

their efforts to divert him from his purpose. The man who had once been highly esteemed by all went on missions to other courts mounted on an ass, an object of sorrow or derision to different people for his mode of transport and for the humility of his service, for he was afraid of becoming entangled in the world, nor wished any longer to ride horses, serving on the back of an ass the lord from whom he was unwilling to depart without permission. And as he was not at all ashamed to humble himself for the sake of God, so God was not ashamed of him and rendered unto him even upon earth a still greater reward. . . .

At length [the count] granted to his beloved vassal (*cliens*) the desired release of himself and of all his possessions.

63 *Pp. 95–8* There arose at this time in Italy[3] a man whom the whole Latin world, restored by him to its ancient state of learning, acknowledged with due love and honour as master: his name was Lanfranc. . . . Having left his own country with several scholars of high renown, he arrived in Normandy. However, this wisest of men came to realize that to win fame among mortals is vanity, and because all is worthless save only He who is eternal and those who seek after Him, he applied his heart and mind to gaining His love. So therefore he seized upon the most perfect policy for pleasing God which he could find in books, in order that, giving up all things and even abandoning his own free will, he might follow Him who said, 'If any man will come after Me, let him deny himself and take up his cross and follow Me.'[4] And because he desired to humble himself in proportion to the great reputation which he once had, he sought out a place where there would be no learned man to treat him with honour and reverence. So he came to Bec, which was considered to be the poorest and most humble of all religious houses. It chanced that the abbot at the time of his arrival was working with his own hands constructing an oven, and, moved by respect and love for his humility of spirit and dignity of speech, Lanfranc became a monk in that place.

. . . Thus for three years he lived in solitude away from the world of men. He rejoiced that he was unknown there, ignored by all except the few with whom he sometimes talked. Then rumour betrayed him and spread far and wide, and the outstanding fame of the man soon made Bec and abbot Herluin famous throughout the world. There flocked thither clerks, the sons of princes, and the most renowned masters of the schools of Latin Christendom; secular magnates and many men of high nobility for love of him made numerous grants of land to the church; and Bec became endowed with ornaments and possessions from noble and distinguished benefactors. . . .

Lanfranc was taken up by William duke of Normandy as his chief councillor in the affairs of the entire duchy. It is worth recording how, when one day dark clouds suddenly obscured the light of his favour, God swiftly and unexpectedly restored a clear sky. Violently embittered towards him by the accusations of certain informers, the duke gave orders that he should be banished both from the monastery and the country. . . . Lamentation accompanied the departure of him who had been the entire joy and consolation of

[3] Lanfranc came from Pavia in north Italy.
[4] Matthew, 16: 24.

the brethren. Because there was nothing better, a horse lame in one leg was given him, and one servant. . . . But almost at once as he departed, his horse bending its head to the ground with every step, he met the duke coming in the opposite direction, and saluted his lord. He knew he was innocent and, if given the chance to speak, did not despair of the outcome. The duke, concerned for his dignity, at first averted his gaze, but soon, by the intervention of divine clemency, looked at him sympathetically, and with a friendly nod motioned him to speak. Then Lanfranc uttered a becoming jest: 'At your command I am leaving your province on foot, thanks to this useless quadruped: I pray you, give me a better horse that I may obey you more effectively'. . . . The duke laughed: Lanfranc stated his case with his accustomed eloquence; and was soon received back into full favour. . . .

64 *Pp. 98–9, 104–8* Herluin is reluctantly persuaded by Lanfranc to build a new and larger church[5] and monastery to accommodate Bec's growing numbers:

Convinced at last, with assured hope in the grace of God, and trusting absolutely in the help of his adviser [Lanfranc] whose efforts on his behalf always prospered, he began work on a new monastery and offices on a much more salubrious site, an extensive and impressive complex whose splendour was not rivalled by many richer abbeys. In undertaking this work he was relying not so much upon his own resources, which were modest, as upon his complete trust in God, which supplied everything that was needed so that from the day when the foundations were first laid to the putting in place of the last stone neither material nor money was ever wanting. Those who were in charge of the finances bear witness that often they did not have enough to pay the workmen at the end of the week and from some source God provided sufficient money when it was due.

After three years, when only the church remained to be completed, the venerable Lanfranc who was responsible for the work's having been begun, was constrained by the lord and magnates of Normandy to become abbot of Caen.[6] For a while the work in hand was delayed, but whenever necessary his advice and active assistance was always at hand. . . .

Meanwhile the oft mentioned William duke of the Normans acquired by inheritance the English kingdom, and imposed his right by force of arms upon that rebellious realm according to his will. Then he turned his attention to the reformation of the [English] Church. To this task he appointed the aforesaid doctor [Lanfranc][7]. . . .

The new church was not yet consecrated, and Herluin prayed earnestly to God that he might see this done by him with whose advice it had been begun and by whose help it had been completed. And God who had shown his favour to him in other matters granted that

---

[5] This is the third and final church of Bec, begun *c.*1060, finished in 1073, and consecrated in 1077 (see below). It was later much rebuilt and enlarged, so that none of the remains now visible are of this date.

[6] *I.e.* of St Stephen's, the Conqueror's own foundation. Lanfranc was appointed the first abbot in 1063.

[7] Lanfranc was appointed archbishop of Canterbury in 1070.

this prayer might come to pass. . . . For the apostle of the island race [*i.e.* Lanfranc] came on both secular and ecclesiastical business to the court of the most eminent king of the English, William, when he was resident in his Norman duchy.

But when he [Lanfranc] first came to the said monastery he behaved towards the brethren with the utmost humility, as it is written 'In as much as thou art mighty, humble thyself in all things'.[8] Drawing near to exchange kisses with the abbot now bowed down with years, this most eminent archbishop sought to prostrate himself at his feet . . . . the archbishop sat in the cloister just like any of them; he called to himself individually the old, the young and the oblates, and exorted them with suitable encouragement. At table the brethren sat on the right and the left of the archbishop and were constrained to partake with him from the common cup and bowl . . .

Under pressure from them all to consecrate their church, and ready to give way to their wishes, he sought and obtained their leave to refer the question to the [king's] court. For he knew that so important a matter must depend upon the royal edict and counsel. . . .

So the day approached which had been anticipated with such longing by so many for so long. High-ranking persons and the foremost ecclesiastical dignitaries came from far-off regions; a large concourse was expected and eagerly received; huge expenses were incurred in the reception of all manner of men.

So on 23 October 1077 the reverend Lanfranc, primate of the Church of all the island races, came to celebrate the consecration of that church which by God's grace he had begun and in the laying of whose foundation he had set the second stone with his own hands. There were assembled all the bishops and abbots of Normandy and other men of religion, together with the magnates of the kingdom, though the king himself could not be present because of other business. Queen Mathilda would have willingly been present had she not been detained by royal affairs, but she was there in spirit by the liberal bestowal of her gifts. . . . There were present also the foremost magnates and many other nobles of the kingdom of France, and clerks and monks of all the neighbouring provinces. . . . The dedication[9] was carried out with the most joyful ceremony and the festive joy of all, the very air was sweet and a radiant day smiled upon the celebration of men. The choir was scarcely audible because of the tumult of those thronging about them. . . . When the procession was over the bishops could scarcely enter through the press. The crush of people following broke down all the doors, though no one was injured, and as many crowded in as the great church could hold. . . . The ceremony ended with even greater joyfulness than that with which it had begun; and so to refreshment. There was no shortage of dishes from morning until into the night for the successive crowds of brethren who had come to the feast. . . .

On the third day the aforesaid archbishop of Canterbury, mindful of his worldly cares, sought leave from all the brethren to depart. Who of all those who had met with so much magnanimous kindness from him could view his departure with dry eyes? All wept and the young novices could not be consoled. He deliberately hastened his departure so that

[8] Ecclus. iii, 20.
[9] To Our Lady.

they might contain their sorrow at least after he had gone. Abbot Herluin, who loved him above all mortals and was loved by him in return, accompanied for two miles his departing friend, whom in this life he would never see again. What bitterness of heart, what tears although they tried to fight them back, at that final farewell and ultimate departure. After his return he sat alone in his chamber with the one brother who was closest to him of all the community, and gave way to his flowing tears, lifting up his hands to Heaven and uttering these words: 'Lord, now lettest Thou Thy servant depart in peace, for mine eyes have seen what I dearly wished to see before I died and that for which I continuously prayed. Thou hast fulfilled my desire. Now will Thy servant joyfully come to Thee at whatever hour Thou choosest.' Thus he ceased speaking but could not stop his tears, until the brother who was with him could bear it no longer and tried to talk of other things.

Pp. 109–10 Herluin died in the night of Sunday 26 August 1078, and his biography ends with the description of his funeral.

De obitu Willelmi – The death of William, duke of the Normans and king of the English, who brought peace to Holy Church

This short piece is found only in two manuscripts,[1] both of a later edition of William of Jumièges' *Gesta Normannorum Ducum*. The editor of William of Jumièges, Jean Marx, thought that it was written soon after the death of the king by an anonymous monk of St Stephen's at Caen (*i.e.* the Conqueror's own foundation) and was thus of considerable value. Later scholars noted that the description of the Conqueror was derived from Einhard's *Life of Charlemagne* (*Vita Karoli Magni*)[2], and most recently L.J. Engels[3] has shown in a detailed study that the whole is derivative, comprising selected passages almost verbatim from the so-called Astronomers' *Life of Louis the Pious* (*Vita Hludowici imperatoris*) for the death of the king, and from Einhard for the description of him (*i.e.* from the paragraph beginning 'Of all those who ruled in his time'[4] to the end, excluding the epitaph. The epitaph itself contains mistakes). Engels also suggests that the work was written in England in the first decades of the twelfth century. Nevertheless, the author, whoever he was and wherever he wrote, shows himself to be well informed, carefully selects the passages from his sources which suited his purpose (the *Life of Louis the Pious*, thus, was not a well known work), and makes not only the necessary alterations of name and time and place but also such other alterations as are necessary to fit the facts of 1087. Thus the late king's voice is altered from the *clara* (clear or loud) of Einhard to *rauca*

---

[1] B1 and B2 in Marx. See also Elizabeth van Houts in *Battle*, iii, 1980, pp. 108–9.
[2] H.R. Loyn, *The Norman Conquest*, London, 1965, p. 193; F. Barlow, *William I and the Norman Conquest*, London, 1965, pp. 177–8.
[3] In *Mélanges Christine Mohrmann, nouveau receuil offert par ses anciens élèves*, Utrecht-Anvers, 1973, pp. 209–55.
[4] Below, p. 49.

(harsh). Plagiarism itself, of course, was no literary sin in this period, and the question of the resulting value of the *De Obitu Willelmi* is best summed up in the words of the late John Le Patourel: 'It is a nice point to decide how much credence should be given to a text which, though it uses the words and phrases of another and lifts whole passages verbatim, yet makes the changes and omissions necessary for its own purpose.'[5]

Source: *Guillaume de Jumièges, Gesta Normannorum Ducum*, ed. J. Marx, Société de l'histoire de Normandie, Rouen-Paris, 1914, pp. 145–9; revised text by L.J. Engels, *op. cit.*,[6] pp. 223–30.

65   In the year of our Lord's Incarnation 1087, king William of most pious memory, as he was returning from the overthrow or burning of Mantes, began to be afflicted with nausea and his stomach to reject food and drink. He was seized and shaken by repeated retchings and sobs and became increasingly weaker. He realized it was therefore necessary to order some accommodation to be prepared for him at the church of St Gervase, which is situated in the suburb of the city of Rouen, and there, his strength gone, he took to his bed. Thenceforward who can gauge what concern was uttered for the state of the Church or what lamentation for its impending affliction, or who can say what rivers of tears flowed to hasten the divine mercy. He did not grieve at his approaching death but lamented the future which he foresaw, asserting that after his death disaster would fall upon the Norman homeland, as afterwards proved to be the case. Then there arrived for his comfort venerable bishops, and many other servants of God, amongst whom were William, archbishop of the aforesaid city, Gilbert, bishop of Lisieux, John the Doctor (*Medicus*) and Gerard the Chancellor, and also Robert, count of Mortain, brother of the king, whom he trusted in all things as befitted their close kinship. Then he commanded this same respected brother Robert to summon the ministers of his chamber to come before him, and he ordered them to list item by item the royal treasures of his household, that is to say crowns, arms, utensils, books and ecclesiastical vestments. And as he thought fit, he decreed what was to be given to churches, to the poor, and, lastly, to his sons. And he allowed William his son to have the crown, sword and sceptre encircled with gold and jewels. Whereupon the venerable archbishop William and the others who were present were afraid lest he should remain implacable towards his eldest son Robert, for they knew that a wound frequently opened or cauterized causes sharper pain to the wounded. Trusting therefore in the indomitable forbearance which he invariably showed, they sought gently to sway his mind through archbishop William whose advise he valued. At first the king showed the bitterness of his feelings. Pondering a little while, and collecting his waning strength, he seemed to be counting the number and degree of the injuries he had received from him. Then he spoke: 'Because', he said, 'he has no wish to come and scorns to come, I must now do my part: as you and God are my witnesses, I forgive him all the injuries he has done me, and I give him all the duchy of Normandy (which, by the testimony of God and the magnates of the palace he had formerly conferred upon

[5] J. Le Patourel, *The Norman Empire*, Oxford, 1976, p. 183, n. 1.
[6] Above, n. 3.

him).[1] It will be for you to sway him, for he, taking advantage of my repeated forgiveness of his acts, has brought his father's grey hairs in sorrow to the grave, and in so doing has disregarded the commandments and admonishments of God our Father.' Having thus spoken, he asked for blessing and unction, and by the office and hand of the archbishop Holy Communion was given to him according to custom. In this way he gained the end of his mortal life, and went happily, as we believe, to his rest. Thus he died on the tenth day of September,[2] in the fifty-ninth year of his life, and having reigned over England for 22 years.

Of all those who ruled in his time this king was the most prudent and pre-eminent in greatness of spirit. He would never refuse those things which had to be undertaken or accomplished on account of the labour or the danger involved, and he was so experienced in accepting and submitting to the reality of every truth that he would neither yield in adversity nor be misled by the false blandishments of good fortune.[3] In person he was well built and strong, commanding in stature yet not ungainly, moderate in food and drink, more especially the latter; indeed he abhorred drunkeness in any man, more yet in himself and in his household. He was so sparing in wine and every drink that he rarely took more than three draughts after dinner. He was fluent and eloquent in his speech, and could express things with the utmost clarity as necessary, in a voice perhaps harsh[4] but which nevertheless was modulated to suit the occasion. He was diligent in the Christian religion, in which he had been steeped from birth, and when he was in good health assiduously attended church at morning and evening and at Mass. Finally it was decided by all that he could not be more appropriately buried than in the church which he had built at his own expense at Caen for the love and honour of God and St Stephen the proto-martyr, and as he had previously arranged. In that church he was therefore buried and a monument of silver gilt with gold erected above his tomb by his son William, who succeeded him in the English kingdom.

The king's Epitaph. This inscription is written on the tomb in letters of gold.[5]

> Who governed the proud Normans, by his firm hand
> Constrained the Bretons vanquished by his arms;
> The warriors of Maine he curbed by valour,
> Kept in obedience to his rule and right.
> The great king lies here in this little urn,
> So small a house serves for a mighty lord.

[1] The person and tense of *largitus fuerat* in the Latin makes it clear that the words in parenthesis are not the direct speech of the dying king but an inserted observation of the author. The whole passage beginning 'and I give him all the duchy of Normandy' and ending with the parenthesis is not taken from the *Life of Louis the Pious*.

[2] The correct date is 9 September.

[3] The text as emended by Engels at this point (*op. cit.*, p. 228, 11. 126–7) makes this rendering easier to sustain.

[4] The author substitutes *rauca* (harsh) for Einhard's *clara* (clear or loud).

[5] Cf. Orderic Vitalis, *Ecclesiastical History*, ed. M. Chibnall, iv, 110–12, who says the verses were composed by Thomas, archbishop of York.

> The twenty-third day of Scorpio was his birth
> He died on the sixteenth day of Virgo's sign.[6]

Old English

The principal literary and narrative sources for the Norman Conquest on the English side are the various versions of the Anglo-Saxon Chronicle, 'Florence' of Worcester, and the *Vita Edwardi Regis* or *Life of King Edward*. Each is discussed and extracted below. In addition a translation of 'The Song of Maldon' is given especially for the light it throws on Old English military tactics and organization.

The Anglo-Saxon Chronicle and 'Florence' of Worcester

The first thing to say about the Anglo-Saxon Chronicle is that it is not one source but several. Thus Stenton – 'The fundamental authority for Old English history is the series of annalistic compilations known collectively as the *Anglo-Saxon Chronicle*'.[1] Of the common stock of annals distributed to various religious houses by king Alfred, and covering English history from Julius Caesar up to his own day (*c*.892), some remained barren but others grew and flourished to become in the fulness of time, in spite of some common material, effectively independent sources. Eight manuscripts in all have survived until the present day, of which A, B, C, D and E (to use the common labels) are the most important,[2] each of them becoming a distinct version. For the eleventh century and the period covered by this volume those five are reduced in practice to three, for B (made up in the monastery of Abingdon) ends in 977, and A (compiled at Christ Church, Canterbury, after 1101, and before that, at Winchester), though it continues down to 1070, has for our period so many serious gaps in it as to be of little use, and only one extract from it is printed below.[3]

We are left, thus, with C, D and E. C is known to have been compiled at Abingdon and the surviving manuscript is written in a hand or hands of the mid-eleventh century. It has an inconvenient gap between 1056 and 1065, and ends altogether in 1066, towards the end

---

[6] This rendering of the last two lines of very obscure Latin, differing from the version given by Orderic, is very dependent on the scholarly notes of Marx (*op. cit.*, p. 148 n. 1) and Chibnall (*op. cit.*, iv, 112 n. 1). If correct it suggests a date for the birth of William in mid-November (1027) See D.C. Douglas, *William the Conqueror*, 1964, p. 380) and gives 10 September (1087) for his death. See however, Engels, *op. cit.*, pp. 248–9.

[1] *Anglo-Saxon England*, 2nd. ed., p. 679 (Bibliography)
[2] F is a bilingual (English and Latin) version of the original of E; G (sometimes called W) is a copy of the earlier part of A; and H is a mere fragment.
[3] **99**, for 1070.

of its account of the Battle of Stamford Bridge. D and E are very closely related down to 1031, and until then represent a northern recension of the Chronicle probably compiled at York and no longer itself extant. After 1031, D continues to be a northern compilation, presumably York, though it shows also a particular interest in, and knowledge of, the affairs of Worcester and the west midlands – the two sees of York and Worcester being, of course, themselves closely related at that time, with often a common bishop. D ends in 1079. E, however, after 1031, moved to the abbey of St Augustine's at Canterbury, where it remained until 1121, when a copy was sent to Peterborough to help replace the loss of books there in a disastrous fire. This manuscript continued to be made up at Peterborough until 1154 as well as receiving interpolations relating to Peterborough in the annals of its earlier years. It is this version of E, *i.e.* the so-called Peterborough Chronicle, which survives, and is far and away the longest-lived of all branches of the Anglo-Saxon Chronicle.

The advantages to the historian of having several distinct versions of the Chronicle are, of course, considerable, for each may give information not to be found in another. Nor is such variety only geographical, though such differences may well matter in a kingdom far from truly united before 1066. We may also be given our late Old English political history in, so to speak, three dimensions; for in what we see as the great issues of the time, C (from Abingdon) is hostile to the house of Godwine, E (from Canterbury in this period) has a strong bias in favour, and D (from the north) is largely neutral.

The Anglo-Saxon Chronicle in all its versions was compiled simply as a series of annals – 'In this year such and such a thing happened' – which as a form of literary composition was both primitive and somewhat old-fashioned by the mid-eleventh century. This in turn may be thought characteristic of the generally old-fashioned culture of England on the eve of the Norman Conquest, where also the writing of history was in any case at a low ebb.[4] The Chronicle is certainly characteristic of Old English culture in being written in the vernacular, not Latin. While the Old English vernacular is commonly and justifiably praised for its precocious development, it was not yet sufficiently developed, it would seem, for a sustained, supple and sophisticated prose; which accounts for a naivety of style which is echoed in any translation. The value of the Chronicle as a source for the history of pre-Conquest England in the eleventh century the user can decide for himself. It may be the best source that we have; but it scarcely seems always in all its versions well informed, it can at the least be enigmatic (as with the D version's mysterious remarks about the death of the aethling Edward in 1057, **91**), and its silences and prevarications, whether from ignorance or discretion, can be profound (as when no single version gives any annal for 1064).

The *Chronicon ex Chronicis* or composite chronicle which goes under the name of Florence of Worcester, like the work of William of Malmesbury, Eadmer and others, belongs to that distinguished school of Anglo-Norman history of the earlier twelfth century, itself produced in reaction to the cataclysmic events of 1066 and after.[5] It has been called 'the most learned of all contemporary attempts to put the facts of English history

[4] Cf. M. Brett, in *The Writing of History in the Middle Ages* (cited below) p. 101.
[5] For which see especially R.W. Southern in *TRHS* (5), 23, 1973, pp. 246–56.

into a universal chronology',[6] for it was based upon the world history of one Marianus Scotus (d. *c.*1082–3) into which its compiler inserted and integrated notices of English history carefully derived from all the best sources he could find. The work was begun at Worcester on the order of bishop Wulfstan II (d. 1095) and continued as a contemporary history down to *c.*1140. It now seems very likely that its compiler was not the monk Florence (d. 1118) to whom it has traditionally been attributed, but, as Orderic Vitalis implies (**140**), the monk John of Worcester, who has hitherto been regarded as the mere continuator of Florence.[7] Whoever he may have been, it is quite clear that the compiler derived his English history for our period principally from the Anglo-Saxon Chronicle. His version, albeit in Latin, is usually closest to D, yet contains additional material not in D or any other extant manuscript. Since his historical method was to copy almost verbatim the relevant passages he selected from his sources, it looks very much as though John or Florence used a version of the Chronicle now lost,[8] and so preserved much of it for us. This in turn is generally regarded as the chief importance of the text to the historian of the Conquest.

The *Chronicon ex Chronicis* is much in need of the new and critical edition now being prepared by Dr P. McGurk from the preliminary work of the late Professor R.R. Darlington, and that will no doubt make plainer much that remains obscure in an important history hitherto editorially neglected. Meanwhile the fullest commentaries on the text of 'Florence' of Worcester are currently M. Brett, 'John of Worcester and his contemporaries', in *The Writing of History in the Middle Ages. Essays presented to Richard William Southern*, Oxford, 1981; and R.R. Darlington and Patrick McGurk, 'The *Chronicon ex Chronicis* of "Florence" of Worcester and its use of sources for English history before 1066', in *Anglo-Norman Studies, Proceedings of the Battle Conference*, v. 1982. In the much more extensive literature devoted to the Anglo-Saxon Chronicle, the most convenient discussions are those of F.M. Stenton, *Anglo-Saxon England* (2nd ed.) pp. 679ff (Bibliography), and Dorothy Whitelock's Introduction to *The Anglo-Saxon Chronicle. A Revised Translation*, ed. D. Whitelock, D.C. Douglas, S.I. Tucker, London 1961, 1965. For the earliest history of the Chronicle, however, reference must also be made to R.H.C. Davis, 'Alfred the Great: Propaganda and Truth', *History*, lvi, 1971.

The extracts which follow have been drawn from all four versions of the Anglo-Saxon Chronicle relating to the period. Each has been chosen from the version which appeared most informative or convenient to the purpose of this volume, and collated with other versions when necessary. Additional information supplied by 'Florence' of Worcester has been inserted in parenthesis, or on some occasions printed separately under the year concerned. The vernacular text of the Chronicle is conveniently found, with extensive notes, commentary and glossary, in C. Plummer, *Two of the Saxon Chronicles Parallel*, 2 vols.,

---

[6] *Ibid.*, p. 250.
[7] See especially R.R. Darlington in his *Vita Wulfstani*, R.H.S. Camden 3rd. Series xl (1928), p. xvii; B. Brett, *op. cit.*, pp. 104, 110. For Orderic, see *Ecclesiastical History*, ed. Chibnall, ii, 186–8.
[8] Presumably a Worcester version – which would confirm that D is indeed a northern version in spite of its Worcester interests.

Oxford, 1892, 1952. The translation used here is that of Dorothy Whitelock (below), with the occasional alteration of a word in accordance with recent scholarship, or of punctuation and the spelling of proper names in conformity with the rest of the volume.

Sources: *The Anglo-Saxon Chronicle. A Revised Translation*, ed. and trans. D. Whitelock, D.C. Douglas, S.I. Tucker, London, 1961, 1965; B. Thorpe, *Florentii Wigornensis Monachi Chronicon ex Chronicis*, London, 1848–9.

66 1002 C (D, E)   In this year the king [Ethelred] and his councillors determined that tribute should be paid to the fleet[1] and peace made with them on condition that they should cease their evil-doing. . . . And they then accepted that, and 24,000 pounds were paid to them. . . . And then in the spring the queen, Richard's daughter, came to this land. . . . (*F.W.*, i, 156 – In the same year king Ethelred married Emma, in English called Aelfgifu, daughter of Richard I duke of the Normans. . . .)

67 1003 C (D, E)   In this year Exeter was stormed on account of the French *ceorl* Hugh, whom the queen had appointed as her reeve, and the Danish army then destroyed the borough completely and seized much booty there. . . . (*F.W.*, i, 156 – In this year Swein king of the Danes, through the evil counsel, negligence and treachery of the Norman count Hugh, whom queen Emma had put in charge of Devon, broke into Exeter and pillaged, destroying the city wall from the east gate to the west gate and withdrawing to his ships with immense loot.)

68 1011 C (D, E)   In this year the king and his councillors sent to the army[1] and asked for peace, and promised them tribute and provisions on condition that they should cease their ravaging. They had then overrun: (i) East Anglia, (ii) Essex, (iii) Middlesex, (iv) Oxfordshire, (v) Cambridgeshire, (vi) Hertfordshire, (vii) Buckinghamshire, (viii) Bedfordshire, (ix) half Huntingdonshire, (x) much of Northamptonshire, and south of the Thames all Kent, Sussex, Hastings,[2] Surrey, Berkshire, Hampshire, and much of Wiltshire. All those disasters befell us through bad policy, in that they were never offered tribute in time nor fought against; but when they had done most to our injury, peace and truce were made with them; and for all this truce and tribute they journeyed none the less in bands everywhere, and harried our wretched people, and plundered and killed them. . . .

An account of the capture by the Danes of Canterbury and archbishop Aefheah follows, and, under 1012, of the subsequent martyrdom of the archbishop on 19 April. (*F.W.*, i, 164–5 gives more details and atrocities.)

69 1013 C (D, E)   In the year after the archbishop was martyred, the king appointed bishop Lifing to the archbishopric of Canterbury. And in this same year, before the month of August, king Swein came with his fleet up to Sandwich, and then went very quickly

[1] *I.e.* of the Danes.
[2] *I.e.* district of.

round East Anglia into the mouth of the Humber, and so up along the Trent until he reached Gainsborough. And then at once earl Uhtred and all the Northumbrians submitted to him, as did all the people of Lindsey, and then all the people belonging to the district of the Five Boroughs, and quickly afterwards all the Danish settlers north of Watling Street, and hostages were given to him from every shire. When he perceived that all the people had submitted to him, he gave orders that his army should be provisioned and provided with horses, and then he afterwards turned southward (*F.W.*, i, 166 *adds* – against the south Mercians) with his full forces and left the ships and the hostages in charge of his son Cnut. When he had crossed the Watling Street, they did the greatest damage that any army could do. He then turned to Oxford, and the citizens at once submitted and gave hostages; and from there to Winchester, where they did the same. He then turned eastward to London, and many of his host were drowned in the Thames because they did not trouble to find a bridge. When he came to the borough the citizens would not yield, but resisted with full battle, because king Ethelred was inside and Thorkel[3] with him.

Then king Swein turned from there to Wallingford, and so west across the Thames to Bath, where he stayed with his army. Then Aethelmaer ealdorman (*F.W.*, i, 167 – of Devon) came there, and with him the western thegns, and all submitted to Swein, and they gave him hostages. When he had won everything thus, he then turned northward to his ships, and all the nation regarded him as full king. (*F.W.*, i, 167 – if the title of king can be given to one who acted in almost all things as a tyrant). And after that the citizens of London submitted and gave hostages, for they were afraid that he would destroy them. . . .

Then king Ethelred was for a time with the fleet which lay in the Thames, and the queen went across the sea to her brother, Richard, and with her abbot Aelfsige of Peterborough, and the king sent bishop Aelfhun across the sea with the aethlings Edward and Alfred, that he should take care of them. (*F.W.*, i, 167 – . . . king Ethelred hastened to send to Normandy, to her brother Richard II count of the Normans, queen Emma, and her sons Edward and Alfred, with their guardian, Aelfhun bishop of London, and Aelfsige abbot of Peterborough). And the king then went from the fleet to the Isle of Wight at Christmas and spent that festival there; and after the festival went across the sea to Richard [duke of Normandy] and was there with him until the happy event of Swein's death.

70 1014 C (D, E) In this year Swein ended his days at Candlemas, on 3 February, and then all the fleet elected Cnut king. Then all the councillors who were in England, ecclesiastical and lay, determined to send for king Ethelred, and they said that no lord was dearer to them than their natural lord if he would govern them more justly than he did before. Then the king sent his son Edward hither with his messengers, and bade them greet all his people, and said that he would be a gracious lord to them, and reform all the things which they all hated; and all the things that had been said and done against him should be forgiven, on condition that they all unanimously turned to him without

[3] 'the Tall'; a Viking leader who had joined Ethelred.

treachery. And complete friendship was then established with oath and pledge on both sides, and they pronounced every Danish king an outlaw from England for ever. Then during the spring king Ethelred came home to his own people and he was gladly received by them all . . .

71 War for the possession of England, however, continued between Cnut, son of Swein, and Ethelred, with Edmund Ironside, son of Ethelred by his first wife Aelfgifu, playing a leading part in the native resistance to the Danes. In the spring of 1016 Cnut and his ships approached London.

1016 C (D, E) . . . Then it happened that king Ethelred died before the ships arrived. He ended his days on St George's day (23 April), and he had held his kingdom with great toil and difficulties as long as his life lasted. And then after his death, all the councillors who were in London and the citizens chose Edmund as king, and he stoutly defended his kingdom while his life lasted. (*F.W.*, i, 173 [while noticing the election of Edmund by those in London, adds that Cnut was elected at Southampton.[4]] And after his [Ethelred's] death, the bishops, abbots, ealdormen, and all the more important men of England assembled together and unanimously elected Cnut as their lord and king; and coming to him at Southampton and repudiating and renouncing in his presence all the race of king Ethelred, they concluded a peace with him, and swore loyalty to him and he also swore to them that he would be a loyal lord to them, in affairs both of God and man).

[Edmund who had possession of Wessex fought five battles against the Danes, the last of which was] in Essex at the hill which is called Ashingdon . . . There Cnut had the victory and won for himself all the English people . . . and all the nobility of England was there destroyed.

After Ashingdon the two kings[5] met at Alney near Deerhurst in Gloucestershire and divided the kingdom between them, Edmund retaining Wessex and Cnut all England north of the Thames.

Then on St Andrew's day [30 November] king Edmund died (*F.W.*, i, 179 – at London) and his body is buried at Glastonbury along with his grandfather Edgar. . . .

72 1017 C (D,E) In this year king Cnut succeeded to all the kingdom of England and divided it into four, Wessex for himself, East Anglia for Thorkel, Mercia for Eadric, and Northumbria for Eric. . . . And then before I August the king ordered the widow of king Ethelred, Richard's daughter [Emma of Normandy], to be fetched as his wife.

F.W., i, 181, adds that Cnut intended to kill the aethlings Edmund and Edward, the young sons of Edmund Ironside: they went to Hungary where Edmund eventually died and Edward married Agatha, niece of the emperor Henry II,[6] to produce three children, Margaret, Christina and Edgar.

---

[4] F.M. Stenton's interpretation was that the latter election was by 'a more widely representative assembly', *Anglo-Saxon England*, 2nd. edn., p. 385.
[5] Here Cnut as well as Edmund is specifically called 'king' by the Chronicle, though his election previously at Southampton (above) was not there noticed.
[6] For the uncertain identity of Agatha, see F. Barlow, *Edward the Confessor*, London, 1970, p. 216 and n. 2.

73   1020   F. . . And in this year the king went to Ashingdon and had a minster built there of stone and mortar, for the souls of the men who had been slain there, and gave it to a priest of his who was called Stigand. [C and D say that the minster was consecrated in this year.]

74   1031[in error for 1027]   D (E, F)   In this year king Cnut went to Rome. . . .

F.W., i, 185–9, gives more detail of the visit and the text of a letter about it sent by Cnut to England which is also given by William of Malmesbury, *Gesta Regum*, Rolls Series, ed. W. Stubbs, i, 221–4. The translations from the letter printed here are derived from *English Historical Documents*, i, ed. D. Whitelock (London, 1955), pp. 416–18 –

Cnut, king of the English, the Danes and the Norwegians, went with great honour from Denmark to Rome, and bestowed lavish gifts of gold and silver and other precious things upon St Peter, Prince of the Apostles, and obtained from Pope John [XIX] the concession that the English School [at Rome] should be free from all tribute and tax; and both in going and returning he gave liberal alms to the poor, and removed along the way, at great cost to himself, many barriers where at tolls were taken from pilgrims. And there before the tomb of the Apostles he vowed to God the reform of his life and morals. . . .

The text of the letter, said to have been taken by Lifing abbot of Tavistock follows –

Cnut, king of all England, and of Denmark, and of the Norwegians, and of part of the Swedes, sends greeting to Aethelnoth the metropolitan, and to Aelfric archbishop of York, and to all the bishops and leading men, and to the whole race of the English, whether nobles or ceorls. I make known to you that I have recently been to Rome to pray for the remission of my sins and for the safety of the kingdoms and of the peoples which are subjected to my rule. . . . I give most humble thanks to my Almighty God, who has granted me in my lifetime to visit his holy Apostles Peter and Paul, and every sacred place which I could learn of within the city of Rome and outside it, and in person to worship and adore there according to my desire. . . . Be it known to you that there was there a great assembly of nobles at the celebration of Easter, with the lord Pope John and the emperor Conrad, namely all the princes of the nations from Monte Gargarno to the sea nearest to us;[7] and they all both received me with honour and honoured me with precious gifts; and especially was I honoured by the emperor with various gifts and costly presents, with vessels of gold and silver and silk robes and very costly garments. I therefore spoke with the emperor and the lord Pope and the princes who were present, concerning the needs of all the peoples of my whole realm, whether English or Danes, that they might be granted more equitable law and greater security on their way to Rome, and that they should not be hindered by so many barriers on the way and so oppressed by unjust tolls; and the emperor and king Rodulf [of Hungary], who chiefly had dominion over those barriers, consented to my demands; and all the princes confirmed by edicts that my men, whether merchants or others travelling for the sake of prayer, shall go and return from Rome in safety with firm peace and just law, free from hindrances by barriers and tolls.

[7] Probably the North Sea.

Again, I complained before the lord Pope and said that it displeased me greatly that my archbishops were so much oppressed by the immensity of the sums of money which were exacted from them when, according to custom, they came to the apostolic see to receive the *pallium*. It was decided that this should not be done in future. . . . Now, therefore, be it known to you all that I have humbly vowed to Almighty God to amend my life from now on in all things, and to rule justly and faithfully the kingdoms and peoples subject to me and to maintain equal justice in all things; and if hitherto anything contrary to what is right has been done through the intemperance of my youth or through negligence, I intend to repair it all henceforth with the help of God. For this reason I implore and command my councillors . . . that from now on they shall not in any way, either for fear of me or for the favour of any powerful person, consent to any injustice, or suffer it to flourish in any part of my kingdom. I command also all the sheriffs and reeves over my whole kingdom, as they wish to retain my friendship and their own safety, that they employ no unjust force against any man, neither rich nor poor, but that all men, of noble or humble birth, rich or poor, shall have the right to enjoy just law. . . . And therefore I wish to make known to you that, returning by the same way that I went, I am going to Denmark. . . . Then, when peace has been concluded with the nations which are round about us. . . . I intend to come to England as early in the summer as I can get a fleet equipped. . . . Now, therefore, I command and implore all my bishops and reeves of the kingdom, by the faith which you owe to God and to me, that you bring it about before I come to England that all the dues which according to ancient law we owe to God, shall be paid in full, namely plough-alms and tithe of livestock born that same year, and the pence which we owe to St Peter at Rome . . . and in the middle of August tithe of the fruits of the earth, and at the feast of St Martin [11 November] the first fruits of the grain which are called church-scot in English to the church of the parish where each man resides. . . . Farewell.

75 1035 E (F) In this year king Cnut died at Shaftesbury (C, D – on 12 November) and he is buried at Winchester in the Old Minster and he was king over all England for very nearly 20 years. And immediately after his death there was an assembly of all the councillors at Oxford. And earl Leofric [of Mercia] and almost all the thegns north of the Thames and the shipmen (*lithsmen*) in London chose Harold[8] to the regency of all England, for himself and for his brother Harthacnut[9] who was then in Denmark. And earl Godwin [of Wessex] and all the chief men in Wessex opposed it as long as they could, but they could not contrive anything against it. And it was then determined that Aelfgifu [Emma], Harthacnut's mother, should stay in Winchester with the housecarls (*huscarlum*) of her son the king,[10] and they should keep all Wessex in his possession; and earl Godwin was their most loyal man. Some men said about Harold that he was the son of king Cnut and of Aelfgifu [of Northhampton], daughter of ealdorman Aelfhelm, but it seemed

---

[8] 'Harefoot', son of Cnut and Aelfgifu of Northampton.
[9] Son of Cnut and queen Emma.
[10] *I.e.* Hardacnut.

incredible to many men (*F.W.*, i, 190 – many others said he was the son of Aelfgifu and a cobbler); and yet he was full king over all England.

76 1036 C (D) In this year the innocent aethling Alfred, the son of king Ethelred, came into this country, wishing to go to his mother who was in Winchester, but earl Godwin did not allow him, nor did the other men who had great power (D omits specific reference to Godwin – but those who had much power in the land did not permit it), because feeling was veering much towards Harold, although this was not right.

But Godwin [D has 'But he', *i.e.* again suppressing Godwin's name] then stopped him and put him into captivity, and he dispersed his companions and killed some in various ways; some were sold for money, and some were cruelly killed, some were put in fetters, some were blinded, some were mutilated, some were scalped. . . . The aethling still lived. He was threatened with every evil, until it was decided to take him thus in bonds to Ely. As soon as he arrived, he was blinded on the ship, and thus blind was brought to the monks, and he dwelt there as long as he lived. Then he was buried as well befitted him, very honourably, as he deserved, in the south chapel at the west end, full close to the steeple. His soul is with Christ.

F.W., i, 191–2 has significant differences –

The innocent aethlings Alfred and Edward, the sons of Ethelred late king of the English, came to England from Normandy, where they had long been with Richard their uncle, accompanied by a few ships and many Norman knights (*milites*), to confer with their mother then residing at Winchester. Because, however unjustly, they favoured Harold rather than the aethlings many magnates reacted angrily and violently to this, especially, it is said, Godwin. Thus he then seized Alfred, as the latter was hastening on his orders to London to speak with king Harold, and held him in close captivity: he dispersed his companions . . . and put six hundred of them to death at Guildford. . . . As soon as she heard of this, queen Aelfgifu [Emma] sent her son Edward, who had remained with her, back to Normandy with all speed. Then at the command of Godwin and certain others the aethling Alfred was taken in bonds to Ely . . . [was blinded, died and was buried, as in C and D].

77 1037 C (D) In this year Harold (*F.W.*, i, 192 – king of the Mercians and Northumbrians) was chosen as king everywhere, and Harthacnut was deserted because he was too long in Denmark; and then his mother, queen Aelfgifu, was driven out without any mercy to face the raging winter. And then she went across the sea to Bruges, and earl Baldwin[11] received her well there and maintained her there as long as she had need. . . .

78 1040 C (D) In this year king Harold died (E and F – on 17 March, and he was buried at Westminster . . .) Then they sent to Bruges for Harthacnut, thinking that they were acting wisely, and he then came here with 60 ships (*F.W.*, i, 194 – and manned

[11] Baldwin V, count of Flanders.

them with Danish troops) before midsummer, and then imposed a very severe tax . . . namely eight marks to each rowlock (*F.W.*, i, 194 – and twelve to each steersman). And all who had wanted him before were then ill-disposed towards him. And also he did nothing worthy of a king as long as he ruled. He had the dead Harold dug up and thrown into the fen.

F.W., i, 194–5 [amongst other details adds] – At this time he [Harthacnut] was inflamed with a great rage against earl Godwin and Lifing bishop of Worcester because of the murder of his brother Alfred, of which they were accused by Aelfric archbishop of York and others . . . Godwin, to gain the king's benevolence, gave him a splendid trireme manned by 80 superbly equipped warriors . . . In addition he swore, with the support of the magnates and leading thegns of almost all England, that it was not by his counsel or his will that his [Harthacnut's] brother had been blinded but that his [Godwin's] lord, king Harold, had ordered him to do what he did.

79 1041 C (D) . . . And soon in that year there came from beyond the sea (E and F – from France. *F.W.*, i, 196 – from Normandy where he had been living in exile many years) Edward, his [Harthacnut's] brother on the mother's side, the son of king Ethelred, who had been driven from his country many years before – and yet he was sworn in as king; and he thus stayed at his brother's court as long as he lived . . .

80 1042 C (D) In this year Harthacnut died in this way: he was standing at his drink and he suddenly fell to the ground with fearful convulsions, and those who were near caught him, and he spoke no word afterwards. He died on 8 June. And all the people then received Edward as king, as was his natural right. (*F.W.*, i, 196 – Edward was elevated to the kingship at London, chiefly by the exertions of earl Godwin and Lifing bishop of Worcester.)

81 1043 D In this year Edward was consecrated king at Winchester on the first day of Easter [3 April]. And this year . . . the king was advised to ride from Gloucester, together with earl Leofric[12] and earl Godwin and earl Siward[13] and their retinue, to Winchester. And they came unexpectedly upon the lady[14] and deprived her of all the treasures which she owned . . . because she had formerly been very hard to the king, her son, in that she did less for him than he wished both before he became king and afterwards as well. And they allowed her to stay there afterwards.

C . . . And soon after this Stigand[15] was deprived of his bishopric, and all that he owned was placed in the king's control, because he was closest in his mother's counsel, and because it was suspected that she did as he advised.

---

[12] Of Mercia.
[13] Of Northumbria.
[14] Queen Aelfgifu – Emma.
[15] A royal chaplain, recently made bishop of East Anglia (Elmham) that same year.

82 1044   E. . . And Stigand [re-] obtained his bishopric.

83 1045   C [under 1044]   And in the same year king Edward married Edith, daughter of earl Godwin, ten nights before Candlemas.

84 1047   D [under 1048]   This year was the severe winter, and in the course of this year Aelfwine bishop of Winchester died, and bishop Stigand was raised to his see . . .

85 1049   E [under 1046]   In this year was the great synod held at Rheims. Pope Leo [IX] was there and the archbishop of Burgundy, and the archbishop of Besançon, and the archbishop of Trèves, and the archbishop of Rheims, and many others both clerks and lay. And king Edward sent there bishop Dudoc [of Wells], and Wulfric abbot of St Augustine's [Canterbury], and abbot Aelfwine [of Ramsey], so that they might inform the king of whatever was there decided in the interests of Christendom. . . .

86 1051[16]   D [under 1052]   . . . And in the same year king Edward abolished the army-tax (*heregyld*) which king Ethelred had imposed, that is in the thirty-ninth (*F.W.*, i, 204 – thirty-eighth) year after it had been instituted.   . . . In the same year Eustace (*ibid.* – count of Boulogne), who had married king Edward's sister (*ibid.* – called Goda), landed at Dover (*ibid.* – in September). Then his men went foolishly looking for billets and killed a certain man of the town (*porte*), and another of the townsmen [killed] their comrades, so that seven of his comrades were struck down. And great damage was done on either side with horses and with weapons until the people assembled, and then Eustace's men fled to the king at Gloucester, who granted them protection. Then earl Godwin was indignant that such things should happen in his earldom, and he began to gather his people from all over his earldom (*F.W.*, i, 205 – Kent, Sussex and Wessex) and earl Swein his son did the same over all his (*ibid.* – Oxfordshire, Gloucestershire, Herefordshire, Somerset and Berkshire), and Harold his other son over all his (*ibid.*-Essex, East Anglia, Huntingdonshire and Cambridgeshire). And they all assembled in Gloucestershire at Langtree,[17] a great and innumerable force all ready to do battle against the king unless Eustace were surrendered and his men handed over to them, as well as the Frenchmen who were in the castle (*castelle. F.W.*, i, 205–6 – as well as the Normans, and the men of Boulogne, who held the castle on the hill at Dover). This was done a week before the second Feast of St Mary [8 September]. (*F.W.*, i, 205 – after 8 September). King Edward was then residing at Gloucester. He sent for earl Leofric [of Mercia], and to the north for earl Siward [of Northumbria], and asked for their troops. And they came to him at first with a small force, but after they had understood how things were in the south, they sent north throughout all their earldoms and had a great army called out for

---

[16] For this important year the two fullest annals, D and E, are printed here almost completely. 'Florence' of Worcester is closest to D, and his more significant additions and variations are there noted.

[17] The hundred in which Beverstone is situated. Cf. E below.

the help of their lord, and Ralph[18] did the same throughout his earldom [Hereford]; and they all came to Gloucester to the help of the king, though it was late. They were all so much in agreement with the king that they were willing to attack the army of Godwin if the king had wished them to do so. Then some of them (*F.W.*, i, 206 – earl Leofric and some others) thought it would be a great piece of folly if they joined battle, for in the two hosts there was most of what was noblest in England, and they considered that they would be opening a way for our enemies to enter the country and to cause great ruin among ourselves. They advised the exchange of hostages, and they issued summonses for a meeting at London. . . . And earl Godwin and his sons were to come there to defend themselves. Then they came to Southwark, and a great number with them from Wessex, but his force dwindled more and more as time passed. And all the thegns of Harold his son were transferred to the king's pledge (*borhfaeste*), and earl Swein his other son was outlawed. Then it did not suit him to come to defend himself against the king and against the force that was with the king. Then Godwin went away by night and next morning the king held a meeting of his council (*witenagemot*) and he and all the army declared him an outlaw, and all his sons with him. And he went south to Thorney, and so did his wife (*F.W.*, i, 206 – Gytha) and his sons Swein and Tostig with his wife who was a kinswoman of Baldwin of Bruges (*ibid.* – Judith, daughter of Baldwin count of the Flemings), and his son Gyrth. And earl Harold and Leofwine went to Bristol to the ship which earl Swein had equipped and provided for himself. And the king sent bishop Ealdred from London with a force, and they were to intercept him before he got on board, but they could not – or would not. And he went out from the estuary of the Avon, and had such stiff weather that he escaped with difficulty, and he suffered great losses there. He continued his course to Ireland when sailing weather came. And Godwin and those who were with him went from Thorney to Bruges, to Baldwin's country, in one ship with as much treasure for each person as they could stow away. It would have seemed remarkable to everyone in England if anybody had told them it could happen, because he had been exalted so high, even to the point of ruling the king and all England, and his sons were earls and the king's favourites, and his daughter was married to the king. She was brought to Wherwell and they entrusted her to the abbess (*F.W.*, i, 207 – The king, however, because of the anger which he bore to her father, Godwin, repudiated queen Edith, and sent her without honour and with one female attendant to Wherwell and placed her in the custody of the abbess). Then forthwith count William[19] came from overseas with a great force of Frenchmen, and the king received him and as many of his companions as suited him, and let him go again. (*F.W.*, i, 207 – Then the Norman count William came to England with a large following of Normans, and king Edward and his companions received him honourably and sent him back to Normandy with many and rich gifts.) This same year William the priest[20] was given the bishopric of London which had been given to Sparrowhawk.

[18] King Edward's nephew, son of his sister Goda and Drogo, count of the Vexin.
[19] *I.e.* William duke of Normandy.
[20] A Norman.

E [under 1048]   In this year in Lent king Edward appointed Robert of London[21] to be archbishop of Canterbury, and in the course of the same Lent Robert went to Rome for his pallium. And the king gave the bishopric of London to Sparrowhawk, abbot of Abingdon, and he gave the abbey to bishop Rothulf his kinsman. Then the archbishop came from Rome one day before the eve of the Feast of St Peter and occupied his archiepiscopal throne at Christ Church on St Peter's Day [29 June], and soon after he went to the king. The abbot Sparrowhawk met him on the way with the king's writ and seal (*ge write and insegle*) to the effect that he was to be consecrated bishop of London by the archbishop. But the archbishop refused and said the Pope had forbidden it him. Then the abbot went to the archbishop again about it and asked for ordination as bishop, and the archbishop refused him resolutely and said that the Pope had forbidden it him. Then the abbot went back to London and occupied the bishopric that the king had given him; he did this with the king's full permission all that summer and autumn. Then Eustace came from overseas soon after the bishop, and went to the king and told him what he wished, and then went homewards. When he came east to Canterbury, he and his men took refreshment there, and went to Dover. When he was some miles or more on this side of Dover he put on his hauberk (*byrnan*) and all his companions did likewise. So they went to Dover. When they got there, they wished to lodge where it suited their own convenience. Then one of Eustace's men came and wished to stay at the home of a householder against his will, and he wounded the householder, and the householder killed him. Then Eustace got upon his horse and his companions upon theirs, and went to the householder and killed him upon his own hearth, and afterwards they went up towards the borough (*burge*) and killed, within and without, more than 20 men. And the townsmen (*burh men*) killed 19 men on the other side and wounded they did not know how many. And Eustace escaped with a few men and went back to the king and gave him a prejudiced account of how they had fared, and the king grew very angry with the townsmen (*burhware*). And the king sent for earl Godwin and ordered him to carry war into Kent to Dover because Eustace had informed him that it was more the townsmen's (*burhwaru*) fault than his. But it was not so. And the earl would not consent to this expedition because he was reluctant to injure his own province. Then the king sent for all his council (*witan*) and ordered them to come to Gloucester near the later Feast of St Mary [8 September]. The foreigners then had built a castle (*castel*) in Herefordshire in earl Swein's province, and had inflicted every possible injury and insult upon the king's men in those parts. Then earl Godwin and earl Harold came together at Beverstone, and many men with them, intending to go to their royal lord and to all the councillors who were assembled with him, so that they should have the advice and support of the king and of all the councillors as to how they should avenge the insult to the king and all the people. Then the foreigners went beforehand to the king and accused the earls, so that they were not allowed to come into his sight, because they said, they meant to betray the king. Earl Siward and earl Leofric had come there to the king and a large company with them from the north, and earl Godwin and his sons were informed

[21] *I.e.* Robert 'Champart', abbot of Jumièges, formerly appointed bishop of London by the king in 1044.

that the king and the men who were with them meant to take measures against them. And they strengthened themselves firmly in reply, though they were reluctant to have to stand against their royal lord. Then the councillors gave advice that evil doing should cease on both sides, and the king gave the peace of God, and his complete friendship to both sides. Then the king and his councillors decided that there should be a meeting of all the councillors a second time at London at the autumnal equinox, and the king ordered the army (*here*) to be called out both south of the Thames and in the north, all the best of them. Then earl Swein was declared an outlaw and earl Godwin and earl Harold were ordered to come to the meeting as quickly as ever they could make the journey. When they got there they were summoned to the meeting. Then Godwin asked for safe-conduct and hostages, so that he could come to the meeting, and leave it, without being betrayed. Then the king asked for all those thegns that the earls had had, and they were all handed over to them. Then the king sent to them again and ordered them to come with 12 men into the king's council. Then the earl again asked for a safe-conduct and hostages so that he might be allowed to exculpate himself of all the charges that were brought against him. But he was refused hostages and granted five days' safe-conduct to leave the country. Then earl Godwin and earl Swein went to Bosham and there launched their ships and went overseas and sought Baldwin's[22] protection, and stayed there all the winter. Earl Harold went west to Ireland, and was there all the winter under the king's protection.[23] And as soon as this had happened the king put away the lady who was consecrated his queen, and deprived her of all that she owned, land and gold and silver and everything; and entrusted her to his sister at Wherwell. And abbot Sparrowhawk was expelled from the bishopric of London, and William the king's priest was consecrated to it; and Odda[24] was appointed earl over Devon and Somerset and Dorset and Cornwall; and Aelfgar, son of earl Leofric, was granted the earldom which Harold had possessed.[25]

87   1052[26]   **D**   This year on 6 March the lady Aelfgifu [Emma], the widow of king Ethelred and of king Cnut, died (*F.W.*, 1, 207 – at Winchester where she was buried). In the same year Griffith the Welsh king[27] was ravaging in Herefordshire so that he came quite close to Leominster, and people gathered against him, both natives and the Frenchmen (*ibid.* – many Normans) from the castle (*castele: F.W. castellum*) . . .

C, D   In this year forthwith earl Harold (*F.W.*, i, 208 – and his brother Leofwine) came from Ireland with his ships to the mouth of the Severn near the boundary of Somerset and Devon, and there did much damage, and the local people gathered together against him out of Somerset and Devon and he put them to flight and killed more than 30 good

[22] Baldwin V, count of Flanders.
[23] Diarmaid king of Leinster.
[24] The builder of the surviving church of Deerhurst.
[25] East Anglia.
[26] For this second important year C and D have a full and more or less common text (to which 'Florence' comes closest, as noted) which, together with the full annal of E, is printed below as completely as necessary.
[27] Gruffydd ap Llewelyn, king or prince of Gwynedd and Powys.

thegns, apart from other people, and immediately after that he went round Land's End. Then king Edward had 40 small boats manned which lay at Sandwich in order that they might keep watch for earl Godwin, who was in Bruges that winter. But despite this, he got into this country (*F.W.*, i, 208 – with a few ships) without their knowing anything about it. And . . . he enticed all the men of Kent and all the sailors (*butsecarlas*) from the district of Hastings and from the region round about there by the sea-coast, and all Essex and Surrey and much else beside. (*F.W.*, i, 208 ¬ he landed in Kent and by secret messengers enticed to his cause first the men of Kent, then those of Sussex, Essex and Surrey, all the seamen (*butsecarlas*) of Hastings and everywhere along by the coast, and many others.) Then they all said that they would live and die with him. When the fleet that was lying at Sandwich found out about Godwin's expedition, they set out after him; and he escaped them, and the fleet turned back to Sandwich, and so homeward to London. When Godwin found out that the fleet that had been lying at Sandwich was on its way home, he went back again to the Isle of Wight, and lay off the coast there long enough for earl Harold his son (*F.W.*, i, 208 – and Leofwine with their fleet) to join him. And they would not do any great harm afterwards except that they lived off the countryside. But they enticed all the local people to their side, both along the sea-coast and inland also. And they went towards Sandwich and kept on collecting all the sailors (*butsecarlas*) that they met, and so they came to Sandwich with an overwhelming force. When Edward found out about this, he sent inland for more help, but it came very slowly, and Godwin kept on advancing towards London with his fleet, until he came to Southwark (*F.W.*, i, 209 – 14 September), where he waited some time until the tide came up. In that interval he treated with the citizens so that they nearly all wanted what he wanted. When Godwin had arranged all his expedition the tide came in, and they forthwith weighed anchor and proceeded through the bridge (*F.W.*, i, 209 – meeting no opposition at the bridge) always keeping to the southern bank, and the land force came from above and drew themselves up along the shore, and they formed a wing with their ships (C – towards the north shore; *F.W.*, i, 209 – the fleet turned towards the north shore) as if they meant to encircle the king's ships. The king also had a large land force on his side in addition to the sailors. But it was hateful to almost all of them to fight against men of their own race, for there was little else that was worth anything apart from Englishmen on either side; and they also did not wish the country to be laid the more open to foreigners through their destroying each other. Then it was decided that wise men should go between the parties, and they made a truce on both sides. And Godwin and his son Harold went ashore and as many of their sailors (*lith*) as suited them, and then there was a meeting of the council, and Godwin was given his earldom unconditionally and as fully and completely as he had ever held it, and all his sons all that they had held before (*F.W.*, i, 209 – except Swein . . .[28]), and his wife and his daughter as fully and completely as they had held it before. And they confirmed full friendship with them, and promised the full benefits of the laws to all the people. And they outlawed all the Frenchmen (*F.W.*, i, 210 – all the Normans) who had promoted injustices and passed unjust judgements and given bad counsel in this country,

[28] For Swein see C below.

with the exception, as they decided, of as many as the king should wish to have with him, who were loyal to him and to all the people. (*F.W.*, i, 210 particularizes the few (*sic*) as – Robert the deacon and his son-in-law Richard son of Scrob,[29] Alfred the king's equerry, Anfrid called Ceocesfot and certain others whom the king loved more than the rest). And archbishop Robert and bishop William and bishop Ulf escaped with difficulty with the Frenchmen (*ibid.* – Normans) who were with them and so got away overseas (*ibid.* – but William, on account of his goodness, was soon afterwards recalled and received back in his see. Osbern called Pentecost, and his companion Hugh, gave up their castles (*castella*),[30] and with the licence of earl Leofric they passed through his earldom and went into Scotland, where they were received by Macbeth king of Scots.)

C   And earl Godwin and Harold and the queen stayed on their estates. Swein had gone to Jerusalem from Bruges, and died on the way home at Constantinople . . . [Godwin] did all too little reparation about the property of God which he had from many holy places . . .

E   In this year Aelfgifu Emma (*sic*), mother of king Edward and of king Harthacnut died. And in the same year the king and his council decided that ships should be sent to Sandwich, and they appointed earl Ralph and earl Odda as their captains. Then earl Godwin went out from Bruges with his ships to the Isere, and put out to sea a day before the eve of the mid-summer festival [24 June], so that he came to Dungeness, which is south of Romney. Then it came to the knowledge of the earls out at Sandwich, and they went out in pursuit of the other ships, and a land force was called out against the ships. Then meanwhile earl Godwin was warned; and he went to Pevensey, and the storm became so violent that the earls could not find out what had happened to earl Godwin. And then earl Godwin put out again so that he got back to Bruges, and the other ships went back again to Sandwich. Then it was decided that the ships should go back again to London, and that other earls and other oarsmen (*hasaeton*) should be appointed to them. But there was so long a delay that the naval expedition was quite abandoned and all the men went home. Earl Godwin found out about this and hoisted his sail – and so did his fleet – and they went westward direct to the Isle of Wight and there landed, and ravaged there so long that the people paid them as much as they imposed upon them, and then they went westward until they came to Portland and landed there, and did whatever damage they could. Then Harold had come from Ireland with nine ships, and he landed at Porlock, and there was a great force gathered there to oppose him, and he did not hesitate to obtain provisions for himself, and he landed and killed a great part of the force that opposed him and seized for himself what came his way . . . and then he went east to his father, and they both went eastward until they came to the Isle of Wight . . . Then they went on to Pevensey and took with them as many ships as were serviceable and so proceeded to Dungeness. And he took all the ships that were at Romney and Hythe and Folkestone, and then they went east to Dover and landed and seized ships for themselves

[29] Evidently the lord of Richard's Castle.
[30] Ewyas Harold and an unknown castle of Hugh. Cf. E below and n.

and as many hostages as they wished. So they came to Sandwich and there they did exactly the same. . . . They went on to the Northmouth,[31] and so towards London, and some of the ships went within Sheppey and did much damage there, and they went to King's Milton and burnt it down to the ground. Thus they proceeded on their way to London in pursuit of the earls. When they came to London, the king and the earls were all lying there with 50 ships ready to meet them. Then the earls [*i.e.* Godwin and Harold] sent to the king and asked him loyally to return to them all those things of which they had been unjustly deprived. But the king refused for some time – for so long that the men who were with the earl were so incensed against the king and against his men that the earl himself had difficulty in calming those men. Then bishop Stigand with the help of God went there and the wise men both inside the city and without, and they decided that hostages should be arranged for on both sides. And so it was done. Then archbishop Robert found out about this, and the Frenchmen, so that they took horses and departed, some west to Pentecost's castle (*castele*), and some north to Robert's castle (*castele*).[32] And archbishop Robert and bishop Ulf and their companions went out at the east gate and killed or otherwise injured many young men, and went right on to Eadulfesness,[33] and he[34] there got on board a broken-down ship, and went right on overseas, and left behind him his pallium and all the Church in this country. This was God's will, in that he had obtained the dignity when it was not God's will. Then a big council was summoned outside London, and all the earls and the chief men who were in the country were at the council. Then earl Godwin expounded his case, and cleared himself before king Edward, his lord, and before all his countrymen, declaring that he was guiltless of the charges brought against him, and against Harold his son and all his children. Then the king granted the earl and his children his full friendship and full status as an earl, and all that he had had. And all the men who were with him were treated likewise. And the king gave the lady[35] all that she had had. And archbishop Robert was declared utterly an outlaw, and all the Frenchmen too, because they were most responsible for the disagreement between earl Godwin and the king. And bishop Stigand succeeded to the archbishopric of Canterbury . . .

88 1053 D . . . And in the course of this same year earl Godwin died, and he was taken ill while he was sitting with the king at Winchester. And Harold his son succeeded to the earldom his father had had, and Aelfgar succeeded to the earldom that Harold had had.[36]

C . . . In this year there was no archbishop in the land, but bishop Stigand held the bishopric in Canterbury at Christ Church and Kynsige at York. And Leofwine and Wulfwig went overseas and had themselves consecrated there . . .

[31] *I.e.* the northern mouth of the Kentish river Stour.
[32] Usually identified respectively as Ewyas Harold, the castle of Osbern Pentecost in Herefordshire, and Clavering, the castle of Robert fitz Wimarch in Essex.
[33] The Naze, Essex.
[34] *I.e.* archbishop Robert.
[35] *I.e.* queen Edith.
[36] East Anglia.

89 1054 D . . . In the course of this same year bishop Ealdred (*F.W.*, i, 212 – of Worcester) went overseas to Cologne on the king's business, and there was received with great honour by the emperor, [37] and he stayed there for nearly a year, and the bishop of Cologne and the emperor both gave him entertainment. (*ibid.* – and he requested the emperor on the king's behalf that messengers should be sent to Hungary to bring back Edward the king's nephew, son of king Edmund Ironside, and send him to England).

90 1055 C In this year earl Siward died at York . . . (D – And Tostig succeeded to the earldom he had had). [38] Then after that within a short space there was a council at London, and earl Aelfgar, son of earl Leofric, was outlawed without any guilt; and then he went to Ireland and there got himself a fleet . . . and then they went to Wales to king Griffith with that force, and he took him into his protection. And then they gathered a large force with the Irishmen and with the Welsh, and earl Ralph gathered a large force against them at Hereford town, and there battle was joined. But before any spear had been thrown the English army fled because they were on horseback (*F.W.*, i, 213 – Against them earl Ralf 'the Timid', son of king Edward's sister, raised an army and, two miles from the city of Hereford, on 24 October, came against them, commanding the English to fight on horseback contrary to their custom . . .) . . . And then they went back to the town and burnt it with the glorious minster. . . . [Earl Harold leads an army against the Welsh and earl Aelfgar is reinstated].

91 1057 D This year the aethling Edward came to England who was the son of king Edward's brother, king Edmund who was called Ironside because of his valour (*F.W.*, i, 215 – For the king had decided to make him his heir to the kingdom.) . . . We do not know for what reason it was brought about that he was not allowed to see [39] [the face?] of his kinsman king Edward. . . .

92 1058 D In this year earl Aelfgar [40] was banished but he came back forthwith by violence through Griffith's help. And a naval force came from Norway. [41] It is tedious to relate fully how things went.

93 1063 E In this year earl Harold and his brother earl Tostig went into Wales with both a land force and a naval force and subdued the country. And that people gave hostages and surrendered, and then went out and killed their king, Griffith, [42] and brought his head to Harold. . . .

[1064 No version of the Chronicle has any entry for this year.]

[37] Henry III
[38] Northumbria.
[39] The text is evidently corrupt at this point.
[40] Now earl of Mercia.
[41] A large invasion force led by Magnus, son of Harold Hardrada king of Norway. See F.M. Stenton, *Anglo-Saxon England* (2nd ed.)., p. 567.
[42] Gruffydd ap Llewelyn.

94 1065 D[43] . . . And soon after this all the thegns in Yorkshire and in Northumberland came together and outlawed their earl Tostig and killed his bodyguard (*hired menn*) and all they could get at, both English and Danish, and took all his weapons in York, and gold and silver and all his treasure they could hear about anywhere. And they sent for Morcar, son of earl Aelfgar, and chose him as their earl, and he went south with all the people of the shire, and of Nottinghamshire, Derbyshire and Lincolnshire, until he came to Northampton. And his brother Edwin came to meet him with the men that were in his earldom, and also many Welsh came with him. Thereupon earl Harold came to meet them, and they entrusted him with a message to king Edward, and also sent messengers with him, and asked that they might be allowed to have Morcar as their earl. And the king granted this and sent Harold back to them at Northampton on the eve of St Simon and St Jude [28 October]. And he proclaimed this to them and gave them surety for it, and he renewed there the law of king Cnut. And the northern men did much damage round Northampton while he was gone . . . so that that shire and other neighbouring shires were the worse for it for many years. And earl Tostig and his wife and all those who wanted what he wanted went south overseas to count Baldwin,[44] and he received them all and there they remained all the winter.

F.W., i, 223-4 . . . Then, after the feast of St Michael Archangel, on Monday 3 October, the Northumbrian thegns Gamelbearn, Dunstan son of Aethelnoth, and Glonieorn son of Heardwulf, came to York with 200 soldiers (*milites*), to avenge the death of the noble Northumbrian thegns Gospatrick – whom queen Edith, for her brother's sake, had ordered to be treacherously slain at the king's court on the fourth night of Christmas [28 December] – and Gamel son of Orm, and Ulf son of Dolfin, both of whom earl Tostig had ordered treacherously to be slain, while under pledge of peace, in his chamber at York the previous year; and also because of an immense tax which Tostig had wrongly taken from all Northumbria, they first seized his Danish housecarls (*huscarlas*) Amund and Ravenswart as they tried to escape, and slew them outside the city walls, and the next day slew more than 200 of his household on the north side of the Humber; in addition they broke into his treasury and carried off all that was his. Almost the entire county went in one body to meet Harold, earl of Wessex, and others whom the king at Tostig's request had sent to restore peace; and first there, and afterwards at Oxford on the feast of St Simon and St Jude [28 October], though Harold and many others sought to make peace between them and Tostig, they unanimously refused, and outlawed him with all those who incited him to enact bad law; and after the feast of All Souls [1 November], with the aid of earl Edwin, they expelled Tostig from England. He shortly after went with his wife to Baldwin count to the Flemings, and spent the winter at St Omer.

C (D) And king Edward came to Westminster at Christmas and had the minster consecrated which he had himself built to the glory of God and of St Peter and of all God's

---

[43] In this annal and the next, D is a combination of C and E.
[44] Baldwin V, count of Flanders. Tostig's wife, Judith, was Baldwin's daughter.

saints. The consecration of the church was on Holy Innocents' Day [28 December]. And he died on the eve of the Epiphany and was buried on the Feast of the Epiphany [6 January 1066], in the same minster – as it says below: [verses followed which include the following lines]

-Yet the wise ruler entrusted the realm
To a man of high rank, to Harold himself

And earl Harold was now consecrated king[45] and he met little quiet in it as long as he ruled the realm.

F.W., i, 224 has a very carefully worded sentence bringing together all points justifying Harold's succession, and follows with a brief eulogy of the reign –

After the burial the underking [*subregulus*] Harold, earl Godwin's son, whom the king before his death had appointed successor to the kingdom, was elected to the royal dignity by the magnates of the whole realm and on the same day was honourably consecrated as king by Aldred archbishop of York.

95 1066 C[46] ... Then over all England there was seen a sign in the skies such as had never been seen before. Some said it was the star 'comet' which some call long-haired star; and it first appeared on the eve of the Greater Litany, that is 24 April, and so shone all the week. And soon after this earl Tostig came from overseas (*F.W.*, i, 225 – from Flanders) into the Isle of Wight with as large a fleet as he could muster and both money and provisions were given him. And then he went away from there and did damage everywhere along the sea-coast wherever he could reach, until he came to Sandwich. When king Harold, who was in London, was informed that Tostig his brother was come to Sandwich, he assembled a naval force and a land force (*F.W.*, i, 225 - a large fleet and a horsed army) larger than any king had assembled before in this country, because he had been told as a fact that count William from Normandy, king Edward's kinsman, meant to come here and subdue this country. This was exactly what happened afterwards. When Tostig found that king Harold was on his way to Sandwich, he went from Sandwich and took some of the sailors (*butse karlon*) with him, some willingly and some unwillingly, and then went north to [blank] and ravaged in Lindsey and killed many good men there. When earl Edwin[47] and earl Morcar[48] understood about this, they came there and drove him out of the country; and then he went to Scotland, and the king of Scots[49] gave him protection, and helped him with provisions, and he stayed there all the summer. Then king Harold came to Sandwich and waited for his fleet there, because it was long before it could be assembled; and when his fleet was assembled, he went into the Isle of Wight, and

[45] On 6 January, the day of Edward's funeral.
[46] For this year 'Florence' is closest to C down to Stamford Bridge and then is close again to D for that battle.
[47] Of Mercia.
[48] Of Northumbria.
[49] Malcolm Canmore.

lay there all that summer and autumn; and a land force was kept everywhere along by the sea, though in the end it was no use. When it was the Feast of the Nativity of St Mary [8 September], the provisions of the people were gone, and nobody could keep them there any longer. Then the men were allowed to go home, and the king rode inland, and the ships were brought up to London, and many perished before they reached there. When the ships came home, Harold, king of Norway, came by surprise north into the Tyne with a very large naval force . . .[50] (F.W., i, 226 – more than 500 large ships). And earl Tostig came to him with all those he had mustered, just as they had agreed beforehand, and they both went with all the fleet up the Ouse towards York.

D and E both say that Tostig appeared first in the Humber with 60 ships, was driven off by Edwin earl of Mercia and, deserted by many of his men, joined Harold Hardrada in Scotland with only 12 ships. *F.W.*, i, 226 has the combined force land at Riccall.

Then king Harold in the south was informed when he disembarked that Harold, king of Norway and earl Tostig were come ashore near York. Then he went northwards day and night as quickly as he could assemble his force. Then before Harold could get there earl Edwin and earl Morcar assembled from their earldom as large a force as they could muster, and fought against the invaders. (F.W., i, 226 – on the north bank of the river Ouse near York) and caused them heavy casualties, and many of the English host were killed and drowned and put to flight, and the Norwegians remained masters of the field. And this fight[51] was on the eve of St Matthew the Apostle, and that was a Wednesday [20 September]. And then after the fight Harold, king of Norway, and earl Tostig went into York[52] with as large a force as suited them, and they were given hostages, and also helped with provisions, and so went from there on board ship and settled a complete peace, arranging that they should all go with him southwards and subdue this country. (F.W., i, 226 – They took 150 hostages from York and returned to their ships leaving 150 of their men in York as hostages.) Then in the middle of these proceedings Harold, king of the English, came on the Sunday [24 September] with all his force to Tadcaster, and there marshalled his troops, and then on Monday [25 September] went right on through York. And Harold, king of Norway, and earl Tostig and their divisions were gone inland beyond York to Stamford Bridge, because they had been promised for certain that hostages would be brought to them there out of all the shire. Then Harold, king of the English, came against them by surprise beyond the bridge, and there they joined battle, and went on fighting strenuously until late in the day. And there Harold king of Norway was killed, and earl Tostig, and numberless men with them both Norwegians and English, and the Norwegians [the original text of C stops at this point. A well-known addition in a much later hand reads as follows and finally ends the C version: –] fled from the field. There was one of the Norwegians there who withstood the English host so that they could not cross the bridge nor win victory. Then an Englishman shot an arrow, but it

---

[50] The text is here corrupt.
[51] The battle at Gate Fulford, now a suburb of York.
[52] On Sunday 24 September.

was no use, and then another came under the bridge and stabbed him under the coat of mail. Then Harold king of the English came over the bridge and his host with him, and there killed large numbers of both Norwegians and Flemings, and Harold let the king's son . . . go home to Norway with all the ships.)

D . . . Then Harold our king came upon the Norwegians by surprise at Stamford Bridge (*F.W.*,[53] i, 226 – on Monday 25 September) with a large force of the English people; and that day there was a very fierce fight on both sides. There was killed Harold Hardrada[54] and earl Tostig, and the Norwegians who survived took to flight; and the English attacked them fiercely as they pursued them until some got to the ships. Some were drowned, and some burned, and some destroyed in various ways so that few survived, and the English remained in command of the field. The king gave quarter to Olaf, son of the Norse king, and their bishop and the earl of Orkney (*F.W.*, i, 226 – called Paul, who had been detailed with part of the army to guard the ships) and all those who survived on the ships, and they went up to our king and swore oaths (*ibid*. – and gave hostages) that they would keep peace and friendship with this country; and the king let them go home with 24 (*ibid*. – 20) ships. These two pitched battles were fought within five nights. Then count William came from Normandy to Pevensey on Michaelmas Eve [28 September][55] and as soon as they were able to move on they built a castle (*castel*) at Hastings. King Harold was informed of this and he assembled a large army and came against him at the hoary apple-tree. And William came against him by surprise before his army was drawn up in battle array. But the king nevertheless fought hard against him, with the men who were willing to support him, and there were heavy casualties on both sides. There king Harold was killed and earl Leofwine his brother, and earl Gyrth his brother, and many good men, and the French remained masters of the field, even as God granted it to them because of the sins of the people. Archbishop Ealdred and the citizens of London wanted to have Edgar *Cild*[56] as king, as was his proper due, and Edwin and Morcar promised him that they would fight on his side; but always the more it ought to have been forward the more it got behind, and the worse it grew from day to day, exactly as everything came to be at the end. The battle took place on the festival of Calixtus the pope [Saturday, 14 October]. And count William went back to Hastings, and waited there to see whether submission would be made to him. But when he understood that no one meant to come to him, he went inland with all his army that was left to him, and that came to him afterwards from overseas, and ravaged all the region that he overran (*F.W.*, i, 228 – Sussex Kent, Hampshire, Surrey, Middlesex, Hertfordshire) until he reached Berkhampstead.[57] There he was met by archbishop Ealdred and Edgar *Cild*, and earl Edwin and earl Morcar, and all the chief men from London. [*F.W.*, i, 228 adds to those named Wulfstan, bishop of Worcester, and Walter, bishop of Hereford.] And they

---

[53] 'Florence' at the end of C comes close again to D.
[54] MS 'Harold Fairhair' in error.
[55] Cf. E below.
[56] *I.e.* son of the aethling Edward who died in 1057.
[57] Possibly Little Berkhampstead.

submitted out of necessity after most damage had been done – and it was a great piece of folly that they had not done it earlier, since God would not make things better, because of our sins. And they gave hostages and swore oaths to him, and he promised them that he would be a gracious lord, and yet in the meantime they ravaged all that they overran. Then on Christmas Day, archbishop Ealdred consecrated him king at Westminster (*F.W.*, i, 228 – because Stigand, the primate of all England, stood accused of not having received the pallium canonically from the papacy). And he promised Ealdred on Christ's book and swore moreover (before Ealdred would place the crown on his head) that he would rule all this people as well as the best of the kings before him, if they would be loyal to him. All the same he laid taxes on people very severely, and then went in spring [*i.e.* 1067] overseas to Normandy, and took with him archbishop Stigand, and Aethelnoth, abbot of Glastonbury, and Edgar *Cild* and earl Edwin and earl Morcar, and earl Waltheof (*F.W.*, ii, 1 – and the noble leader Aethelnoth the Kentishman), and many other good men from England. And bishop Odo[58] and earl William[59] stayed behind and built castles (*castelas*) far and wide throughout this country, and distressed the wretched folk, and always after that it grew much worse. May the end be good when God wills!

E . . . Meanwhile count William landed at Hastings on Michaelmas Day [29 September], and Harold came from the north and fought with him before all the army had come, and there he fell and his two brothers Gyrth and Leofwine; and William conquered this country, and came to Westminster, and archbishop Ealdred consecrated him king, and people paid taxes to him, and gave him hostages and afterwards bought their lands.[60] And Leofric abbot of Peterborough was at that campaign and fell ill there, and came home and died soon after. . . . In his day there was every happiness and every good at Peterborough. . . . Then the Golden Borough became a wretched borough. Then the monks elected Brand, the provost, as abbot, because he was a very good man and very wise, and sent him to the aethling Edgar because the local people expected that he would be king and the aethling gladly gave assent to it. When king William heard about this he grew very angry, and said the abbot had slighted him. Then distinguished men acted as intermediaries and brought them into agreement, because the abbot was of good family. Then he gave the king 40 marks of gold as settlement. . . .

F.W., i, 227–8[61] [following the account of Stamford Bridge –] While these things were happening, and the king was proclaiming the destruction of all his enemies, news was brought to him that William, count of the Norman race, had invaded with a great force of horse and foot, slingers (*fundibalii*) and archers, made innumerable by the recruitment of powerful auxiliary troops from all Gaul, and had brought his fleet to land at a place called Pevensey. Whereupon the king at once marched his army towards London with all speed; and although he knew very well that many of the better warriors in all England had fallen

[58] *I.e.* Odo bishop of Bayeux, half-brother to the Conqueror.
[59] William fitz Osbern, soon to be earl of Hereford.
[60] What follows is a later Peterborough interpolation in E.
[61] 'Florence's' account of Hastings differs from that of D or any other surviving version of Chronicle.

in the two battles, and that half his army had not yet come in, nevertheless he did not hesitate to meet his enemy in Sussex as quickly as he could, and nine miles from Hastings he gave them battle, before a third of his army was drawn up, on Saturday 22 October[62]: but because the English were drawn up in a confined position, many deserted from the line, and a very few stood firm with him: yet from the third hour of the day until evening he resisted his foes with the utmost courage, and so bravely and vigorously did he defend himself that it seemed he was invulnerable to his adversaries. But alas! after so many had fallen on both sides, he himself was slain as the evening shadows lengthened. Earls Gyrth and Leofwine, his brothers, were also slain, and almost all the nobility of England: and William returned to Hastings with his army. Harold had reigned for nine months and as many days: when they heard of his death, earls Edwin and Morcar, who with their forces had withdrawn from the battle, went to London, and sent their sister, queen Ealdgyth[63] to the city of Chester. Then Ealdred archbishop of York and the same earls, with the citizens and mariners (*butsecarle*) of London, wished to make the aethling Edgar, grandson of Edmund Ironside, king, and promised that they would fight for him; but when many prepared themselves to do that, the earls withdrew their support and went home with their army. . . .

96 1067 D In this year the king came back to England on St Nicholas's Day [6 December]. And that day Christ Church at Canterbury was burnt down. . . . And Edric *Cild*[64] (*F.W.*, ii, 1 – the son of Aelfric who was the brother of Edric Streona) and the Welsh became hostile, and fought against the men of the castle (*castel*) at Hereford.[65]. . . And the king imposed a heavy tax on the wretched people, and nevertheless caused all that they overran to be ravaged. And then he went to Devon and besieged the city of Exeter for 18 days, and there a large part of his army perished. . . . Edgar *Cild* went abroad with his mother Agatha and his two sisters, Margaret and Christina . . . and came to Scotland under the protection of king Malcolm [III], and he received them all. Then the aforesaid king Malcolm began to desire his sister Margaret for his wife.[66] And soon after that the lady Maud [Mathilda] came to this country and archbishop Ealdred consecrated her as queen at Westminster on Whitsunday [11 May 1068]. Then the king was informed that the people in the north were gathered together and meant to make a stand against him if he came. He then went to Nottingham and built a castle (*castel*) there, and so went to York and there built two castles (*F.W.*, ii, 2 – and placed 500 knights in them), and in Lincoln and everywhere in that district. . . .

97 1068 D[67] In this year king William gave earl Robert[68] the ealdormanry of

---

[62] An error for Saturday 14 October. October 22 in 1066 was a Sunday.

[63] Whom Harold married in 1066.

[64] An error for Edric 'the Wild'.

[65] These events and all others which follow from this annal in fact took place in 1068.

[66] The marriage duly took place in 1069 or 1070 in spite of the reluctance of both Margaret and her brother, Edgar. This is queen, and subsequently Saint, Margaret.

[67] The following events from this annal in fact took place in 1069.

[68] Robert de Commines, now made earl of Northumbria.

Northumberland; but the local people surrounded him in the city of Durham and killed him and 900 men with him. And soon after that the aethling Edgar came to York with all the Northumbrians, and the citizens made peace with him. And king William came on them by surprise from the south with an overwhelming army and routed them, and killed those who could not escape . . . and the aethling went back to Scotland.

98 1069 D . . . Soon after that [the death of archbishop Ealdred[69]] three sons of king Swein came from Denmark with 240 ships (E – 300) into the Humber, together with earl Osbern and earl Thorkil. And there came to meet them the aethling Edgar and earl Waltheof and Merleswein and earl Gospatric with the Northumbrians and all the people, riding and marching with an immense army rejoicing exceedingly; and so they all went resolutely to York, and stormed and razed the castle (*castel*) and captured an incalculable treasure in it and killed many hundreds of Frenchmen and took many with them to the ships. And before the shipmen got there the Frenchmen had burned the city, and had also thoroughly ravaged and burnt the holy minster of St Peter. When the king found out about this, he went northward with all his army that he could collect, and utterly ravaged and laid waste that shire. . . . And the king was in York on Christmas Day, and so was in the country all the winter.

99 1070 D [under 1071] In this year earl Waltheof made peace with the king. And in the following spring the king had all the monasteries that were in England plundered (*F.W.*, ii, 4–5 – During Lent, on the advice of William earl of Hereford and certain others, king William commanded that the monasteries of all England were to be searched and the money which rich Englishmen had deposited there . . . taken away and paid into his treasury). Then in the same year king Swein came from Denmark into the Humber,[70] and the local people came to meet him and made a truce with him – they expected that he was going to conquer the country. Then there came to Ely Christian the Danish bishop,[71] and earl Osbeorn and the Danish housecarls (*hus carles*) with them, and the English people from all the Fenlands came to them and expected that they were going to conquer all the country. Then the monks of Peterborough heard it said that their own men meant to plunder the monastery – that was Hereward and his following. That was because they heard it said that the king had given the abbacy to a French abbot called Turold,[72] and he was a very stern man, and had then come to Stamford with all his Frenchmen. . . .

A long account of the sacking of Peterborough by Hereward the Wake and his Danish friends then follows in this version of the Chronicle, which in its final form is, of course, of Peterborough provenance.

[69] The date of Ealdred's death is given as 11 September. 'Florence' (ii, 3) has it follow the arrival of the Danes on 8 September and caused by grief at their coming.
[70] *I.e.* to join the Danish fleet of 1069 still lying there.
[71] Of Aarhus.
[72] Turold of Fécamp, whom the Conqueror translated from Malmesbury to Peterborough with the splendid remark that if he was going to behave more like a knight than an abbot he might as well go where the fighting was (William of Malmesbury, *Gesta Pontificum*, Rolls Series, 1870, ed. N.E.S.A. Hamilton, p. 420).

F.W., ii, 5 – A great council was held at Winchester in the octaves of Easter [4 April], king William present and presiding, with the assent of the lord Pope Alexander [II] and with his authority exercised through his legates Ermenfrid cardinal bishop of Sion and the cardinal priests John and Peter. At which council Stigand archbishop of Canterbury was deposed on three counts, *viz* because he had uncanonically held the bishopric of Winchester with the archbishopric; and because, during the lifetime of archbishop Robert, he had not only assumed the archbishopric, but also had for some time, in celebrating mass, made use of his pallium, which he had left behind at Canterbury when wrongfully driven out of England; and later had accepted a pallium from Benedict [X], whom the Roman Church had excommunicated for obtaining the apostolic see by simony. [Aethelmaer bishop of East Anglia[73] and several abbots were also deposed.]

A In this year Lanfranc, who was abbot of Caen, came to England and after a few days he became archbishop of Canterbury. He was consecrated on 29 August at his own see. . . . In that year Thomas, who was bishop-elect of York, came to Canterbury to be consecrated there according to the ancient custom. When Lanfranc demanded the confirmation of his obedience by oath, he refused and said that he ought not to do it. Then archbishop Lanfranc got angry, and ordered the bishops . . . and all the monks to unrobe, and at his orders they did so. So Thomas went back that time without consecration. Then immediately after this it happened that archbishop Lanfranc went to Rome, and Thomas along with him. When they arrived there, and had spoken about other things . . . Thomas brought forward his case, how he had gone to Canterbury and how the archbishop had asked for his obedience on oath, and he had refused it. Then archbishop Lanfranc began to explain with clear reasoning that what he had demanded he had demanded legitimately, and he established the same with firm argument before Pope Alexander [II] and all the council that was assembled there. And so they went home. After this, Thomas came to Canterbury and humbly fulfilled all that the archbishop demanded of him, and then received the consecration. [74]

100 1071 D [under 1072] In this year earl Edwin and earl Morcar fled away and travelled aimlessly in woods and moors until Edwin was killed by his own men and Morcar went to Ely by ship. And bishop Aethelwine[75] and Siward Bearn (*F.W.*, ii, 9 – and Hereward) came there and many hundred men with them. But when king William found out about this, he called out a naval force and a land force, and invested that part of the country from outside, and made a bridge (*F.W.*, ii, 9 – two miles long) and placed a naval force on the seaward side. And they then all surrendered to the king . . . except Hereward alone and those who could escape with him, and he led them out valiantly.

101 1072 D [under 1073] In this year king William led a naval force and a land

[73] Stigand's brother.
[74] The A version of the Chronicle ends here.
[75] Of Durham.

force to Scotland, and blockaded that country from the sea with ships. And he went himself with his land force in over the Forth, and there he found nothing that they were any the better for. And king Malcolm came and made peace with king William and was his vassal and gave him hostages, and afterwards went home with all his force. . . .[76]

102 1073 D,E In this year king William led an English and French force overseas and conquered the county of Maine. . . .

103 1074 E In this year king William went overseas to Normandy. And Edgar *Cild* came from Scotland to Normandy, and the king reversed his outlawry and that of all his men. And he was in the king's court and received such dues as the king granted him.

D (under 1075) has a much fuller annal (though confined to these same events) in which Edgar, at the latter's suggestion, first sought to join king Philip in France against the Normans but was prevented by ship-wreck. It ends: –

And again king Malcolm and [his wife] Edgar's sister gave him and all his men immense treasure, and again very honourably sent him out of their jurisdiction. And the sheriff of York came to meet them at Durham and went all the way with them and had them provided with food and fodder at every castle (*castelle*) they came to, until they got overseas to the king. And king William received him with great honour and he stayed there at court and received such dues as were appointed him.

104 1075 D [under 1076] In this year king William gave to earl Ralph[76] the daughter of William fitz Osbern [Emma]. (*F.W.*, ii, 10 – Roger earl Hereford, son of William earl of Hereford, against the king's command, gave his sister in marriage to Ralph earl of the East Anglians.) This same Ralph was a Breton on his mother's side, and Ralph his father was English and was born in Norfolk, and the king gave the earldom there and Suffolk as well to his son. He then took the lady to Norwich (*F.W.*, ii, 10 has the wedding feast at Exning in Cambridgeshire – now Suffolk.) Earl Roger[78] was there and earl Waltheof[79] and bishops and abbots, and there they plotted to drive their royal lord out of his kingdom. And the king in Normandy was soon informed about this. Earl Ralph and earl Roger were the ringleaders in this conspiracy; and they lured the Bretons to their side; and they also sent to Denmark for a naval force (*F.W.*, ii, 10 – and they compelled earl Waltheof, who was won over by their treachery, to join their confederacy). And Roger went west to his earldom and assembled his people for the king's undoing, as he thought, but it turned out to his own great harm. Ralph also wanted to go forward with the men of his earldom, but the castle men (*castel menn*) who were in England and also the local people came against them and prevented them all from doing anything; but he was glad to escape to the ships. And his wife remained behind in

[76] E makes it clear that it was William, not Malcolm, who 'went home with all his force'.
[77] Ralph 'Guader', earl of Norfolk, lord of Gael in Brittany.
[78] Earl of Hereford in succession to his father William fitz Osbern.
[79] Son of Siward, former earl of Northumbria.

the castle (*castele*), and held it until she was given safe-conduct. . . . And the king afterward came to England (*F.W.*, ii, 10 – in the autumn) and captured earl Roger, his kinsman, and put him into prison. And earl Waltheof went overseas and accused himself and asked for pardon and offered treasure. But the king made light of it until he came to England and then had him captured. And soon after this 200 ships came from Denmark. . . . And they dared not fight against king William but went to York and broke into St Peter's Minster . . . and so departed. . . . And the lady Edith who was king Edward's widow died at Winchester a week before Christmas, and the king had her brought to Westminster with great honour and laid her near king Edward her husband.

105 1076 D [under 1077] . . . And in this year earl Waltheof was beheaded at Winchester on St Petronella's Day [31 May]; and his body was taken to Crowland, and he is buried there. . . .

106 1079 E[80] In this year king Malcolm came from Scotland into England between the two feasts of St Mary[81] with a great army, and ravaged Northumbria as far as the Tyne. . . . And in the same year king William fought against his son Robert outside Normandy near a castle (*castele*) called Gerberoi (*F.W.*, ii, 13 – which king Philip had given him) and king William was wounded there. . . .

107 1081 E In this year the king led an army into Wales and there liberated many hundreds of men.

108 1082 E In this year the king seized bishop Odo. And in this year there was a great famine.

109 1083 E In this year the discord arose at Glastonbury between the abbot Thurstan (*F.W.*, ii, 16 – whom king William, ill advised, had appointed as abbot there from Caen) and his monks . . . [A detailed account of that notorious affair then follows.] . . . And in the same year Mathilda, William's queen, died the day after All Saint's Day [2 November]. And in the same year, after Christmas, the king had a great and heavy tax ordered all over England – it was 72d. for every hide.[82]

110 1085 E In this year people said and declared for a fact, that Cnut, king of Denmark, son of king Swein, was setting out in this direction and meant to conquer this country with the help of Robert, count of Flanders, because Cnut was married to Robert's daughter. When William king of England, who was then in Normandy . . . found out about this, he went to England (*F.W.*, ii, 18 – in the autumn) with a larger force of mounted men and infantry from France and Brittany than had ever come to this

[80] D ends with the annal for 1079. 'Florence' is now closer to E, which after 1079 becomes the sole remaining version of the Chronicle.
[81] August 15 and September 8.
[82] This gold was taken early in 1084.

country, so that people wondered how this country could maintain all that army. And the king had all the army dispersed all over the country among his men (*mannon*), and they provisioned the army each in proportion to his land. And people had much oppression that year, and the king had the land near the sea laid waste, so that if his enemies landed, they should have nothing to seize on so quickly. . . .

Then at Christmas the king was at Gloucester with his council, and held his court there for five days, and then the archbishop and clerics had a synod for three days. There Maurice was elected bishop of London, and William for Norfolk, and Robert for Cheshire – they were all clerics of the king.

After this, the king had much thought and very deep discussion with his council about this country – how it was occupied or with what sort of people. Then he sent his men over all England into every shire and had them find out how many hundred hides there were in the shire, or what land and cattle the king himself had in the country, or what dues he ought to have in 12 months from the shire. Also he had a record made of how much land his archbishop had, and his bishops and his abbots and his earls – and though I relate it at too great length – what or how much everybody had who was occupying land in England, in land or cattle, and how much money it was worth. So very narrowly did he have it investigated, that there was no single hide nor virgate of land, nor indeed (it is a shame to relate but it seemed no shame to him to do) one ox nor one cow nor one pig which was there left out, and not put down in his record (*ge-writ*), and all these records (*ge-writa*) were brought to him afterwards.

F.W., ii, 18–19 – king William caused the whole of England to be surveyed, how much land each of his barons possessed, how many enfeoffed knights (*feudatos milites*), how many ploughs, how many villeins, how many animals and what livestock everybody had from the highest to the lowest in all his kingdom, and what rent could be obtained from every estate. . . .

111 1086 E [under 1085] In this year the king wore his crown and held his court at Winchester for Easter, and travelled so as to be at Westminster for Whitsuntide, and there dubbed his son Henry a knight (*dubbade . . . to ridere.*) (*F.W.*, ii, 19 – honoured with the arms of knighthood: *armis militaribus honoravit*). Then he travelled about so as to come to Salisbury at Lammas [1 August]; and there his councillors (*witan*) came to him, and all the people occupying land who were of any account over all England, no matter whose men they were; and they all bowed to him (*bugon to him*) and became his men and swore hold oaths (*hold athas*) to him, that they would be loyal to him against all other men. . . .

F.W., ii, 19 – Not long afterwards he commanded that the archbishops, bishops, abbots, earls, barons, sheriffs, should come to him at Salisbury on 1 August, with their knights (*milites*); and when they had come he made their knights (*milites*) swear fealty (*fidelitatem*) to him against all men. . . .

112 1087 E. . . it became a very severe and pestilential year in this country. Such a disease came on people that very nearly every other person was ill . . . and that so severely that many people died of the disease. Afterwards . . . there came so great a famine over all England that many hundreds of people died a miserable death. . . . Alas! how miserable and pitiable a time it was then. . . . There was little righteousness in this country in anyone, except in monks alone where they behaved well. The king and the chief men loved gain much and over-much – gold and silver – and did not care how sinfully it was obtained provided it came to them. The king sold his land on very hard terms – as hard as he could. Then came somebody else and offered more than the other had given, and the king let it go to the man who had offered him more . . . and did not care how sinfully the reeves had got it from poor men, nor how many unlawful things they did. But the more just laws were talked about, the more unlawful things were done. They imposed unjust tolls and did many other injustices which are hard to reckon up. . . .

Also in the same year before the Assumption of St Mary [15 August] king William went from Normandy into France . . . and burnt down the city of Mantes. . . . He fell ill. . . . He died in Normandy on the day after the Nativity of St Mary [9 September], and he was buried at Caen in St Stephen's monastery: he had built it, and afterwards had endowed it richly. . . .

If anyone wishes to know what sort of man he was, or what dignity he had or of how many lands he was lord – then we will write of him even as we, who have looked upon him, and once lived at his court, have perceived him to be.

This king William of whom we speak was a very wise man, and very powerful and more worshipful and stronger than any predecessor of his had been. He was gentle to the good men who loved God, and stern beyond all measure to those people who resisted his will. In the same place where God permitted him to conquer England, he set up a famous monastery[83] and appointed monks for it, and endowed it well. In his days the famous church at Canterbury was built, and also many another over all England. Also, this country was very full of monks, and they lived their life under the rule of St Benedict, and Christianity was such in his day that each man who wished followed out whatever concerned his order. Also, he was very dignified: three times every year he wore his crown, as often as he was in England. At Easter he wore it at Winchester, at Whitsuntide at Westminster, and at Christmas at Gloucester, and then there were with him all the powerful men over all England, archbishops and bishops, abbots and earls, thegns and knights (*cnihtas*). Also, he was a very stern and violent man, so that no one dared do anything contrary to his will. He had earls in his fetters, who were against his will. He expelled bishops from their sees, and abbots from their abbacies, and put thegns in prison, and finally he did not spare his own brother, who was called Odo; he was a very powerful bishop in Normandy, his cathedral church was at Bayeux, he was the foremost man next the king, and had an earldom in Kent. And when the king was in Normandy, then he was master in this country; and he [the king] put him in prison. Amongst other things the good security he made in this country is not to be forgotten – so that any honest man could travel over his kingdom without injury with his bosom full of gold; and no one dared strike (or kill)

[83] Battle, Sussex.

another, however much wrong he had done him. And if any man had intercourse with a woman against her will, he was forthwith castrated.

He ruled over England, and by his cunning it was so investigated that there was not one hide of land in England that he did not know who owned it, and what it was worth, and then set it down in his record (*ge-writ*). Wales was in his power, and he built castles (*casteles*) there, and he entirely controlled that race. In the same way he also subdued Scotland to himself, because of his great strength. The land of Normandy was his by natural inheritance, and he ruled over the county called Maine; and if he could have lived two years more, he would have conquered Ireland by his prudence and without any weapons. Certainly in his time people had much oppression and very many injuries:

The memorial then turns to verses which begin –

> He had castles (*castelas*) built
> And poor men hard oppressed

and end

> May Almighty God show mercy on his soul
> And grant unto him forgiveness for his sins.

The Vita Edwardi Regis: The Life of King Edward who rests at Westminster

This work shares some of the enigma of the Anglo-Saxon Chronicle. To begin with, it is anonymous. Though we include it among our 'English' sources, there is general agreement (from internal evidence) that it was written by a foreigner, in England and with access to information from the royal court, probably from Flanders, probably from St Omer, and probably a monk from St Bertin in that town. Though Marc Bloch argued for its being a mere literary exercise – in fact, a fraud – composed in the early twelfth century, most scholars now agree that it has to be taken seriously as written early, at least before Sulcard, the historian of Westminster, used it in about 1080, and presumably (from internal evidence again) before the death of queen Edith in 1075 and the deposition of Stigand in 1070. Its most recent and thorough editor, Professor Frank Barlow, argues for the very early overall date of 1065–7.[1] In his view, the work is clearly composed of two parts (which he thus calls Parts I and II), each preceded by a verse prologue and the second very different from the first. Part I, which is a kind of history of Edward the Confessor's reign, he dates 1065–6, and Part II, which is much more a religious life of the dead king, he dates 1067, arguing also that the change of plan and purpose between the two parts was caused by the drama of 1066 itself. While there is not a universal acceptance that the first part of the *Life* was written before Hastings, Professor Barlow's arguments have won a wide support.[2] There is no doubt of the complete change of character as between the first

[1] See Barlow's introduction to his *Life of King Edward the Confessor* (cited below), pp. xxvff.
[2] Cf. Antonia Gransden, *Historical Writing in England c. 550 to c. 1307* (also cited below) pp. 60–6.

and second parts, which it is difficult to account for except by the explanation of the author himself that he was overtaken by events[3] which statement is, in turn, one of the foundations of Barlow's argument.

The whole is more or less explicitly dedicated to queen Edith, and the work is amongst other things the earliest life of king Edward,[4] written, if its early date be accepted, before the cult of the Confessor's sanctity had gone so far as to banish all reality. Part I is not a full chronological history of Edward's reign but, rather, a series of seven episodes or subjects, forming in effect chapters separated by verses. Thus (i) concerns the rise of Godwin in the time of Cnut, and the accession of Edward; (ii) (missing from the MS as we have it) concerns Godwin's children, including Edith and her marriage to the king; (iii) Edward's Norman friends in England, especially Robert, abbot of Jumièges, first made bishop of London and then archbishop of Canterbury, and whose pre-eminence in the king's counsels and hostility to earl Godwin lead straight into the crisis of 1051; (iv) the come-back of Godwin and his sons in 1052; (v) the death of Godwin is followed by a discussion and appreciation of his sons Harold and Tostig; (vi) the saintly rule of Edward while Harold and Tostig defend his realm to west and north respectively: the building of Westminster by the king and Wilton by the queen; (vii) the Northumbrian revolt of 1065 against Tostig, his banishment and the king's death. Part II is very different: after its verse prologue, itself obliquely referring to the double tragedy of Tostig's death, fighting against Harold at Stamford Bridge, and Harold's death at Hastings –

> . . . For whom shall I write now?
> This murderous page will hardly please the queen
> Their sister . . .[5]

it is a religious life of Edward, an embryonic saint's *Life*, relating the miracles worked in his lifetime, his edifying death, and briefly referring to the subsequent miracles at his tomb. 'You will paint', says the Muse to the author in the prologue to this Part,

> 'King Edward fair in form and work, what he
> Did in his life and what when dying said'[6]

– and so he does.

The text survives in a single manuscript (now in the British Library[7]) lacking sections from both Parts I and II.[8] The principal claimants to authorship are both monks of St Bertin at St Omer: Goscelin, who was in the household of Herman (another St Bertin

---

[3] Ed. Barlow, pp. 56–60.
[4] 'You shall be first to sing king Edward's song', pp. 3, 60.
[5] Ed. Barlow, p. 58.
[6] *Ibid.*, p. 59.
[7] Harley 526, ff. 38–57.
[8] The section or chapter (ii) dealing with the children of Godwin in Part I (see above), and much relating to Edward's miracles in his lifetime from Part II. In Barlow's edition the substance of what is missing is printed from later sources themselves borrowing from this work, notably the *Life of Edward the Confessor* by Osbert of Clare (*c.*1138).

monk) bishop of Sherborne (1058-78) and was at one time chaplain at Wilton; and Folcard, who is known to have been acting-abbot of Thorney from *c*.1067 to *c*.1083. Both were notable hagiographers. The extracts below include something from each of the extant sections or chapters of Part I, and from Part II. The value of the work is considerable, though it needs to be used with some discretion and as a supplement to one's knowledge of the framework of events derived from other sources. Each of the select sections of the book, court orientated, is written up in detail, the whole thus often supplying information not to be found elsewhere; *e.g.* the disputed election to Canterbury in 1051 (**116**), Harold's pilgrimage to Rome (**118**), the remarkable description of Edward's new church at Westminster (**120**), or, most notably, the only detailed account we have of Edward's death-bed (**123**) – (which, however, is very close indeed to the silent depiction on the Bayeux Tapestry (**200**). Again, though this is the earliest *Life* of king Edward, containing also the earliest description of him, the fact that the book was written for his queen, the author's patron, makes it, in its first part, in effect a history of the house of Godwin, and gives us in consequence an unusual slant upon the happenings chosen to be recounted. But there are snags. The pro-Godwin stance of the author in the relevant sections of Part I produces more absurdity than anything in the oft maligned panegyric of William of Poitiers upon duke William. And king Edward is already fading into the mists of hagiography, most obviously, of course, in Part II, but even in Part I where we find, amongst other things, that uncertainty of time and place characteristic of the *genre*.

Finally, the book is without question a conscious and self-conscious literary work, educated and skilful, written in sophisticated, not to say inflated, Latin, replete with high-flown verses.

The fullest discussion of every aspect of the *Vita Edwardi* will be found in the introduction and appendices of its most recent and best edition by Professor Frank Barlow (see below) from whom the following translations are taken with grateful acknowledgement. There is another full discussion by Antonia Gransden in her *Historical Writing in England c.550 to c.1307*, London, 1974, pp. 60–6.

Source and translation: *The Life of King Edward who rests at Westminster*, ed. and trans. Frank Barlow, Nelson's Medieval Texts, London, 1962. Professor Barlow's divisions into Parts and Chapters are noted in parenthesis with the page references.

(Part I)

After a lengthy verse prologue, in which the author dedicated his book to queen Edith (and is told by his Muse, 'You shall be first to sing king Edward's song'), the work begins at once in praise of Godwin –

113 (c.1) pp. 5–7   When God's rod of justice had swept away by the oppression of the Danes what had displeased Him among the people, and the kingdom, as a result of the vicissitudes of war, had passed to Cnut,[1] among the new nobles of the conquered

[1] 1016.

kingdom attached to the king's side that Godwin, whom we have just mentioned,[2] was judged by the king himself the most cautious in counsel and the most active in war. . . . He also found out how profound he was in eloquence, and what advantage it would be to him in his newly acquired kingdom if he were to bind him more closely to him by means of some fitting reward. Consequently he admitted the man . . . to his council and gave him his sister as wife.[3] And when Godwin returned home, having performed all things well, he was appointed by him earl and office-bearer of almost all the kingdom. Having obtained this pre-eminent honour, Godwin did not carry himself high, but showed himself to all good men as much as he could like a father. . . . There were born anon sons and daughters not unworthy of such a sire . . . and in their education attention was paid specially to those arts which would prepare them to be a strength and help to future rulers. . . . In the reign of this king Cnut Godwin flourished in the royal palace, having the first place among the highest nobles of the kingdom. . . .

114 (c.i) p. 9   When by God's gracious mercy there came for the English, who had suffered so long under the yoke of the barbarians, the jubilee of their redemption, that earl Godwin, whom I have already mentioned, took the lead in urging that they should admit their king [*i.e.* Edward] to the throne that was his by right of birth; and since Godwin was regarded as a father by all, he was gladly heard in the witenagemot. . . .

115 (c.i) p. 12   And not to omit his attitude and appearance, he [king Edward] was a very proper figure of a man – of outstanding height, and distinguished by his milky white hair and beard, full face and rosy cheeks, thin white hands, and long translucent fingers; in all the rest of his body he was an unblemished (*integer*) royal person. Pleasant, but always dignified, he walked with eyes down-cast, most graciously affable to one and all. If some cause aroused his temper, he seemed as terrible as a lion, but he never revealed his anger by railing. To all petitioners he would either grant graciously or graciously deny, so that his gracious denial seemed the highest generosity. In public he carried himself as a true king and lord; in private with his courtiers as one of them, but with royal dignity unimpaired. . . .

116 (c.iii) pp. 17–23   When king Edward of holy memory returned from Francia quite a number of men of that nation, and they not base-born, accompanied him. And these, since he was master of the whole kingdom, he kept with him, enriched them with many honours, and made them his privy-counsellors and administrators of the royal palace. Among them had come a certain abbot named Robert, who overseas had ruled the monastery of Jumièges,[4] and who, they say, was always the most powerful confidential adviser of the king. . . . Moreover, on the death of the bishop of London he succeeded by

---

[2] *I.e.* in the verses above.
[3] Sister-in-law, Gytha, the daughter of Thurgils Sprakaleg and the sister of Ulf the husband of Cnut's sister Estrith. The marriage was in 1019.
[4] Abbot of Jumièges from 1037.

royal favour to the see of his pontifical cathedral,[5] and with the authority derived from this promotion intruded himself more than was necessary in directing the course of the royal councils and acts; so much so, indeed, that . . . through his assiduous communication with him the king began to neglect more useful advice. Hence . . . he offended quite a number of the nobles of his kingdom. . . . And for such reasons his realm gradually became disturbed, because, when the holders of dignities died, one set of men wanted the vacant see for their own friends, and others were alienating them to strangers.[6] While the royal court was being shaken by this storm, Eadsi, archbishop of Kent [*i.e.* Canterbury] died.[7] There had grown up, however, in that Church of Christ, from childhood educated in the monastic discipline, one who sprang from the stock of that Godwin whom I have already mentioned, a monk named Aelric, a man active in secular business and endowed with much wisdom in the ways of the world, and not less beloved in the ways of that community. Both the whole body of the clergy and the monks of his monastery asked for his appointment as archbishop, and they elected him to the office both by general consent and by petition according to the rule. They also sent to Godwin, who was by royal favour ruling in that part of the kingdom, reminded him of his family, and entreated him for the love of his relative to approach the king and to approve this man as their pontiff since he was a nursling of that church and elected according to canon law. The famous earl loyally engaged himself as far as in him lay, and, approaching the king, informed him of the petition and election of the ecclesiastical community. But since . . . in those days the good king lent his ear more to the rival party, the earl suffered a defeat in pressing his request. Indeed, Robert left the see of London and, archbishop by royal grant, migrated to the Kentish church,[8] while all the clergy protested with all their might against the wrong.

His ambition satisfied at last, the archbishop in the office of high honour he had obtained began to provoke and oppose the earl [Godwin] with all his strength and might. . . . However, that certain lands of the earl ran with some that belonged to Christ Church, served to direct the hostile movements into a cause in which right was on the bishop's side. There were, also, frequent disputes between them, because he said that Godwin had invaded the lands of his archbishopric and injured him by keeping them to his own use. . . . And . . . Robert . . . adding madness to madness, tried to turn the king's mind against him, and brought Edward to believe that Godwin was guilefully scheming to attack him, just as once upon a time he had attacked his brother. That business was not related before because the matter did not arise. King Edward had had a full brother named Alfred. When their step-father king Cnut died and, at the instigation of the Danes (at that time very powerful and mighty in the kingdom), one of Cnut's sons, Harold[9] (born to him, they say, left-handedly, an arrogant fellow of bad character) succeeded to the kingdom, Alfred had entered Britain inadvisedly with a few armed Frenchmen. Then, when

[5] Robert was appointed bishop of London in 1044.
[6] The details of the disputed election to Canterbury which follow are unique to this source.
[7] 29 October, 1050.
[8] Mid-Lent 1051.
[9] 'Harefoot', son (probably) of Cnut and Aelfgifu of Northampton, regent for Harthacnut. *c.*1035–7, king 1037–40 Died 1040.

Alfred acted rashly about getting possession of the paternal kingdom, he was, by order of king Harold, they say, wrongfully arrested and tortured to death, and his comrades, they say, were disarmed by guile and then some murdered and the rest given in slavery to the victors. And so archbishop Robert asserted to king Edward, as we have just said, that the crime of his brother's death and of the massacre of his men was perpetrated on the advice of the glorious earl, since at that time also, as in the previous reign, he was the king's chief counsellor; and he persuaded him as much as he could that Godwin was now planning in the same way the ruin of even Edward himself, his son-in-law; and with continual persuasion he got the king to give more credence to this than was right.

As the king was moved by these accusations more than was just, all the nobles and earls from the whole of Britain assembled in the royal palace at Gloucester;[10] and there, after Edward had complained of these things, the guiltless earl was formally charged with the crime. When Godwin learned of this . . . he asked . . . for the king's peace, and offered to purge himself of the crime. But in vain. For the king had so convinced himself of the truth of this crime that he would not hear even one word of the purgation that was offered. Gathered there were Siward, earl of the Northumbrians . . . Earl Leofric[11] . . . and Alfgar, Earl Leofric's son. And after they had all struggled in vain to get the foul charge put to the ordeal, the royal court moved from that palace to London . . . [Godwin and his forces took up position on the opposite side of the Thames at his manor (of Southwark) and the earl again offered to satisfy the king in any way he chose. By the mediation of Stigand, then bishop of Winchester, judgement was deferred while the king took counsel.] Meanwhile archbishop Robert stood fiercely in the way of the earl, and at length at his instigation there was declared by the king against the earl this irrevocable judgement in the case at issue: that he could hope for the king's peace when and only when he gave him back his brother alive together with all his men and all their possessions intact which had been taken from them quick or dead . . . [Godwin was thus forced into banishment, 'rode hard for Bosham on Sea' and took ship with his wife and children to Flanders. The archbishop, still unsatisfied –] used every device to secure that even the queen herself, the earl's daughter, should be separated from the king, against the law of the Christian religion. This plan the king, although not opposing, yet did mitigate, giving out as reason for the separation this honourable pretext, that she was to await the subsidence of the storms over the kingdom in the monastery of Wilton,[12] where she had been brought up. And so with royal honours and imperial retinue, but with grief at heart, she was brought to the walls of Wilton convent, where for almost a year in prayers and tears she awaited the day of salvation. . . .

117 (c.iv) pp. 25–8 . . . This disturbance in the English kingdom happened about the beginning of October [1051]; and the one party[13] was received into Flanders for the

[10] September, 1051
[11] Earl of Mercia.
[12] An evident error for Wherwell. Cf. No. **86**.
[13] *I.e.* earl Godwin and those who went with him.

winter by count Baldwin [V] and the other[14] into Ireland by king Dermot.[15] And since, as we said before, Godwin was revered by all Englishmen as a father, when the unexpected news of his departure was known, the heart of the people was sore afraid. They considered his absence . . . the ruin of the English people. . . . Some hurried after him, some sent messages that they were ready . . . to fight for him. . . . And although this man so admirable in his loyalty and courage . . . was sought by the whole kingdom with so much love and yearning, he sent again to ask for peace and mercy from the king, his lord, that he might with his permission come before him and lawfully purge himself. Also the king of the French[16]. . . asked through ambassadors for this; and the marquis[17] of Flanders . . . urged the same. . . .

But when the active earl saw that he was wrongfully overthrown and that by the intrigue of evil men he was barred from a legal trial, he remembered his old valour and the many achievements of his early youth, assembled a large fleet in the River Yser, and in the middle of the next summer [1052] put to sea; and with a favourable wind blowing from due east, entered a port on the shore of Britain.[18] All the eastern and southern English who could manage it met his ship; all came to meet him, I repeat, like children their long-awaited father. At the same time, and stirred by the same news, his two sons[19] mentioned before came with large naval forces from Ireland to meet him; and they wasted with sword, fire and the seizure of booty all the kingdom from the farthest limits of the western Britons or English to the place where the earl was stationed. . . . The sea was covered with ships. The sky glittered with the press of weapons. And so at length, with the soldiers made more resolute by mutual exhortation, they crossed the Kentish sea, as it is called, and, with the ships in long line astern, entered the mouth of the river Thames.

When the king heard of this hostile and unlicensed entry into the kingdom, although he did not believe his informers, he nevertheless came with such military force as he could muster to London; and, as he was of passionate temper and a man of prompt and vigorous action, he tried to deny them entry into the city where he was encamped. But the whole city went out to help and protect the earl, and all with one voice joyfully applauded his coming. And since opportunity was bringing him superior strength from all directions, many urged that he should make an attack even on the king himself. But the earl, loyal and devoted to God, drew back in horror from these words and purpose. . . . When he had vigorously deterred them all from such an action, and had come into the king's presence, he immediately cast away his weapons and threw himself at his feet, and begged as a suppliant that in the name of Christ . . . he would grant him permission to purge himself of the crime with which he was charged, and bestow the peace of his favour on him when cleared. The king was constrained both by his mercy and the satisfaction offered by the

---

[14] Godwin's sons Harold and Leofwine, as the author had stated above.

[15] Diarmaid, king of Leinster and Dublin.

[16] Henry I.

[17] Evidently here an alternative title to count.

[18] The fact that the port is not named shows that the author is not always well informed. Cf. Wilton for Wherwell, No. **116** above.

[19] Harold and Leofwine, as above.

86

earl — who in any case appeared much superior in arms, if he chose to use them — and also indeed because he had been deserted, especially by the flight of the archbishop and of many of his men who feared to face the earl, since it was they who had been responsible for that storm of trouble. He was, moreover, overcome by the prayers of the suppliants. So he returned them their arms and entered the palace with the earl. There he gradually calmed the boiling tumult of his mind, and, with the advice of his council, gave the earl the kiss of peace, condoned all offences, and also granted his full favour both to him and all his sons. A short time after a party was properly sent with royal pomp, as was right, to the monastery of Wilton. And . . . so after all the kingdom's turmoil had abated, the queen, that earl's daughter, was brought back to the king's bed-chamber. And so, after this great evil had been checked without bloodshed by the wisdom of the earl, there was deep joy both at court and in the whole country. [More verses follow.]

118 (c.v) pp. 30–7 [Earl Godwin died (15 April 1053) at Winchester and was buried in the Old Minster of which he was a benefactor.] His son Harold, eldest in birth as in wisdom, was, by the king's favour, appointed to the earldom in his place; and at this the whole English host breathed again and was consoled for its loss. In the strength of his body and mind Harold stood forth among the people like a second Judas Maccabeus: a true friend of his race and country, he wielded his father's powers even more actively, and walked in his ways, that is, in patience and mercy, and with kindness to men of good will. But disturbers of the peace, thieves and robbers this champion of the law threatened with the terrible face of a lion. Not long afterwards also died Siward, earl of the Northumbrians . . . and he was buried in the church he had built from its foundations in honour of St Olave, king and martyr.[20] And Tostig, a man of courage, and endowed with great wisdom and shrewdness of mind, with the aid of his friends, and especially, and deservedly, his brother, earl Harold, and his sister the queen, and with no opposition from the king because of innumerable services faithfully performed, assumed his earldom. And since the occasion offers, we wish, to the best of our small powers, to inform posterity about the life, habits, and deeds of these two brothers. And we do not think our wish to do this unreasonable, both on account of the plan of the work, and also so that their posterity shall have models for imitation. Both had the advantage of distinctly handsome and graceful persons, similar in strength, as we gather; and both were equally brave. But the elder, Harold, was the taller, well practised in endless fatigues and doing without sleep and food, and endowed with mildness of temper and a more ready understanding. He could bear contradiction well, not readily revealing or retaliating — never, I think, on a fellow citizen or compatriot. With anyone he thought loyal he would sometimes share the plan of his project, sometimes defer this so long, some would judge — if one ought to say this — as to be hardly to his advantage. Indeed, the fault of rashness or levity is not one that anybody could charge against him, or Tostig, or any son born of Godwin, or anyone brought up under his rule or instruction. And earl Tostig himself was endowed

[20] This church was at Galmanho in York. The dedication to the Norwegian king Olave is worth noting.

with very great and prudent restraint – although occasionally he was a little over-zealous in attacking evil – and with bold and inflexible constancy of mind. He would first ponder much and by himself the plans in his mind, and when he had ascertained by an appreciation of the matter the final issue, he would set them in order; and these he would not readily share with anyone. Also sometimes he was so cautiously active that his action seemed to come before his planning; and this often enough was advantageous to him in the theatre of the world. When he gave, he was lavish with liberal bounty, and, urged by his religious wife,[21] it was done more frequently in honour of Christ than for any fickle favour of man. In his word, deed, or promise he was distinguished by adamantine stead-fastness. He renounced desire for all women except his wife of royal stock, and chastely, with restraint, and wisely he governed the use of his body and tongue. Both persevered with what they had begun; but Tostig vigorously, Harold prudently; the one in action aimed at success, the other also at happiness. Both at times so cleverly disguised their intentions that one who did not know them was in doubt what to think. And to sum up their characters for our readers, no age and no province has reared two mortals of such worth at the same time. The king appreciated this, and with them thus stationed in his kingdom, he lived all his life free from care on either flank, for one drove back the foe from the south and the other scared them off from the north. Also the king did not suffer their younger brother, Gyrth . . . to be left out of the honours, but gave him a shire at the extremity of East Anglia, and promised to increase this when he was older and had thrown off his boyhood years.

The senior brother studied the character, policy and strength of the princes of Gaul not only through his servants but also personally; and adroitly and with natural cunning and at great length observed what he could get from them if he needed them in the manage-ment of any business. And he acquired such an exhaustive knowledge of them by these means that he could not be deceived by any of their proposals. Having carefully observed the Frankish customs, and being himself famous by name and reputation in that country, he made his way to the relics of the Apostles at Rome.[22] And when he had worshipped there with fitting bounty the threshold of the saints, by God's grace he came home, passing with watchful mockery through all ambushes, as was his way.

Earl Tostig and his younger brother Gyrth also made the pilgrimage to Rome (1061), which was visited at this time also by Ealdred, bishop of Worcester and would-be archbishop of York, Giso, bishop of Wells, and Walter, bishop of Hereford, on ecclesiastical business[23]. The first went for his pallium and the other two for the consecration they would not receive from Stigand the schismatical archbishop of Canterbury. In the verse interlude which follows, the author bewails the coming fatal quarrel between Tostig and Harold – 'Ah, vicious discord sprung from brother's strife!' etc.

119 (c.vi) pp. 40–2   And so, with the kingdom made safe on all sides by these princes,

[21] Judith, daughter of Baldwin IV of Flanders and his second wife, Eleanor of Normandy. According to this source they married in the autumn of 1051 (pp. 24–5).
[22] Harold's pilgrimage to Rome is known almost exclusively from this source. The date may be 1056. See F. Barlow n. 5 to p. 33 of this *Life*.
[23] The relevant section has very full notes by Barlow.

the most kindly king Edward passed his life in security and peace, and spent much of his time in the glades and woods in the pleasures of hunting. . . . In these . . . activities he sometimes spent the day, and it was in these alone that he seemed naturally inclined to snatch some worldly pleasure. Otherwise this man, of his free will devoted to God, lived in the squalor of the world like an angel. . . . What tongue or what page could unfold, in accordance with reality and truth, how kindly he received religious abbots and monks, above all foreign. . . . Moreover, . . . he exhibited such men as models to the abbots and monks of his own kingdom, for monastic discipline had come to these more recently, and was on that account less strict. . . . Moreover, it was quietly and only for the occasion . . . that he displayed the pomp of royal finery in which the queen obligingly arrayed him. . . . Although by custom and law a royal throne was always prepared for her at the king's side, she preferred, except in church and at the royal table, to sit at his feet, unless perchance he should reach out his hand to her, or with a gesture of the hand invite or command her to sit next to him. . . .

120 (c.vi) pp. 43–6 . . . But now let us turn again[24] to king Edward and his royal consort Edith – the illustrious mistress whom we chiefly serve in this present account – and display with all the power and understanding we have, and with the aid of God's grace and favour, with what zeal they showed their devout faith in the church of Christ.

Outside the walls of London, upon the river Thames, stood a monastery dedicated to St Peter, but insignificant in buildings and numbers, for under the abbot only a small community of monks served Christ. Moreover the endowments from the faithful were slender, and provided no more than their daily bread. The king, therefore, being devoted to God, gave his attention to that place, for it both lay hard by the famous and rich town and also was a delightful spot, surrounded with fertile lands and green fields and near the main channel of the river, which bore abundant merchandise of wares of every kind for sale from the whole world to the town on its banks. And, especially, because of his love of the Prince of the Apostles, whom he worshipped with uncommon and special love, he decided to have his burial place there. Accordingly he ordered that out of the tithes of all his revenues should be started the building of a noble edifice, worthy of the Prince of the Apostles.[25] . . . And so, at the king's command the work, nobly begun is being prepared successfully; and neither the outlay nor what is to be expended are weighed, so long as it proves worthy and acceptable to God and blessed Peter. The house of the principal altar, raised up with very high arches (or vaults – *fornicibus*), is surrounded with squared work and even jointing; moreover the periphery of the building itself is enclosed on either side

[24] The author has briefly referred to campaigns against the Welsh by earl Harold and against the Scots by earls Siward and Tostig, pp. 42–3.
[25] The translation from here to the end of the paragraph is taken from R.D.H. Gem, 'The Romanesque rebuilding of Westminster Abbey', *Battle*, iii, 1980, p. 36. That important article, on what is, in fact, the building by Edward the Confessor of the first Norman church in England, should certainly be consulted. The church was begun perhaps about 1050 and consecrated (unfinished) at Christmas 1065.

by a double arch of stones, strongly consolidated with a joining together of work from different directions. Further on is the crossing of the temple; which might surround the central quire of those singing to God, and with its twin abutment from different directions might support the lofty apex of the central tower; it rises simply, at first, with a low and strong vault (*or* arch – *fonice*); grows, multiple in art, with very many ascending spiral stairs; then, indeed, reaches with a plain wall right up to the wooden roof, carefully roofed with lead; indeed, disposed below and above, lead out chapels, fit to be consecrated by means of their altars to the memories of the apostles, martyrs, confessors and virgins. Moreover, this multiplicity of so vast a work is set out so great a space from the east [end] of the old temple that, of course, in the meantime the brethren staying therein might not cease from the service of Christ; and furthermore so that some part of the nave to be placed between might advance.

121 (c.vi) pp. 46–8 But so that the king should not labour alone, the queen . . . was drawn to emulate that project of his[26]. . . For at Wilton at that time, although there was a convent of the handmaidens of Christ, a choir, too, of the greatest antiquity, and her namesake saint,[27] adequately housed, was worshipped there – Edith, from whose stock king Edward himself was descended – the church was still of wood. And she judged no place more deserving her devoted labour and zeal than that which, she recalled, had taken pains with her education . . . and began here royally to build a monastery in stone. Impetuously she urged the workmen to make haste. Thus here the king and there the queen strove in a contest which was pleasing to God. . . . But the prudent queen's building, because it was more modestly planned, was complete more quickly . . . [Some account of the dedication to St Benedict in 1065 follows.]

122 (c.vii) pp. 50–5. . . At this time [1065] the earl of the Northern Angles . . . Tostig, was at the king's court. . . . Meanwhile, a party of nobles, whom he had repressed with the heavy yoke of his rule because of their misdeeds, conspired among themselves against him.[28]. . . To give them authority for their savage rashness, they made the younger son of earl Aelfgar[29] their leader and lord, and invited his elder brother[30] to join their mad conspiracy. . . . And all that region, which had for so long rested in the quietness of peace through the strength and justice of the famous earl [Tostig], by the wickedness of a few nobles was turned upside down for his own personal undoing. . . . The Northumbrians advanced as far south as Oxford where the king sought to conciliate them. . . . But those in revolt against their God and king rejected the conciliatory message, and replied to the king that either he should straightway dismiss that earl of his

[26] *I.e.* Westminster, above.
[27] St Edith, natural daughter of king Edgar the Peaceable, brought up by her mother, who became a nun, at Wilton, and died aged 23 in 984. Of her it was written, 'She did not leave the world; she never knew it'.
[28] *I.e.* in Northumbria. This is the Northumbrian revolt of 1065.
[29] Morcar.
[30] Edwin.

from his person and the whole kingdom, or he himself would be treated as an enemy and have all them as enemies. And when the most gracious king had a second and third time through messengers and by every kind of effort of his counsellors tried to turn them from their mad purpose, and failed, he moved from the forests, in which he was as usual staying for the sake of regular hunting, to Britford, a royal manor near the royal town of Wilton. And when he had summoned the magnates from all over the kingdom, he took counsel there on what was to be done in this business. Not a few charged that glorious earl with being too cruel; and he was accused of punishing disturbers more for desire of their property . . . than for love of justice. It was also said, if it be worthy of credence, that they had undertaken this madness against their earl at the artful persuasion of his brother, earl Harold (which heaven forbid!). But I dare not and would not believe that such a prince was guilty of this detestable wickedness against his brother. Earl Tostig himself, however, publicly testifying before the king and his assembled courtiers charged him with this; but Harold, rather too generous with oaths (alas!), cleared this charge too with oaths.

When the rebels . . . would not agree, but rather raged more furiously in their mad purpose, Edward stirred up the whole population of the rest of England by a royal edict and decided to crush their impudent contumacy by force. But because changeable weather was already setting in from hard winter, and it was not easy to raise a sufficient number of troops for a counter-offensive, and because in that race horror was felt at what seemed civil war, some strove to calm the raging spirit of the king and urged that the attack should not be mounted. And after they had struggled for long time, they did not so much divert the king from his desire to march as wrongfully and against his will desert him. Sorrowing at this, he fell ill, and from that day until the day of his death he bore a sickness of the mind. He protested to God with deep sorrow, and complained to Him, that he was deprived of the due obedience of his men in repressing the presumption of the unrighteous; and he called down God's vengeance upon them.

The queen was on the other hand, confounded by the quarrel of her brothers and, on the other, bereft of all support by the powerlessness of her husband the king . . . she plainly showed her foreboding of future evils by her tears . . . [and] all men deduced future disasters from the signs of the present. But the king, the beloved of God, when he could not save his earl, graciously heaped on him many gifts and let him depart, profoundly, distressed at the powerlessness that had come upon him. And a short time after that, Tostig took leave . . . and with his wife and infant children and a goodly company of his thegns (*nobilium*) crossed the Channel and came to that old friend of the English people, count Baldwin. . . . He [Baldwin] received the husband of his sister honourably . . . and bade him dwell . . . in a town which is named after the famous St Omer. . . . This happened a few days before Christmas; and soon, within the festal days, king Edward, the beloved of God, languishing from the sickness of soul he had contracted, died indeed to the world, but was joyfully taken up to live with God.[31]

[31] At this point Barlow's 'Part I' ends. 'Part II', which is much more a religious and hagiographical life of Edward the Confessor and much of which is lost, opens with a long and lamenting poetic section.

(Part II)

123 Pp. 74–81 [The dying king Edward lies at his new palace of Westminster –]
. . . While he slept those in attendance felt in his sleeping body the travail of his unquiet soul, and, woken by them in their terror, he spoke these words (Up till then, for the last two days or more, weakness had so tired him that when he spoke scarcely anything he said had been intelligible) . . . 'Just now,' he said, 'two monks stood before me, whom I had once known very well when I was a young man in Normandy, men of great sanctity, and for many years now relieved of earthly cares. And they addressed me with a message from God. "Since," they said, "those who have climbed to the highest offices in the kingdom of England, the earls, bishops and abbots, and all those in holy orders are not what they seem to be, but, on the contrary, are servants of the devil, on a year and a day after the day of your death God has delivered all this kingdom, cursed by him, into the hands of the enemy, and devils shall come through all this land with fire and sword and the havoc of war.". . .

When those who were present had heard these words – that is to say, the queen, who was sitting on the floor warming his feet in her lap, her brother, earl Harold, and Robert,[1] the steward of the royal palace and a kinsman of the king, also archbishop Stigand and a few more whom the blessed king when roused from sleep had ordered to be summoned – they were all sore afraid as men who had heard a speech containing many calamities and a denial of the hope of pity. And while all were stupefied and silent from the effect of terror, the archbishop himself, who ought either to have been the first to fear or give a word of advice, with folly at heart whispered in the ear of the earl that the king was broken with age and disease and knew not what he said. But the queen and those who had been wont to know and fear God in their hearts, all pondered deeply the words they had heard and understood them quite otherwise, and correctly. For these knew that the Christian religion was chiefly dishonoured by men in holy orders, and that both the Pope of Rome by means of legates and letters, and the king and queen by frequent admonition had often proclaimed this ⸱ . . [A passage on the moral depravity of England and its clergy follows] . . . If God looks down upon us, he will find, alas, nothing in us to cause Him to cease from smiting. That man will repent too late or not at all who thought that the blessed king, filled with prophetic spirit by virtue of his auspicious life, rambled owing to age and disease. . . .

But leaving this sorrow for a while, let us return to the other, and describe how this gem of God stripped off the corruption of his earthly body and obtained a place of eternal splendour in the diadem of the heavenly king. When he was sick unto death and his men stood and wept bitterly, he said, 'Do not weep, but intercede with God for my soul, and give me leave to go to Him.' . . . Then he addressed his last words to the queen who was sitting at his feet, in this wise, 'May God be gracious to this my wife for the zealous solicitude of her service. For she has served me devotedly, and has always stood close by my side like a beloved daughter. And so from the forgiving God may she obtain the reward of eternal happiness.' And stretching forth his hand to his governor (*nutricium*), her brother,

---

[1] Identified as Robert fitz Wimarch and a staller or steward of the king.

Harold, he said, 'I commend this woman and all the kingdom to your protection. Serve and honour her with faithful obedience as your lady and sister, which she is, and do not despoil her, as long as she lives, of any due honour got from me. Likewise I also commend those men who have left their native land for love of me, and have up till now served me faithfully. Take from them an oath of fealty, if they should so wish, and protect and retain them, or send them with your safe conduct safely across the sea to their own homes with all that they have acquired in my service. Let the grave for my burial be prepared in the minster[2] in the place which shall be assigned to you' . . . Now and then he also comforted the queen . . . to ease her natural grief. 'Fear not', he said, 'I shall not die now, but by God's mercy regain my strength.' Nor did he mislead . . . by these words, for he has not died but has passed from death to life, to live with Christ.

. . . They bore his holy remains from his palace home into the house of God. . . . And so, before the altar of St Peter the Apostle, the body, washed by his country's tears, is laid up in the sight of God.[3] . . .

The Song of the Battle of Maldon

This heroic poem concerning the Battle of Maldon (Essex) fought against the Vikings in August 991 survives only in part (352 lines), lacking its beginning and probably its end. In the past generally accepted as a contemporary and authentic account, it may be in its details literary fiction of the earlier eleventh century, composed especially to extol the heroic virtues in contrast to the tribute-paying weakness and divisions of Ethelred's reign (979–1016). The crucial point has been succinctly put – 'As we have it, the text of Maldon equates survival with infamy; if it is history, what living man could tell its story?'; though it may equally be argued that a survivor to relate his experience to the unknown poet could have been a fallen warrior recovered from his wounds, or even one who fought on relatively unscathed until the bitter end and the Danes' withdrawal. The question matters less to us because the principal reason for the poem's inclusion here is its vivid portrayal of late Old English military tactics, whether actual at Maldon in 991 or assumed then to have been adopted – the dismounting of all before the fight, and the defensive formation of the shield-wall – which are those also of Hastings in 1066 (No. **48**)

A good and full discussion of the general significance of the poem is that of George Clark, 'The Battle of Maldon: *A Heroic Poem*', in *Speculum*, xliii, 1968. The relevant entry for 991 in the 'A' version of the Anglo-Saxon Chronicle reads: 'In this year Olaf came with 93 ships to Folkestone, and ravaged round about it, and from there went to Sandwich, and so from there to Ipswich, and overran it all, and so to Maldon. And ealdorman Brihtnoth came against him there with his army and fought against him; and they killed the ealdorman there and had control of the field. . . .' The 'C' version (together

---

[2] Westminster Abbey.
[3] King Edward died on 4 or 5 January 1066 and was buried on 6 January in his new church at Westminster. There is no mention in this source of Harold's coronation, also at Westminster, which took place on the day of the funeral.

with 'D' and 'E') reads: 'In this year Ipswich was ravaged and very soon afterwards ealdorman Brihtnoth was killed at Maldon. And in that year it was determined that tribute should first be paid to the Danish men. . . .'

Source and translation: *English Historical Documents*, i, ed. and trans. D. Whitelock (1955), No. 10.

124   Then he bade each warrior leave his horse, drive it afar and go forth on foot, and trust to his hands and to his good intent.

Then Offa's kinsman first perceived that the earl would suffer no faintness of heart; he let his loved hawk fly from his hand to the wood and advanced to the fight. By this it might be seen that the lad would not waver in the strife now that he had taken up his arms.

With him Eadric would help his lord, his chief in the fray. He advanced to war with spear in hand; as long as he might grasp his shield and broad sword, he kept his purpose firm. He made good his vow, now that the time had come for him to fight before his lord.

Then Brihtnoth began to array his men; he rode and gave counsel and taught his warriors how they should stand and keep their ground, bade them hold their shields aright, firm with their hands and fear not at all. When he had meetly arrayed his host, he alighted among the people where it pleased him best, where he knew his bodyguard to be most loyal.

Then the messenger of the Vikings stood on the bank, he called sternly, uttered words, boastfully speaking the seafarers' message to the earl, as he stood on the shore. 'Bold seamen have sent me to you, and bade me say, that it is for you to send treasure quickly in return for peace, and it will be better for you all that you buy off an attack with tribute, rather than that men so fierce as we should give you battle. There is no need that we destroy each other, if you are rich enough for this. In return for the gold we are ready to make a truce with you. If you who are richest determine to redeem your people, and to give to the seamen on their own terms wealth to win their friendship and make peace with us, we will betake us to our ships with the treasure, put to sea and keep faith with you.'

Brihtnoth lifted up his voice, grasped his shield and shook his supple spear, gave forth words, angry and resolute, and made him answer: 'Hear you, searover, what this folk says? For tribute they will give you spears, poisoned point and ancient sword, such war gear as will profit you little in battle. Messenger of the seamen, take back a message, say to your people a far less pleasing tale, how that there stands here with his troop an earl of unstained renown, who is ready to guard this realm, the home of Ethelred my lord, people and land; it is the heathen that shall fall in the battle. It seems to me too poor a thing that you should go with our treasure unfought to your ships, now that you have made your way thus far into our land. Not so easily shall you win tribute; peace must be made with point and edge, with grim battle-play, before we give tribute.'

Then he bade the warriors advance, bearing their shields, until they all stood on the river bank. Because of the water neither host might come to the other. There came the tide, flowing in after the ebb; the currents met and joined. All too long it seemed before they might clash their spears together. Thus in noble array they stood about Pante's stream, the flower of the East Saxons and the shipmen's host. None of them might harm another, unless a man should meet his death through javelin's flight.

The tide went out, the seamen stood ready, many a Viking eager for war. Then the bulwark of heroes appointed a warrior, hardy in war, to hold the bridge, Wulfstan was his name, accounted valiant among his kin. It was he, Ceola's son, who with his javelin shot down the first man that was so hardy as to set foot upon the bridge. There with Wulfstan stood warriors unafraid, Aelfhere and Maccus, a dauntless pair; they had no thought of flight at the ford, but warded themselves stoutly against the foe, as long as they might wield their weapons. When the Vikings knew and saw full well that they had to deal with grim defenders of the bridge, the hateful strangers betook themselves to guile,[1] craved leave to land, to pass over the ford and lead their men across. Then the earl, in his pride,[2] began to give ground all too much to the hateful folk; Brihthelm's son called over the cold water (the warriors gave ear): 'Now is the way open before you; come quickly, men, to meet us in battle. God alone knows to whom it shall fall to hold the field.'

The wolves of slaughter pressed forward, they recked not for the water, that Viking host; west over Pante, over the gleaming water they came with their bucklers, the seamen came to land with their linden shields.

There, ready to meet the foe, stood Brihtnoth and his men. He bade them form the war-hedge with their shields, and hold their ranks stoutly against the foe. The battle was now at hand, and the glory that comes in strife. Now was the time when those who were doomed should fall. Clamour arose; ravens went circling, the eagle greedy for carrion. There was a cry upon earth.

They let the spears, hard as files, fly from their hands, well-ground javelins. Bows were busy, point pierced shield; fierce was the rush of battle, warriors fell on either hand, men lay dead. Wulfmaer was wounded, he took his place among the slain; Brihtnoth's kinsman, his sister's son, was cruelly cut down with swords. Then was payment given to the Vikings; I heard that Edward smote one fiercely with his blade, and spared not his stroke, so that the doomed warrior fell at his feet. For this his lord gave his chamberlain thanks when time allowed.

Thus the stout-hearted warriors held their ground in the fray. Eagerly they strove, those men at arms, who might be the first to take with his spear the life of some doomed man. The slain fell to the earth.

The men stood firm; Brihtnoth exhorted them, bade each warrior, who would win glory in fight against the Danes, to give his mind to war.

Then came one, strong in battle; he raised his weapon, his shield to defend him, and bore down upon the man; the earl, no less resolute, advanced against the 'churl'. Each had an evil intent toward the other. Then the pirate sent a southern spear, so that the lord of warriors was stricken. He pushed with his shield so that the shaft was splintered, and shivered the spear so that it sprang back again. The warrior was enraged; he pierced with his lance the proud Viking who had given him the wound. The warrior was deft; he drove his spear through the young man's neck; his hand guided it so that it took the life of his

---

[1] Not all agree with 'guile' (and the implication that Brihtnoth was tricked) but would prefer e.g. 'prudence'. See G. Clark, *op. cit.*, pp. 58, 68.
[2] *Or* the uncritical 'high courage', *ibid.*, pp. 58, 68–71.

deadly foe. Quickly he shot down another, so that his corselet burst asunder; he was wounded through his mail in the breast, a poisoned point pierced his heart. The earl was the more content; then the proud man laughed, and gave thanks to his Creator for the day's work that the Lord had granted him.

Then one of the warriors let a dart fly from his hand, so that it pierced all too deeply Ethelred's noble thegn. By his side stood a warrior not yet full grown, a boy in war. Right boldly he drew from the warrior the bloodly spear, Wulfstan's son, Wulfmaer the young, and let the weapon, wondrous strong, speed back again; the point drove in so that he who had so cruelly pierced his lord lay dead on the ground. Then a man, all armed, approached the earl, with intent to bear off the warrior's treasure, his raiment and his rings and his well-decked sword. Then Brihtnoth drew his blade, broad and of burnished edge, and smote upon his mail. All too quickly one of the seamen checked his hand, crippling the arm of the earl. Then his golden-hilted sword fell to the earth; he could not use his hard blade nor wield a weapon. Yet still the white-haired warrior spoke as before, emboldened his men and bade the heroes press on. He could no longer now stand firm on his feet. The earl looked up to heaven and cried aloud: 'I thank thee, Ruler of Nations, for all the joys that I have met with in this world. Now I have most need, gracious Creator, that thou grant my spirit grace, that my soul may fare to thee, into thy keeping, Lord of Angels, and pass in peace. It is my prayer to thee that fiends of hell may not entreat it shamefully.'

Then the heathen wretches cut him down, and both the warriors who stood near by. Aelfnoth and Wulfmaer, lay overthrown; they yielded their lives at their lord's side.

Then those who had no wish to be there turned from the battle, Odda's sons were first in the flight; Godric for one turned his back on war, forsook the hero who had given him many a steed. He leapt upon the horse that had been his lord's, on the trappings to which he had no right. With him his brothers both galloped away, Godwine and Godwig, they had no taste for war, but turned from the battle and made for the wood, fled to the fastness and saved their lives, and more men than was fitting at all, if they had but remembered all the favours that he had done them for their good. It was as Offa had told them on the field when he held a council, that many were speaking proudly there, who later would not stand firm in time of need.

Now was fallen the people's chief, Ethelred's earl. All the retainers saw how their lord lay dead. Then the proud thegns pressed on, hastened eagerly, those undaunted men. All desired one of two things, to lose their lives or to avenge the one they loved.

With these words Aelfric's son urged them to go forth, a warrior young in years, he lifted up his voice and spoke with courage. Aelfwine said: 'Remember the words that we uttered many a time over the mead, when on the bench, heroes in hall, we made our boast about hard strife. Now it may be proved which of us is bold! I will make known my lineage to all, how I was born in Mercia of a great race. Ealhhelm was my grandfather called, a wise ealdorman, happy in the world's goods. Thegns shall have no cause to reproach me among my people that I was ready to forsake this action, and seek my home, now that my lord lies low, cut down in battle. This is no common grief to me, he was both my kinsman and my lord.'

Then he advanced (his mind was set on revenge), till he pierced with his lance a seaman from among the host, so that the man lay on the earth, borne down with his weapon.

Then Offa began to exhort his comrades, his friends and companions, that they should press on. He lifted up his voice and shook his ashwood spear: 'Lo! Aelfwine, you have exhorted all us thegns in time of need. Now that our lord lies low, the earl on the ground, it is needful for us all that each warrior embolden the other in war, as long as he can keep and hold his weapon, hard blade, spear and trusty sword. Godric, Odda's cowardly son, has betrayed us all. Too many a man, when he rode on that horse, on that proud steed, deemed that it was our lord. So was our host divided on the field, the shield-wall broken. A curse upon his deed, in that he has put so many a man to flight!'

Leofsunu lifted up his voice and raised his shield, his buckler to defend him, and gave him answer: 'This I avow, that I will not flee a foot-space hence, but will press on and avenge my lord in the fight. About Sturmer the steadfast heroes will have no need to reproach me now that my lord has fallen, that I made my way home, and turned from the battle, a lordless man. Rather shall weapon, spear-point and iron blade, be my end.' He pressed on wrathful and fought sternly, despising flight.

Dunhere spoke and shook his lance; a simple churl, he cried above them all, bade each warrior avenge Brihtnoth: 'He that thinks to avenge his lord, his chief in the press, may not waver nor reck for his life.' Then they went forth, and took no thought for life; the retainers began to fight hardily, those fierce warriors. They prayed God that they might take vengeance for their lord, and work slaughter among their foes.

The hostage began to help them eagerly; he came of a stout Northumbrian kin, Aescferth was his name, Ecglaf's son. He did not flinch in the war-play, but urged forth the dart unceasingly. Now he shot upon a shield, now he hit his man; ever he dealt out wounds, as long as he could wield his weapons.

Still in the van stood Edward the Long, bold and eager; he spoke vaunting words, how that he would not flee a foot-space or turn back, now that his lord lay dead. He broke the shield-wall and fought against the warriors, until he had taken due vengeance upon the seamen for his lord. Then he himself lay among the slain.

So too did Aethelric, Sigebriht's brother, a noble companion, eager and impetuous, he fought right fiercely, and many another. They clove the hollow shield and defended themselves boldly. The buckler's edge burst and the corslet sang a fearful song.

Then Offa smote a seaman in the fight, so that he fell to the earth. Gadd's kinsman too was brought to the ground, Offa himself was quickly cut to pieces in the fray. Yet he had compassed what he had promised his chief, as he bandied vows with his generous lord in days gone by, that they should both ride home to the town unhurt or fall among the host, perish of wounds on the field. He lay, as befits a thegn, at his lord's side.

Then came a crashing of shields; seamen pressed on, enraged by war; the spear oft pierced the life-house of the doomed. Wigstan went forth, Thurstan's son, and fought against the men. Wighelm's child was the death of three in the press, before he himself lay among the slain.

That was a fierce encounter; warriors stood firm in the strife. Men were falling, worn out with their wounds the slain fell to the earth.

Oswold and Eadwold all the while, that pair of brothers, urged on the men; prayed their dear kinsmen to stand firm in the hour of need, and use their weapons in no weak fashion.

Brihtwold spoke and grasped his shield (he was an old companion); he shook his ash-wood spear and exhorted the men right boldly: 'Thoughts must be the braver, heart more valiant, courage the greater as our strength grows less. Here lies our lord, all cut down, the hero in the dust. Long may he mourn who thinks now to turn from the battle-play. I am old in years; I will not leave the field, but think to lie by my lord's side, by the man I held so dear.'

So too Godric, Aethelgar's son, emboldened them all to battle. Often he launched his javelin, his deadly spear, upon the vikings; thus he advanced in the forefront of the host; he hewed and laid low, until he too fell in the strife. It was not the same Godric that fled from the battle.

Anglo-Norman

When we turn to the Anglo-Norman literary sources of the earlier twelfth century we turn also to one of the most distinguished periods of historical writing in England or rather, as we should now say, the Anglo-Norman realm.[1] Names like those of Orderic Vitalis or William of Malmesbury are names to conjure with. Unfortunately limitations of space must mean that we draw on them here more briefly, and thus adhere to the golden rule of history that the more contemporary sources are the more important. Nevertheless for the student of the Norman Conquest and of contemporary England and Normandy the versions of events and commentary contributed by well–informed and well–read historians of the next generation, or, it may be, the traditions and living history of his house set down by some less ambitious monk compiling a cartulary or register, can be of great value, and our knowledge of our subject would not be the same without them. In fact, 'Florence' or John of Worcester has already been extensively used above in association with the Anglo-Saxon Chronicle, and extracts of varying quantity and length and now given below from Orderic Vitalis, William of Malmesbury, Hugh the Chantor, the Abingdon Chronicle, the Liber Eliensis and the Battle Abbey Chronicle.

Orderic Vitalis, The Ecclesiastical History

Amongst Anglo-Norman historians Orderic Vitalis is incomparable by the sheer scale and detail of his canvas, on which he worked for over 30 years. No one, it might be said, and

---

[1] See R.W. Southern, 'Aspects of the European tradition of historical writing: 4, The sense of the past'. *TRHS* (5), xxiii, 1973; M. Brett, in *The Writing of History in the Middle Ages*, pp. 101ff.

certainly no one now in print, knew the Anglo-Norman world as he did. Not only was he dedicated and indefatigable, but he was also very well informed indeed, researching, as we would say, all the extant histories he could find (and telling us about them in invaluable asides, **137–40**) and the charters and archives of his own house and others, as well as collecting oral testimony in his well connected abbey of St Evroul or on his occasional travels.

He was born in 1075 near Shrewsbury (**141**), and of mixed parentage, *i.e.* an English mother and a French father, Odelerius of Orleans who was a priest in the household of Roger of Montgomery earl of Shrewsbury. At the age of 10 he was given by his parents as an oblate to the monastery of St Evroul in Normandy, and though he was subsequently happy there this may possibly account for his pro-English and anti-Norman bias which is most certainly to be noted. His first known historical work comprised the so-called Interpolations in William of Jumièges, *i.e.* his edition and continuation of the *Gesta Normannorum Ducum*, 'The Deeds of the Dukes of Normandy', dating from after 1013.[1] This work is not represented in the extracts printed below as being overtaken by his larger work of *The Ecclesiastical History*. This, comprising in all thirteen books, was written and revised between c. 1109 and 1141 when he laid down his pen (**141**). It began, at the command of his abbot, as a history of the abbey of St Evroul and soon expanded into something vastly more ambitious, both a history of the Church and a history of the Normans.[2] Orderic's Book III, dealing mainly with St Evroul, was thus the first to be written, between c.1109 and c.1123–4. It was followed by Book IV in c.1125.

With the exception of the epilogue of No. **141** most of the extracts printed below are taken from Orderic's Books III and IV as dealing most particularly with the period of the Conquest. Even so, Orderic, like Domesday, scarcely lends himself to brief anthologizing. There is no substitute for reading him properly, and this may now be easily done by means of the splendid edition and translation of Marjorie Chibnall. Amongst the few extracts printed here, those relating to events in England from 1068 to 1071 seemed a priority as in effect supplying the lost end of William of Poitiers who was Orderic's principal source for them (**125–30**). Some extracts relating to the foundation and early history of St Evroul seemed irresistible as unique. (**133**) So, as particularly informative, did Orderic's section on the distribution of fiefs and honours in England after 1071 and his remarks about William of Jumièges, William of Poitiers and John of Worcester amongst others (**131, 137, 139 40**), all of whose works he used for this period as we do. Certain other extracts relating to Bec and to the deaths respectively of queen Mathilda and king William make up a collection which, though short, is intended to be representative.

Source: For English-speaking readers the recent edition of Marjorie Chibnall, with translation, supersedes all others, *viz The Ecclesiastical History of Orderic Vitalis*, Oxford Medieval Texts, 6 vols., 1969–80. Behind it lies the edition (Latin only) of Auguste le Prévost, *Orderici Vitalis*

---

[1] See p. 2 above and especially Elizabeth M.C. Van Houts, in *Revue d'Histoire des Textes*, viii, 1978, 213–22.
[2] The change occurs on p. 169 of the second volume of Marjorie Chibnall's edition, cited below. Cf. *ibid.*, ii, xvi.

Ecclesiasticae Historiae Libri Tredecim, Soc. de l'histoire de France, 5 vols., Paris, 1838–55. The translations used below are those of Marjorie Chibnall and the references for each extract are to her edition (with Orderic's Book references in parenthesis).

125   ii, 210–15 (Bk. IV)   After the king's return from Normandy, 1068 – He was at great pains to appease everyone. . . . Every city and district which he had visited in person or occupied with his garrisons obeyed his will. But in the marches (*terminos*) of his kingdom, to the west and north, the inhabitants were still barbarous, and had only obeyed the English king in the time of king Edward and his predecessors when it suited their ends.

Exeter was the first town to fight for liberty, but fell vanquished before the valiant forces that fiercely assaulted it. It is a wealthy and ancient city built in a plain, strongly fortified and only two miles away from the sea shore and the shortest routes to Ireland and Brittany. A great force of citizens held it, young and old seething with anger against every inhabitant of Gaul. Further, they had repeatedly sent for allies from the neighbouring districts and had detained foreign merchants with any aptitude for war, and had built or restored their towers and battlements as they judged necessary. They sent envoys urging other cities to combine with them in similar measures and prepared to fight with all their strength against the foreign king, with whom they had had no dealings before that time. When the king knew the truth of this he commanded the leading citizens to swear fealty to him. But they sent back the following message: 'We will neither swear fealty nor admit him within our walls; but we will pay tribute to him according to ancient custom.' The king in his turn replied as follows: 'It is not my custom to have subjects on such terms.' Thereupon he marched on them in force, and for the first time called out Englishmen in his army. When the chief citizens heard that the king was approaching with an army they went to meet him, begged for peace, offered to open their gates to him, promised to obey all his commands, and brought him all the hostages he demanded. But in spite of this, on returning to their fellow citizens, who were terrified of punishment for their previous disloyalty, they continued their hostile preparations, encouraging each other to fight for many reasons. On learning of this the king, now only four miles from the city, was filled with rage and astonishment.

First of all he rode nearer with 500 knights (*equitatibus*) to reconnoitre the ground, examine the fortifications, and learn what measures the enemy were taking. The gates were closed, and a great force had manned the ramparts and the whole circuit of the walls. So by the king's command the whole army closed in on the city, and one of the hostages was blinded within sight of the gates. But neither fear nor pity for the remaining hostages could shake the resolution of the angry citizens; instead their obstinate determination to defend themselves and their homes grew all the stronger. The king, however, closely besieged the city, attempting to storm it, and for many days he fought relentlessly to drive the citizens from the ramparts and undermine the walls. Finally the citizens were compelled by the unremitting attacks of the enemy to take wiser counsel and humbly plead for pardon. The flower of their youth, the older men, and the clergy bearing their sacred books and treasures went out to the king. As they humbly threw themselves on his mercy that just prince graciously granted them pardon and forgave their guilt, deliberately overlooking the fact that they had wantonly resisted him, and had insulted and ill-treated certain knights sent by him from Normandy, who had been driven by storm into their harbour. . . . The king refrained from seizing their goods and posted a strong and trust-worthy guard at the gates, so that the rank and file of the army could not suddenly break in and loot the city. He chose a spot within the walls where a castle was to be built, and left there Baldwin of Meules, son of count Gilbert,[3] and other leading knights to complete the building of the castle and remain as garrison. He himself went on further into Cornwall. After putting down every disturbance that came to his notice he disbanded his army, and returned to Winchester to celebrate the feast of Easter there.

126 ii, 214–15 (Bk. IV) In the year of Our Lord 1068 King William sent ambassadors to Normandy to summon his wife Mathilda to join him. At once she gladly obeyed her husband's commands, and crossed with a great company of vassals and noble women. Among the clergy who ministered to her spiritual needs the most eminent was Guy bishop of Amiens, who had already celebrated the battle between Harold and William in verse.[4] Ealdred archbishop of York, who had anointed her husband, now anointed Mathilda as queen consort on Whit Sunday [11 May] in the second year of King William's reign . . .

127 ii, 214–19 (Bk. IV) [The further disturbances of 1068[5] –] In the same year the noble youths Edwin and Morcar, sons of earl Aelfgar, rebelled, and many others with them. . . . For when king William had made his peace with earl Edwin, granting him authority over his brother and almost a third of England, he had promised to give him his daughter in marriage; but later, listening to the dishonest counsels of his envious and greedy Norman followers, he withheld the maiden from the noble youth, who greatly desired her and had long waited for her. At last his patience wore out, and he and his brother were roused to rebellion, supported by a great many of the English and Welsh.[6] . . . All were ready to conspire together to recover their former liberty, and bind themselves by weighty oaths against the Normans. In the regions north of the Humber violent disturbances broke out. . . . The city of York was seething with discontent and showed no respect for the holy office of its archbishop when he tried to appease it. . . .

To meet the danger the king rode to all the remote parts of his kingdom and fortified strategic sites (*opportuna loca*) against enemy attacks. For the fortifications (*munitiones*) called castles (*castella*) by the Normans were scarcely known in the English provinces, and so the English – in spite of their courage and love of fighting – could put up only a weak resistance to their enemies. The king built a castle (*castrum*) at Warwick and gave it

---

[3] Gilbert count of Brionne.
[4] Sometimes taken to refer to the extant *Carmen de Hastingae Proelio*, 'The Song of the Battle of Hastings', for which see above p. 1.
[5] Marjorie Chibnall (n. 5 to p. 214) observes at this point, 'Orderic, incorporating much material from William of Poitiers, gives the most detailed account we have of king William's campaigns when he carried the conquest of England to the west and north in 1068–9'.
[6] Orderic specifies Bleddyn, king of Gwynedd and Powis, as joining in.

into the keeping of Henry, son of Roger of Beaumont. After this Edwin, Morcar, and their men, unwilling to face the doubtful issue of a battle, and wisely preferring peace to war, sought the king's pardon and obtained it at least in outward appearance. Next the king built Nottingham castle (*castrum*) and entrusted it to William Peverel.

When the men of York heard this they were terrified, hastened to surrender lest worse befell, and sent the king hostages and the keys of the city. As he was very doubtful of their loyalty he fortified a castle in the city (*in urbe ipsa munitionem firmauit*), and left trustworthy knights to guard it. . . . [Malcolm king of Scots makes peace.] . . . When this was done the king retired, building castles (*castra*) at Lincoln, Huntingdon and Cambridge on his way, and garrisoning them strongly.

128 ii, 220–37 (Bk. IV) [The disturbances of 1069 and the devastation of the North –] In the third year of his reign king William bestowed the county of Durham on Robert of Commine, who shortly afterwards came to the city with 500 knights (*milites*), suspecting nothing. But during the first night the citizens fell upon them in a body, slaughtering him and all his knights (*milites*) except two who managed to escape. . . .

Not long afterwards Robert son of Richard, guardian of the castle (*praesidium*) at York was slaughtered with many of his men.[7] The English now gained confidence in resisting the Normans, whom they saw as oppressors of their friends and allies. . . .

Marleswein, Gospatric, Edgar Aethling, Archill, the four sons of Karl, and other powerful rebels met together, and joining forces with the citizens and men of the district dared to launch an attack on the royal castle (*munitio*) in York. William called Malet, who was castellan there, sent word to the king that he would be compelled to surrender unless his beleaguered forces were speedily relieved. Swift was the king's coming; he fell on the besiegers and spared no man. . . . The king remained a further eight days in the city, built a second castle[8] (*praesidium*), and left earl William fitz Osbern[9] as castellan there. . . .

The king returned to Winchester for Easter and sent Mathilda back to Normandy. Two sons of Harold from Ireland raided the south coast about Exeter and were defeated. Gytha, the mother of Harold fled to France with a great treasure.

At this time Swein king of Denmark fitted out a great fleet of Danes and English; and giving command to his two sons, Osbern his brother, two bishops, and three earls whom he held in high esteem, sent it to England. He had received many messengers from the English begging for help and sending subsidies; and he was moved by the death and disaster that had overtaken his men in Harold's war; but he was influenced even more by his desire for the kingdom to which . . . he had a claim of inheritance. . . . The Danes raided, and were driven off from Dover, Sandwich, Ipswich and Norwich . . . King William at the time was enjoying one of his regular hunting expeditions in the Forest of Dean. The moment he heard of the coming of the Danes he sent a messenger to York to tell his men

[7] On 28 January, 1069.
[8] *I.e.* the second of York's two castles, later the Old Baile. The first (see above) now has the thirteenth-century Clifford's Tower on its motte.
[9] Now earl of Hereford amongst other things.

to prepare for an attack and send for him if they were hard-pressed. The custodians of the castles (*praesidia*) there replied that they could hold out without help for a year. But already the aethling, Waltheof, Siward, and the other English leaders had joined the Danes. The enemy reached the wide estuary of the Humber. . . .

The Danes reached York, and a general rising of the inhabitants swelled their ranks. Waltheof, Gospatric, Marleswein, Elnoc, Archill, and the four sons of Karl were in the advance guard and led the Danish and Norse forces. The garrison made a rash sally to attack them and engaged them ill-advisedly within the city walls. Unable to resist such numbers they were all slain or taken prisoner.[10] The castles (*castella*) were left undefended. . . . The king marched north and attacked the Danes south of the Humber whereupon they recrossed to the other side.

There were local attacks by native rebels upon Montacute, Shrewsbury and Exeter and the king crushed other rebels at Stafford. He then advanced towards York but was held up for three weeks by the river at Pontefract until a courageous knight, Lisois of Montiers, found a ford

. . . Their route now lay through woods, marshes, mountains, valleys, along paths so narrow that two men could not walk abreast. So at last they approached York only to learn that the Danes had fled. The king assigned officers and castellans with armed retainers to repair the castles (*castella*) in the city, and left others on the bank of the Humber to ward off the Danes. He himself continued to comb forests and remote mountain places, stopping at nothing to hunt out the enemy hidden there. His camps were spread over an area of 100 miles. He cut down many in his vengeance; destroyed the lairs of others; harried the land and burned homes to ashes. Nowhere else had William shown such cruelty. Shamefully he succumbed to this vice, for he made no effort to restrain his fury and punished the innocent with the guilty. In his anger he commanded that all crops and herds, chattels and food of every kind should be brought together and burned to ashes with consuming fire, so that the whole region north of Humber might be stripped of all means of sustenance. In consequence so serious a scarcity was felt in England, and so terrible a famine fell upon the humble and defenceless populace, that more than 100,000 Christian folk of both sexes, young and old alike, perished of hunger. . . .

The king sent to Winchester for his regalia to hold his Christmas court at York and then continued his campaign. He advanced as far as the Tees, where Walthcof and Gospatric withdrew. The depleted Danish army returned to Denmark. William, through foul weather and impossible country, encouraging his forces by his own spirit and example, returned to York and restored the castles. He then prepared to cross the Pennines to suppress the Welsh and the rebels of Shropshire. At this there was incipient mutiny in his army by the men of Anjou, Brittany and Maine –

They urged in defence of their conduct that they could not obey a lord who went from one hazard to another and commanded them to do the impossible – The king continued on his way, leaving behind those who would not follow – along a road no horseman had attempted before . . . they were lashed with rain and hail. Sometimes all were obliged to feed on horses which had perished in the bogs. The king himself, remarkably sure-footed,

[10] York fell on 20 September 1069.

led the foot-soldiers, readily helping them with his own hands when they were in difficulties. So at last he brought his army safely to Chester and suppressed all risings throughout Mercia with royal power. He built a castle (*munitio*) at Chester and another at Stafford on his return, garrisoning both and supplying them with abundant provisions. Then going on to Salisbury he distributed lavish rewards to the soldiers for all they had endured, praised those who had shown prowess, and discharged them with warm thanks. But in his anger he kept back those who had wished to desert him for 40 days after the departure of their comrades, and in this way punished a crime that had deserved far more.

129   ii, 236–9 (Bk.IV)   After these events[11] King William celebrated Easter[12] in Winchester, where he was solemnly crowned by cardinals of the Roman Church. For in reply to his petition Pope Alexander [II] had sent three suitable legates to this cherished son of his, Erminfrid bishop of Sion and two cardinal priests. He persuaded these men to stay with him for a year; and listened to their counsels and honoured them as though they had been angels of God. They took part in much business up and down the country, as they found needful in regions which lacked ecclesiastical order and discipline. An important and influential synod was held at Windsor in the year of our Lord 1070. The king and cardinals presided over the council and Stigand, who had already been excommunicated, was deposed there.[13] He had defiled himself with perjury and homicide; and he had not honestly entered into the archbishopric by the right door, but had climbed in from the two bishoprics of Norfolk and Winchester, up the shameful ladder of ambition and intrusion. Some suffragans were deposed at the same time, because their sinful lives and ignorance of the pastoral care made them unworthy of episcopal office. Two Normans, chaplains of the king, were chosen to be nominated as bishops; Walchel in as bishop of Winchester in place of the deposed Stigand, and Thomas as archbishop of York, where the see was vacant through death. Both were men of foresight, full of kindness and humanity, venerable and loveable to men, venerating and loving God in their inmost souls. Others were promoted and brought over from France; all were men of learning and virtuous life, devoted to the divine cult.

King William was justly renowned for his reforming zeal; in particular he always loved true religion in churchmen for on this the peace and prosperity of the world depend. There is evidence of this in the reputation he enjoyed everywhere, and unquestionable proof in the works he performed. For when a bishop or abbot had come to the end of this life and died, and God's widowed church was mourning the loss of its head, this pious prince sent competent officials to the bereaved house and had all the church property inventoried to prevent its dilapidation by sacrilegious keepers. Then he summoned his bishops and abbots and other prudent counsellors, and with their advice tried to find the man most capable of governing the house of God in both spiritual and secular matters. Finally, the

[11] *I.e.* the winter campaign of 1069–70.
[12] 1070.
[13] Dr Chibnall points out that according to 'Florence' of Worcester (**99**) Stigand was deposed at Winchester at Easter, and Orderic is here conflating the two councils.

wise king appointed as administrator and ruler of the abbey or bishopric whoever seemed to his highest counsellors specially distinguished in life and doctrine. . . . The heresy of simony was detestable to him, and so in appointing abbots or bishops he gave less weight to wealth and power than to wisdom and a good life. He appointed abbots of known virtue to the English monasteries, so that by their zeal and discipline monasticism, which for a time had been lax and faltering, revived and was restored to its former strength.

130 ii, 256−7 (Bk.IV)   At this time [*c.* 1070] by the grace of God peace reigned over England; and a degree of security returned to its inhabitants. . . . English and Normans were living peacefully together in boroughs, towns and cities, and were intermarrying with each other. You could see many villages or town markets filled with displays of French wares and merchandise, and observe the English, who had previously seemed contemptible to the French in their native dress, completely transformed by foreign fashions. No one dared to pillage, but everyone cultivated his own fields in safety and lived contentedly with his neighbour. Unhappily this was not to last. Churches were built and restored; and in them pious men devoted their lives to rendering to God the prayers and praises due to Him. The king's passion for justice dominated the kingdom, encouraging others to follow his example. He struggled to learn some of the English language, so that he could understand the pleas of the conquered people without an interpreter, and benevolently pronounced fair judgements for each one as justice required. But advancing age prevented him from acquiring such learning, and the distractions of his many duties forced him to give his attention to other things.

131 ii, 260−7 (Bk. IV)   After William had defeated the leading Mercian earls as I have related[14] − Edwin being dead and Morcar languishing in prison − he divided up the chief provinces of England amongst his followers, and made the humblest of the Normans men of wealth, with civil and military authority. He gave William fitz Osbern, steward (*dapifer*) of Normandy, the Isle of Wight and county of Hereford, and set him up in the marches with Walter de Lacy and other proved warriors to fight the bellicose Welsh. . . . The king had already given the city and county of Chester to the Fleming Gerbod . . . [he returned to Flanders and fell into captivity] . . . Meanwhile the king granted the county of Chester to Hugh of Avranches, son of Richard called Goz,[15] who with Robert of Rhuddlan,[16] Robert of Malpas and other fierce knights (*proceres*), wrought great slaughter amongst the Welsh. He was more prodigal than generous; he went about surrounded by an army instead of a household. He kept no check on what he gave or received. His hunting was a daily devastation of his lands, for he thought more highly of fowlers and hunters than husbandmen or monks. A slave to gluttony, he staggered under a mountain of fat. . . . He was given over to carnal lusts and had a numerous progeny of sons and daughters by his concubines. . . .

---

[14] *I.e.* after the capture of Ely in 1071.
[15] *Vicomte* of the Avranchin.
[16] Son of Humphrey of Tilleul.

King William gave Roger of Montgomery first of all Arundel castle and the town of Chichester; and afterwards granted him the county of Shrewsbury. He was a wise and prudent man, a lover of justice, who always enjoyed the company of learned and sober men. .... He gave positions of authority in the county to William called Pantulf, Picot, Corbet and his sons Roger and Robert, and other brave and loyal men. . . .

King William gave the county of Northampton to earl Waltheof, son of Siward, one of the greatest of the English, and married him to his own niece Judith[17] to strengthen the bonds of friendship between them . . . To Walter called Giffard he gave the county of Buckingham, and to William of Warenne who had taken Gerbod's[18] sister Gundreda to wife he gave Surrey.[19] He also gave the county of Holderness to Eudo of Champagne, nephew of count Theobald,[20] who had married the king's sister, a daughter of duke Robert;[21] and the county of Norfolk to Ralph de Gael, a son-in-law of William fitz Osbern. He appointed Hugh of Grandmesnil castellan of Leicester; and he made a statesmanlike distribution of castellanies, sheriffdoms, great fiefs and rights to other lords. Henry son of Walchelin of Ferrières received the castle (*castrum*) of Tutbury, which Hugh of Avranches had held before; and the king granted many great honours to other adventurers who had supported him, and favoured them so highly that they had many vassals (*clientes*) in England wealthier and more powerful than their own fathers had been in Normandy.

What shall I say of Odo, bishop of Bayeux, who was an earl palatine (*consul palatinus*) dreaded by Englishmen everywhere, and able to dispense justice like a second king? He had authority greater than all earls and other magnates in the kingdom, and gained much ancient treasure, as well as holding Kent. . . . Then there was Geoffrey bishop of Coutances, of noble Norman stock. . . . He received from king William 280 vills, colloquially called 'manors'. . . .

Likewise Eustace count of Boulogne, Robert of Mortain, William of Evreux, and Robert of Eu and Geoffrey son of Rotrou of Mortagne and other earls and magnates too numerous to name received great revenues and fiefs (*honores*) in England from king William. So foreigners grew wealthy with the spoils of England, whilst her own sons were either shamefully slain or driven as exiles to wander hopelessly through foreign kingdoms. . . . King William carefully surveyed his whole kingdom, and had an exact description made of all the dues owed in the time of king Edward. Also he allocated land to knights (*milites*) and arranged their contingents (*ordines*) in such a way that the kingdom of England should always have 60,000[22] knights (*milites*), ready to be mustered at a moment's notice in the king's service whenever necessary.

[17] *c*. 1070.

[18] The earl of Chester, as above.

[19] The principal lands of Warenne were in Norfolk and Sussex and he evidently did not become earl of Surrey until 1088.

[20] Theobald count of Champagne.

[21] Adelaide.

[22] The number is, of course, an exaggeration.

132   Concerning Bec

ii, 296–7 (Bk. IV)   A great store of learning in both the liberal arts and theology was assembled by Lanfranc in the abbey of Bec, and magnificently increased by Anselm so that the school sent out many distinguished scholars and also prudent pilots and spiritual charioteers who have been entrusted by divine providence with holding the reins of the churches in the arena of this world. So by good custom the monks of Bec are so devoted to the study of letters, so eager to solve theological problems and compose edifying treatises, that almost all of them seem to be philosophers; and by association with them, even with those who pass as illiterates and are called rustics at Bec, the most erudite doctors can learn things to their advantage. The whole community is full of joy and charity in the service of God, and because true Wisdom is their teacher, they are unfailing in their devotions. I cannot speak too highly of the hospitality of Bec. . . . The doors of Bec are always open to any traveller, and their bread is never denied to anyone who asks for it in the name of Christ . . .

133   Concerning the foundation and early history of the abbey of St Evroul

ii, 14–21 (Bk. III)   William son of Giroie loved the church of God all his life long. . . . He had twice been on pilgrimage to the Holy Sepulchre at Jerusalem. . . . On his return from the second pilgrimage he renounced the world and took monastic vows at the abbey of Bec, which he piously endowed with the church of St Peter of Ouche. So abbot Herluin sent Lanfranc, who later became archbishop of Canterbury, with three monks to the church of Ouche of restore the service of God which had fallen into decay. The place was then deserted, and a thick growth of ivy covered the outer wall of the church. Two aged clerks, Restold and Ingran, alone remained there, serving God in humble poverty, as best they might in this wilderness.

Hearing that his nephews, Hugh and Robert de Grandmesnil, were planning to found a monastery, he persuaded them to do so here in the forest of Ouche where St Evroul had formerly had his abbey –

'Why not restore this monastery of his which was destroyed by pagans. You will find abundance of water there, and I have a wood near by from which I will supply everything you need for the church. Come and see the place. If you agree, we will combine our resources to built a church, fill it with holy men who will make continual intercession for us, and endow it so liberally that they will be able to devote their whole lives to the worship of God.'. . .

In the year of Our Lord 1050 . . . after deciding to restore the monastery of Ouche, William and Robert [his brother] the sons of Giroie, and Hugh and Robert, the sons of Robert of Grandmesnil, sought out William duke of Normandy and revealed their intentions to him, asking him to give his princely support to so worthy an undertaking. By common consent they gave the chosen site into his protection, free and quit from all customs and dues which anyone might try to exact from the monks or their men, saving only prayers. The duke gladly approved their good intention, and confirmed the charter of gifts which his magnates were giving to St Evroul, passing it on to Mauger, archbishop of Rouen, and his suffragans for corroboration with their subscriptions. When Hugh and Robert had obtained ducal permission to choose an abbot they visited Jumièges and asked abbot Robert[23] to let them have his monk Thierry as the first head of their house. The abbot was very willing to grant so reasonable a request from men of rank, and let his monk, whom he knew to be worthy to undertake care of souls, go with them. Well pleased, they presented him to the duke, who received him with due reverence and invested him with the church of St Evroul by handing him the pastoral staff as the custom is. Afterwards Hugh, bishop of Lisieux, with Osbern the archdeacon and other clerks, brought the good monk Thierry in solemn state to St Evroul and reverently blessed him there on Sunday, 5 October.[24] He did not regard his ordination as a matter for vain glory, but both in word and deed set an example of true religion to the monks under him. Brought up, indeed, from childhood in the house of God, he had learned to lead a life of continual devotion, and never failed in his prayers, fasts and vigils. He forced his body to endure extreme rigours of cold by sometimes going through the whole winter without a cloak. . . .

He obtained permission from his abbot to bring with him his nephew Ralph, Hugh the cantor, and other chosen brethren to help in building up the new community. With their aid, by working devotedly, he established regular life, moderate but firm discipline, and a well-ordered liturgy. He received men of all ages and ranks into the monastery, and patiently taught them to live under the rule of St Benedict. Among the first whom he taught a better way of life through humility in the school of Christ were Gunfrid and Reginald, Fulk the son of Fulk the dean, and other learned grammarians. But Riculf, an old man, and Roger, who were country priests, Durand the gardener, Geoffrey, and Olric and other simple converts were treated with more indulgence. Knowing that they could not understand the more profound books of the Scriptures, he sustained them with colloquies within their grasp, and strengthened their faith and discipline by the example of his own holy life. He himself instructed Herbert and Berengar, Goscelin and Ralph, Gilbert and Bernard, Richard and William, and many other boys of talent in the monastic school; and taught them to excel in reading aloud, singing, writing, and all other studies necessary for the servants of God who seek true knowledge. Soon the countryfolk around began to marvel that a school of such piety had sprung up in a barren wilderness which had been uninhabited for many years. . . .

ii, 48–51 . . . This same abbot [Thierry] was rightly loved by the virtuous and feared by evil-doers Desiring the joys of contemplation he delegated administrative duties as far as possible and gave himself up whole-heartedly to the divine service. He was always at his prayers, and performed the divine office that was proper for him. Being a brilliant calligrapher he left to the young monks at St Evroul some worthy monuments of his

[23] Presumably Robert 'Champart' made by Edward the Confessor bishop of London and archbishop of Canterbury.
[24] There is a minor error here since Sunday did not fall on 5 October in 1050 nor in any year between 1046 and 1057.

skill. . . . By gentle persuasion he induced some of the companions who had accompanied him from Jumièges to copy precious volumes of the divine law. . . .

With the aid of these and other scribes whom he persuaded to undertake the task the reverend father secured in the eight years of his abbacy copies of all the books of the Old and New Testaments and the complete works of Pope Gregory the Great for the library of St Evroul. Many excellent copyists . . . were trained in his school; they filled the monastic library with the treatises of Jerome and Augustine, Ambrose and Isidore, Eusebius and Orosius, and other fathers; and their example was an inspiration to young monks engaged in the same work. The venerable Thierry taught these young men, urging them repeatedly to avoid mental sloth which could harm body and soul alike. He used often to tell them the following story: 'In a certain monastery there dwelt a brother who had committed almost every possible sin against the monastic rule; but he was a scribe, devoted to his work, who had of his own free will completed a huge volume of the divine law. After his death his soul was brought for judgement before the throne of the just judge. Whilst the evil spirits accused him vehemently, bringing forward all his many sins, the holy angels showed in his defence the book he had written in the house of God; and the letters in the huge book were carefully weighed one by one against his sins. In the end one letter alone remained in excess of all the sins; and the demons tried in vain to find any fault to weigh against it. So the judge in his mercy spared this brother, and allowed his soul to return to his body for a little while, so that he might amend his life.[25]

ii, 144–51 (Bk. III) While these preparations were being made[26] Osbern abbot of St Evroul died . . . and the convent asked the prince to provide a successor before he embarked. He took counsel on this matter with his magnates at Bonneville, and . . . chose Mainer the prior. Duke William invested him with the temporalities by means of the pastoral staff, and instructed bishop Hugh[27] to invest him with the spiritual cure . . . he came from the near-by town of Echauffour, was thoroughly learned in grammar, dialectic and rhetoric, and showed himself vigilant and firm in rooting out vice, and eager to inspire the brethren to all good works . . .

He began to build a new church dedicated in the name of Mary, the blessed mother of God, St Peter the Apostle, and St Evroul the Confessor: and there seven altars in honour of the saints were consecrated to God. By this time the old church, which St Evroul had built in honour of the chief apostle . . . had almost crumbled away with age; and in any case it was too small for a community of monks that grew larger every day. Moreover, to build a stone church in the region of Ouche was a heavy labour, for the stone quarry at Merlerault which provided the ashlar blocks (*quadrati lapides*) was six miles away. The overseers whose business it was to procure great piles of stone and other equipment necessary for the works had the greatest difficulty in finding enough horses, oxen and wagons. . . . By the grace of God, and with the help and generous gifts of his brethren and friends, he

---

[25] A little later the abbot duly quotes to the young monks the sentence from St Benedict's Rule, 'Idleness is the enemy of the soul' (c.xl viii).

[26] *I.e.* for the invasion of England. The date is 1066.

[27] Of Lisieux.

completed a fine and spacious church worthy of the celebration of divine service, a cloister and chapter-house, dormitory and refectory, kitchen and store-room, and other buildings necessary for the daily life of the monks. Archbishop Lanfranc gave him 44 pounds of English money and two golden marks when he came to the dedication of the church at Caen[28] . . . and later sent him 40 pounds sterling from Kent. . . . Thanks to these gifts the tower of the church was erected, and a dormitory for the monks. Queen Mathilda gave a costly chasuble and cope for the divine office and 100 Rouen pounds for work on the refectory. . . . So thanks to many benefactors the fabric of the new monastery was raised, and the work begun on the church and monastic buildings worthily completed.

134 Concerning the foundation of churches, including Bec

ii, 10–13 (Bk. III)   Next William[29] his [duke Robert's] son, who was eight years old at the time, was invested with the duchy of Normandy; and in spite of the plots of his many enemies he ruled it indefatigably for 53 years.[30] He strove to imitate the zeal of his ancestors for the Church of God; and God granted him wealth and power to outshine them all. At Caen he built two abbeys, one for monks in honour St Stephen the first martyr, and the other for nuns in honour of the Holy Trinity. The barons of Normandy were inspired by the piety of their princes to do likewise, and encouraged each other to undertake similar enterprises for the salvation of their souls. They vied with each other in the good work, and competed in giving alms generously as befitted their rank. Each magnate would have thought himself beneath contempt if he had not supported clerks and monks on his estates for the service of God.

Orderic then refers to the foundations of Conches by Roger de Tosny, La Trinité-du-Mont at Rouen by Goscelin of Arques, and St Pierre-sur-Dives by William count of Eu. Next, about the foundation of Le Bec Hellouin, he has this to say –

In the time of duke Robert Gilbert count of Brionne invaded the canton of Le Vimeu with 3000 armed men, but the expedition turned out badly for him. For Enguerrand count of Ponthieu opposed him with a strong force, defeated him in a pitched battle, and put his men to flight with heavy losses in killed, maimed and captured. It was there that a certain knight (*miles*) named Herluin, fleeing in terror and fearing for his life, vowed to God that if he escaped alive from such dire peril he would never fight again, save for God alone. By God's will he came unscathed through all perils; and, mindful of his vow, he abandoned the world and built a cell to the honour of the blessed Mary, Mother of God, on his family estate (*in patrimonio suo*) in a place called Bec. The leaders of God's holy Church, recognizing his high birth and piety, made him abbot of the new monastery which he had founded. . . .

135 Concerning the death of Mathilda

iv, 44–7 (Bk. VII)   About this time, in the seventh indiction, Mathilda, queen of

[28] 1077.
[29] *I.e.* the future Conqueror
[30] 2 July 1035–9 September 1087.

England, fell sick; growing apprehensive because her illness persisted, she confessed her sins with bitter tears and, after fully accomplishing all that Christian custom requires and being fortified by the saving sacrament, she died on 3 November.[31] Her body was carried at once to the abbey of the Holy Trinity, which she had founded at Caen for nuns, and was reverently buried by many bishops and abbots between the choir and the altar. Monks and clergy celebrated her obsequies, attended by a great throng of poor people, for in her lifetime she had often been their benefactress in the name of Christ. A monument was erected over her, wonderfully worked with gold and precious stones, and this epitaph engraved in letters of gold.

> The lofty structure of this splendid tomb
> Hides great Mathilda, sprung from royal stem;
> Child of a Flemish duke; her mother was
> Adela, daughter of a king of France,
> Sister of Henry, Robert's royal son.
> Married to William, most illustrious king,
> She gave this site and raised this noble house,
> With many lands and many goods endowed,
> Given by her, or by her toil procured;
> Comforter of the needy, duty's friend;
> Her wealth enriched the poor, left her in need.
> At daybreak on November's second day
> She won her share of everlasting joy.[32]

136 Concerning the death of the Conqueror

iv, 100–1 (Bk. VII) . . . So though king William suffered great internal agony he kept a clear mind and all his powers of speech, and gave sound and practical advice to all who consulted him about the affairs of the kingdom.

At last on Thursday, 9 September, the king awoke as the sun was beginning to shed its clear rays over the earth and heard the sound of the great bell in the cathedral church.[33] When he asked what hour it was sounding, the attendants replied, 'My lord, the hour of prime is being rung in the church of St Mary.' Then the king raised his eyes to heaven with deep devotion, and looking up with outstretched hands said, 'I commend myself to my Lady, the blessed Mary, mother of God, that by her holy prayers she may reconcile me to her most dear Son, our Lord Jesus Christ.' As soon as he had spoken these words he died.

137 Orderic on William of Poitiers

ii, 258–61 (Bk. IV) William of Poitiers has brought his history up to this point,[34]

---

[31] 1083, and in fact on 2 November as on the epitaph, below.
[32] Though no lofty tomb stands over it, the queen's tombstone is still there in her church of the Holy Trinity at Caen, with the epitaph (in Latin) which Orderic records still about it.
[33] Of Rouen.
[34] Orderic has just related the capture of the Isle of Ely and earl Morcar in 1071.

eloquently describing the deeds of king William in a clever imitation of the style of Sallust. He was a Norman by birth, a native of Préaux, and had a sister there who became abbess of the nunnery of St Lèger. We call him 'of Poitiers' because he drank deeply of the fountain of learning there. When he returned home he was conspicuous for his learning in his native parts, and as archdeacon helped the bishops of Lisieux, Hugh and Gilbert, in the administration of their diocese. He had been a brave soldier before entering the church, and had fought with warlike weapons for his earthly prince, so that he was all the better able to describe the battles he had seen through having himself some experience of the dire perils of war. In his old age he gave himself up to silence and prayer, and spent more time in composing narratives and verse than in discourse. He published many subtly linked verses, intended for declamation, and was so free from jealousy that he invited his juniors to criticize and improve them. I have abridged his history of [king] William and his followers for some matters, but I have not tried to include all that he says, or to imitate his artistry.

ii, 184–5 (Bk. III)   His [king William's] virtue and high character, his successes and praiseworthy deeds of valour, have been treated eloquently by William of Poitiers, archdeacon of Lisieux, who has published a book wonderfully polished in style and mature in judgement. He himself was for many years the king's chaplain, and he set out to describe authentically, in detail, all the events which he had seen with his own eyes and in which he himself had taken part. But unfavourable circumstances prevented him from continuing his narrative up to the king's death.

138   Orderic on Guy bishop of Amiens

iii, 184–7 (Bk.III)   Guy bishop of Amiens also wrote a poem describing the battle of Senlac[35] in imitation of the epics of Virgil and Statius, abusing and condemning Harold but praising and exalting William. [See also **126** above.]

139   Orderic on William of Jumièges

ii, 2–5 (Bk.III)   Dudo, dean St Quentin, has eloquently described the warlike deeds of the first three dukes, composing a panegyric full of verbal flourishes and varied metres, which he offered to Richard son of Gunnor[36] to win his favour. This work was next skilfully abbreviated by William called Calculus, a monk of Jumièges, who published a succinct and lucid account of the four dukes next in succession.

ii, 78–9 (Bk. III)   But those who wish to know the details of the conflicts[37] and injuries which each side inflicted on the other may read about them in the books of William called Calculus of Jumièges and William of Poitiers archdeacon of Lisieux, who carefully

[35] *I.e.* Hastings.
[36] Richard II. For Dudo see above p. 2.
[37] *I.e.* between Henry I of France and the Conqueror, marked by the battles of Mortemer, 1054, and Varaville, 1057 (Nos. **21, 22** above).

recorded the deeds of the Normans and, after William became king of England, dedicated their works to him to gain favour.

iii, 305 (Bk. IV)   Dudo dean of Saint-Quentin wrote a careful account of the coming of the Normans and their cruel barbarism, and addressed it to Richard II, son of Gunnor, duke of Normandy. Furthermore, William called Calculus, a monk of Jumièges, skilfully worked over Dudo's material, aptly abbreviated it, added the acts of succeeding dukes up to the conquest of England, completed his narrative after the battle of Senlac, and dedicated it to William, the supreme king of his people.

140   Orderic on John of Worcester

ii, 186–9 (Bk. III)   John, an Englishman by birth who entered the monastery of Worcester as a boy and won great repute for his learning and piety, continued the chronicle of Marianus Scotus and carefully recorded the events of William's reign and of his sons William Rufus and Henry up to the present . . . [Information about Marianus Scotus follows] . . . After him John, at the command of the venerable Wulfstan bishop and monk, added to these chronicles events of about 100 years,[38] by inserting a brief and valuable summary of many deeds of the Romans and Franks, Germans and other peoples whom he knew.

141   Orderic on himself

vi, 550–7 (Bk. XIII, Epilogue)   Now indeed, worn out with age and infirmity, I long to bring this book to an end, and it is plain that many good reasons urge me to do so. For I am now in the sixty-seventh year of my life[39] and service to my Lord Jesus Christ, and while I see the princes of this world overwhelmed by misfortunes and disastrous set-backs I myself, strengthened by the grace of God, enjoy the security of obedience and poverty. . . . I was baptized on Holy Saturday[40] at Atcham on the great river Severn . . . at the hand of Orderic the priest. . . . Afterwards when I was five years old I was put to school in the town of Shrewsbury, and performed my first clerical duties for Thee in the church of St Peter and St Paul the apostles. There Siward, an illustrious priest, taught me my letters for five years, and instructed me in psalms and hymns and other necessary knowledge. . . . It was not Thy will that I should serve Thee longer in that place, for fear that I might be distracted among kinsfolk. . . . And so, O glorious God, who didst command Abraham to depart from his country and from his kindred and from his father's house[41], thou didst inspire my father Odelerius[42] to renounce me utterly, and submit me

---

[38] An inaccurate statement. Orderic was writing only some 50 years after Marianus's death, and the Worcester chronicle (for which see p. 51 above) incorporates notices relating to English history over five or six centuries.

[39] The year is 1141

[40] Orderic was born in 1075

[41] Genesis 12:1

[42] Of Orleans, a priest in the household of Roger of Montgomery earl of Shrewsbury

in all things to thy governance. So, weeping, he gave me, a weeping child, into the care of the monk Reginald, and sent me away into exile for love of Thee and never saw me again. And I, a mere boy, did not presume to oppose my father's wishes, but obeyed him willingly in all things, for he promised me in Thy name that if I became a monk I should taste of the joys of Paradise with the Innocents after my death. So . . . I abandoned my country and my kinsfolk, my friends and all with whom I was acquainted, and they, wishing me well, with tears commended me in their kind prayers to Thee, O Almighty God. . . .

And so a boy of 10, I crossed the English Channel and came into Normandy as an exile, unknown to all, knowing no one. Like Joseph in Egypt, I heard a language which I did not understand. But thou didst suffer me through Thy grace to find nothing but kindness and friendship amongst strangers. I was received as an oblate monk in the abbey of St Evroul by the venerable abbot Mainer in the eleventh year of my age . . . In place of my English name which sounded harsh to the Normans, the name Vitalis was given me, after one of the companions of St Maurice the martyr . . . I have lived as a monk in that abbey by Thy favour for 56 years, and have been loved and honoured by all my fellow monks and companions far more than I deserve. . . .

William of Malmesbury

If Orderic Vitalis is in a class by himself, William of Malmesbury none the less stands very high in the estimation of modern historians, as one of themselves, devoted to the past and writing no mere chronicles or annals but carefully planned histories based on wide research and seeking to reach the unbiased truth. 'In him, to a remarkable degree, the modern student of history finds a kindred spirit.'[1] He like Orderic is an Anglo-Norman in the fullest sense of mixed Norman and English parentage, and he, too, was a Benedictine monk, passing his life in the abbey of Malmesbury where he remained their scholarly librarian, eschewing all other monastic promotion. He has left many works behind him, of which the three most 'important' are the *Gesta Regum Anglorum* ('The Deeds of the Kings of the English', *c.*1125, revised *c.*1140), the *Gesta Pontificum Anglorum* ('The Deeds of the Bishops of the English', *c.*1125, revised *c.*1140), and the *Historia Novella* (1140–2), more or less a history of his own times and of the reign of Stephen. Others include his 'Life of St Dunstan', his 'Life of Wulfstan' and his history of Glastonbury Abbey, all three written probably in the 1120s and 1130s.

The extracts printed below are taken exclusively from the *Gesta Regum* and the *Gesta Pontificum*, the *Historia Novella* being concerned with a period beyond the span of this volume. Nos. **142–3** give at least some of the substance of the missing first part of William of Poitiers whom William of Malmesbury is known to have been using for the events there related.[2] Others provide allegedly new facts relating to the Conquest or William of Malmesbury's reflections upon it (Nos. **144–5**), and others his unusually

[1] R.R. Darlington, *Anglo-Norman Historians* (Inaugural Lecture), Birkbeck College, 1947, p. 10
[2] Cf. R.H.C. Davis in *The Writing of History in the Middle Ages*, ed. R.H.C. Davis and J.M. Wallace-Hadrill, p. 99.

informed interest in architecture, which seem vividly to reflect the revolution in English architecture brought about by the Normans (Nos. **144, 147–8, 150**).[3]

Gesta Regum

Source: *Willelmi Malmesbiriensis Monachi De Gestis Regum Anglorum*, ed. W. Stubbs, 2 vols., Rolls Series, 1887–9.

142 i, 191 (Bk. II) Besides all this[4] he [Ethelred II] behaved so shamelessly towards his wife that he could scarcely bring himself to share his bed with her, but with harlots brought shame upon the royal majesty. She, on the other hand, conscious of her high lineage, began to hate the husband who was indifferent both to her blameless modesty and to her fecundity – for she had borne him two sons, Alfred and Edward. She was the daughter of Richard count of Normandy, the son of William (Longsword). . . .
ibid., p. 219. Thus when all England seemed to be brought under his rule, he [Cnut] bent all his efforts to conciliating the English . . . for which reason he sent to Normandy for the wife of the late king, so that in being subjected to their accustomed lady they would the less resent Danish rule. By the same means he hoped to win the favour of [duke] Richard, who might think less of his nephews if he could hope for others by Cnut. . . .

143 ii, 285–6 (Bk. III) Robert [the Magnificent], the other son of Richard II, after he had held the duchy of Normandy gloriously for seven years, resolved on making the pilgrimage to Jerusalem. He had then a son aged seven, born of his mistress, whose beauty he had seen by chance when she was dancing . . . thenceforth he loved her only, and for some time kept her as his true wife. Of her William was born, named after his great-great-grandfather . . . who, the very moment when he came into the world and touched the ground, seized with both hands the rushes strewn upon the tiled floor, firmly grasping what he had taken up. . . .

When everything was ready for the pilgrimage to Jerusalem, the magnates (*proceres*) were summoned to a council at Fécamp. There, at the father's command, oaths of fealty to William were sworn by all: count Gilbert [of Brionne] was appointed guardian of the boy, and the protection of the guardian was assigned to Henry king of the French. . . . So matters remained until the news of duke Robert's death when everywhere men's affections changed with his [Williams's] fortunes: then everyone fortified his castles (*oppida*), raised towers (*turres agere*) and brought in provisions, and sought the first opportunity of revolting from the boy. . . . William grew up by God's aid uninjured but count Gilbert was slain by his cousin Ralph and fire and slaughter raged on all sides . . . 'Woe to the land whose kingdom is a child!'[5]

144 i, 280 (Bk. II) Thus full of years and glory, he [Edward the Confessor] gave up his

[3] Cf. R. Allen Brown, 'William of Malmesbury as an architectural historian', in *Mélanges d'archéologie et d'histoire médiévales en l'honneur du Doyen Michel de Boüard*, Paris, 1982.
[4] The massacre of the Danes, St Brice's Day 1002.
[5] Eccl. X: 16

pure spirit to the kingdom of heaven and was buried on the day of the Epiphany [6 January] in that same church which he had been the first to build in that style which now almost all seek to emulate at vast expense. The house of Wessex . . . with him forever ceased to reign; for Harold, on the very day of the Epiphany while the grief of the king's death was yet fresh, extorted the consent of the magnates and seized the crown, although the English say it was granted him by the king; but to my mind it is more a matter of bias than judgement to allege that he would have bequeathed his inheritance to a man whose power he had always distrusted. . . .

145 i, 281–2 (Bk. II)   Harold, made overbearing by his triumph,[6] would not share any part of the loot with his comrades in arms, wherefore many, when they got the chance to slip away, deserted him on his march to Hastings; and certainly, though he had with him his stipendiary and mercenary forces (*milites*), he had few local levies (*ex provincialibus*). And so, with those who were with him, overcome by the craft of William, he was vanquished, nine months and a few days after obtaining the kingdom. Yet it was not the art of war but the secret and wondrous determination of God which brought it about that the English never again fought together for liberty in battle, as if the whole strength of England had failed with Harold, who certainly could have and should have paid the price of his perfidy, even at the hands of those less warlike than the Normans. Nor in saying this do I detract from the valour of the Normans, to whom I am bound both by race and benefits received. But they seem to me in error who exaggerate the numbers of the English and underrate their courage, and to dishonour the Normans even while they mean to extol them . . . they were few in number but brave in the extreme, who gave up any thought for their own safety and laid down their lives for their country. . . .

146 ii, 283 (Bk. III, Prologue)   Many both Norman and English have written about king William for different reasons: the former have praised him to excess, lauding both his good and bad deeds to the skies; the latter, out of national hatred, have heaped upon their ruler undeserved reproach. I for my part, as the blood of either people flows in my veins, shall steer a middle course, so that neither may my tale be criticized as false nor may I brand him with notorious censure when almost all his acts can be excused if not applauded. . . .

147 ii, 306 (Bk. III)   . . . They [the Normans] revived by their coming the practice of religion which everywhere was lapsing; throughout the land you might see churches rising in every vill, and monasteries in the towns and cities, built in a style unknown before.

148 ii, 334 (Bk. III)   Thus in his [the Conqueror's] time the goodly company of monks increased on all sides, and monasteries arose ancient in religion but modern in their buildings. But here I perceive the mutterings of those who say that it would have been

---

[6] *I.e.* at Stamford Bridge.

better if the old had been preserved in their original state than new ones raised from their demolition and plunder.

Gesta Pontificum

Source: *Willelmi Malmesbiriensis Monachi De Gestis Pontificum Anglorum* ed. N.E.S.A. Hamilton, Rolls Series, 1870.

149 P. 253 (Bk. III) . . . The sheriff of Worcester appointed by the king was Urse[7], who constructed a castle (*castellum*) at the monks' very throat in that the fosse cut off part of their cemetery. Complaints were made to the archbishop[8] who was the guardian of the bishopric. He, when he had seen Urse, began with these words: 'Hattest thou Urs, have thou Godes kurs.'[9] Thus felicitously spoken but playing harshly upon the euphony of names 'Thou art called Urse', he said, 'and may you have the curse of God, and' – which I have not put in English – 'my curse and the curse of all the priesthood if you do not move that castle (*castellum*) from here. And you may know for sure that your progeny will not long inherit the land of St Mary.' Thus he spoke that those things might be fulfilled which we now see fulfilled. Not many years afterwards his [Urse's] son Roger was driven from the paternal inheritance which he then possessed, by the serious displeasure of king Henry [I], because in hasty rage he had ordered one of the king's officials to be killed.

150   Concerning Wulfstan bishop of Worcester

P. 281–3 (Bk. IV) . . . As I have already said, he was abstemious in food and drink, although in his hall there was drinking to all hours after dinner in the manner of the English. When he sat at table with them he ruminated on the psalms, though pretending to drink in his turn. While others drained great foaming tankards he, holding the smallest goblet in his hand, encouraged them to make merry, though honouring thus the custom of the country rather than the judgement of his heart. Nor did he disregard the customs of the Normans, but was accompanied by a pride of knights (*pompam militum secum ducens*) who were an absolute ruination in their annual stipends and daily food.

 . . . When the work of building a larger church, which he had undertaken from the foundations, had proceeded far enough for the monks to enter into it, orders were given for the old church, which the Blessed Oswald had built, to be unroofed and demolished. Standing thus beneath the sky while this was being done, Wulfstan could not restrain his tears. For this he was gently rebuked by those who were with him, and who said that he should rather rejoice to be witnessing so great an honour about to be done to the church, in that a greater number necessitated more spacious buildings. He replied: 'I think otherwise, that we miserable sinners destroy the works of the saints to win ourselves renown. That age of fortunate men never thought to raise grandiloquent edifices, but under whatever roof offered themselves to God and led all those about them by their example.

[7] Urse d'Abitot.
[8] Ealdred of York.
[9] *I.e.* these words are given in the vernacular in what is otherwise a Latin narrative.

We by contrast labour to pile up stones, neglecting our souls. . . .

The Abingdon Chronicle

This local history of the Abbey of Abingdon dating from the mid-twelfth century is part narrative and part register of deeds, and belongs to that category of narrative cartularies or 'Chronicle-cartularies' peculiar to its period, of which the *Liber Eliensis* (152) from Ely is another example.[1] 'The Abingdon chronicler was particularly interested in the feudalization of the abbey, giving details of the military fees and the abbot's arrangements for the subinfeudation of tenancies.'[2]

Source: *Chronicon Monasterii de Abingdon*, ed. J. Stevenson, 2 vols., Rolls Series, 1858.

151 ii, 3   Concerning the knights (*milites*) of this our church. In the early days of his coming to the abbey [abbot Athelhelm[3]] went nowhere unless surrounded by a force of armed knights (*milites*). And indeed it was necessary to do this. For the many rumours of conspiracies against the king and his realm coming in daily from all parts compelled everyone in England to protect himself. Then castles (*castella*) were raised at Wallingford, Oxford and Windsor, and at many other places, for the defence of the kingdom. Hence this abbey was ordered by royal command to have a guard of knights (*militum excubias*) at that same Windsor castle (*oppidum*). Wherefore in such circumstances knights (*milites*) from overseas coming into England were regarded with special favour.

The affairs of the kingdom being in such a state of uproar, the lord abbot Athelhelm safely guarded with a strong force of knights (*milites*) the place committed to him [i.e. Windsor castle]; and at first, indeed, he used stipendiaries for this purpose. But after the disturbances had died down, since it was noted in the annals (*in Annalibus*)[4] by command of the king how many knights (*milites*) were to be exacted from bishops and abbots for the defence of the realm when need should arise, the abbot, having previously refrained from such grants, thenceforth assigned to kinsmen (*pertinentibus*) manors from the church's possessions, in each case in return for stipulated service from the manor thus given (*edicto cuique tenore parendi de suae portionis mansione*). These lands had been held by those called thegns (*Tahinos*) who had fallen at Hastings.

The Liber Eliensis or Book of Ely

Another mid-twelfth-century chronicle-cartulary, for which see above under Abingdon Chronicle. It is not a very valuable source for its narrative history, but the following extract is at least informative about the imposition of knight-service on English churches after 1066.

[1] Cf. G.R.C. Davis, *Medieval Cartularies of Great Britain*, London, 1958, p. xiii.
[2] Antonia Gransden, *Historical Writing in England c.550 to c.1307*, London, 1974, p. 279.
[3] A monk of Jumièges, appointed *c.* 1071.
[4] Yearly records?

Source: *Liber Eliensis*, ed. E.O. Blake, Royal Historical Society, Camden 3rd Series xcii, London, 1962.

152   Pp. 216–18 (Ch. 134–5)   At this time [1072?] the whole of Scotland with her hordes of warriors sought to rebel against our king William and overthrow him. He, nothing daunted, went against them with a combined force of horse and ships. . . . For he had commanded both the abbots and bishops of all England to send their due knight service (*debita militie obsequia*) and he established that from that time forward contingents of knights (*militum . . . presidia*) should be provided by them to the kings of England in perpetual right for their military expeditions, and that no one, however highly placed, should presume to oppose this edict, and thus he trampled underfoot the just and ancient liberties of the English Church, never ceasing to harass it beyond endurance as though he would extinguish it entirely. And when these things were known to the abbot of Ely, he bitterly bewailed the endless troubles of his house, and sadly took counsel with the brethren as to what he should do, so that in such a crisis they, like good sons, might comfort him, and protect the peace of that place by devout prayer to the mercy of their holy mother Etheldreda, and not refrain from openly declaring what they thought the best course of action. From them he received the advice to go at once to the king's majesty . . . [*i.e.* to plead the liberty of St Etheldreda, not to be violated by new and intolerable exactions] . . . But the king spurned his prayers and gifts alike, would not revoke the evil regulation, but intending rather to increase the burden, commanded him at the royal will (*ex nutu regis*) to keep a garrison of 40 knights (*custodiam xl militum*) in the isle. Whereupon the abbot sorrowfully withdrew, collected knights (*milites*) – who were, however, well-born dependents and adherents of his – bestowed arms on many of them, and maintained according to custom the number predetermined by the king's command within the hall of the church, receiving their daily provisions and wages from the hand of the cellarer, an arrangement which could and did cause intolerable and unendurable disturbances. In consequence therefore the abbot, under compulsion and not as a matter of the influence and favour of the rich or of devotion to his own relatives, allowed the intruders (*invasores*) upon certain of the lands of St Etheldreda to hold them in fee (*in feudum*)[1] – as for example Picot the sheriff, Hardwin de Scalers, Roger Bigod and Hervey de Bourges and others, as the book of lands sets forth[2] – but alienating scarcely any demesne land, so that they would serve the king in all military expeditions and the church be henceforth untroubled. . . .

William surnamed Rufus therefore succeeded his father in the kingdom, but soon a serious discord about the succession arose among the magnates of the realm, some, the minority, supporting the king, the others supporting his brother Robert, on the advice especially of bishops Geoffrey of Coutances, William of Durham and Odo of Bayeux. . . . The king therefore, seeing himself threatened by so great a danger, now

---

[1] *I.e.* he allowed those who had 'invaded' or occupied abbey lands after the Conquest, and more particularly after Hereward's revolt, to retain them, held of the abbey in return for knight-service. See E. Miller, *Abbey and Bishopric of Ely*, Cambridge, 1951, pp. 66–8.

[2] Probably the surviving survey known as the *Inquisitio Eliensis*.

violently exacted from the churches the due service (*debitum servitium*) which his father had imposed, and the English Church was beset on every side with innumerable troubles. He compelled 80 knights of the abbey of Ely to be provided as due to him in the campaign, without any reduction, 40 of whom, that is to say, being those whom his father had ordered to be kept as a garrison in the isle. And when abbot Simeon heard of this he groaned in spirit, calling upon God to be the judge of those things which were done to him.

Hugh the Chantor, History of the Church of York

Hugh the Chantor became a canon of York perhaps as early as 1100 and was subsequently precentor and archdeacon also, dying in *c.*1139. His History covers only the years 1066–1127, begins with the coming of king William to England, and proceeds almost at once to the controversial issue of the subjection of York to Canterbury, which was his consuming interest. 'He understood the political significance of events'[1], and the one extract printed here draws attention to a political reality underlying the famous dispute.

Source and translation: *Hugh the Chantor: The History of the Church of York 1066–1127*, ed. and trans. C. Johnson, Nelson's Medieval Texts, 1961.

153 Pp. 1–3 When the duke had conquered England he became king, and was consecrated and crowned by Ealdred the venerable archbishop of York. But the city of York and the whole district round it, in spite of having given hostages to the king for keeping the peace, was disloyal, wickedly and violently hostile, and was on that account destroyed by the Normans (*Francigenis*) with the sword, famine and flames. The metropolitan church of St Peter was also burned, and its ornaments, charters and privileges consumed or lost. Archbishop Ealdred . . . died.

But the king gave the archbishopric to one of his chaplains, Thomas, treasurer of the church of Bayeux, a distinguished and very learned clerk. . . .

The king gave the archbishopric of Canterbury to an elderly man called Lanfranc, famous for his learning and piety, who had been the master of almost everyone in France, Germany or Italy (including Thomas) who then had any considerable reputation as a man of letters . . .

Lanfranc refused to consecrate Thomas without a profession of subjection – [king] William was annoyed at first, and sent him [Thomas] back to the archbishop with orders to consecrate him without insisting on the profession, but still Lanfranc refused. He came to the king, who asked him why he had not consecrated the archbishop-elect of York. He replied that the church of York ought to be subject to the church of Canterbury. . . . Moreover that it was expedient for the union and solidarity of the kingdom that all Britain should be subject to one primate; it might otherwise happen, in the king's time or that of one of his successors, that some one of the Danes, Norwegians, or Scots, who used to sail up to York in their attacks on the realm, might be made king by the archbishop of York

[1] Antonia Gransden, *Historical Writing in England c.550–c.1307*, p. 124.

and the fickle and treacherous Yorkshiremen, and the kingdom disturbed and divided. Lanfranc's reputation with the Normans was such that whatever he suggested was thought certain to be right. . . .

The Chronicle of Battle Abbey

This text in fact consists of two separate and anonymous chronicles of St Martin's at Battle bound together in the same volume. Both date from the last third of the twelfth century and their principal interest relates to the reign of Henry II. They are represented here by one extract only, because of the obvious connection of Battle Abbey with the Norman Conquest, and because that extract reveals the origin, at the abbey, of what is, alas! the legend of the Conqueror's vow before Hastings to found it. That the victorious king founded Battle Abbey, and did so to alleviate the penances[1] lying upon himself and his vassals for the slaughter and the bloodshed, there is no doubt; but the vow upon the battlefield to do so does not appear before 1155 in a forged Battle charter[2] and is here elaborated.

Source and translation: *The Chronicle of Battle Abbey*, ed. and trans. Eleanor Searle, Oxford Medieval Texts, 1980.

154 Pp. 66–7[3] In the year 1066, the most noble William, duke of the Normans, sailed with a mighty army against England, so that he might wrest the realm of England, left him by his kinsman king Edward, out of the grasp of the deceitful usurper Harold. . . . When Harold learned of the landing he marched against him with his army. The energetic duke faced him . . . at a place today called Battle. Now when the devout duke was armed in martial array, he called together his barons and knights and roused them all to fight faithfully in the battle, by his exhortation and by their hope in his promises. And in order to strengthen their hearts, he made before them and with the approval of all a vow to God, that if the divine mercy granted him victory over his enemies he would offer up that place to God, as wholly free and quit as he might be able to conquer it for himself. And there he would build a monastery, where servants of God might be brought together for the salvation of all, and especially those who should fall in that battle. It would be a place of sanctuary and help to all, paying back for the blood shed there by an unending chain of good works. His speech made the men more courageous; they entered the fight determinedly, and at last, as God had planned, on 14 October they won the victory: the duke's enemy lay fallen and his army fled. . . .

---

[1] Cf. **187**.
[2] Eleanor Searle, *Chronicle of Battle Abbey*, p. 21.
[3] The second of the two versions is chosen as more straighforward. Cf. therefore *ibid.*, p. 37.

II   Documentary Sources

While there may be some superficial overlap, as when, for example, a history or narrative source may contain a copy of some document which the author wishes to include, there are certain essential differences between documentary and literary evidence though both are written. By contrast with a literary source, any document is likely to be produced in the course of administration, an impersonal record of fact such as a conveyance of property, a survey, or a statement of the law, or, it may be, an official mandate or notification, conveying the king's will or act formally in writing. As such it will to a degree lack the subjective element of the literary work, including personal bias or attitude. It is essential to know so far as possible the purpose of any given document before using it, and the means of its production; whereupon its most abundant information for the historian will be under those same two heads. Nevertheless its implicit assumptions, positive and negative, its language and phraseology, even its form and materials, may, if perceptively studied, throw much other light upon the society and circumstances which produced it. There is, moreover, in this early but dynamic period, a fundamental significance to the mere production and proliferation of documents, to the increasing documentary habit, for these things mark at this time an increase in the habit of writing, in the growth of literacy in short, and a marked phase of acceleration in the long transition in the West from a primitive society almost exclusively dependant upon the spoken word and oral custom to one more dependant upon written record.

Charters, Writs and Leases

In the field of administration the conveyance of property is, with law, amongst the first matters to be recorded in writing. A charter may be defined as the written record of the conveyance of property, real or incorporeal (rights, privileges, liberties), in perpetuity. The earliest form of charter, introduced into England, it is thought, by archbishop Theodore or possibly by Augustine himself, is the ancient or solemn diploma (also, in English, land-book). This large and cumbersome document, designed to impress, and even in Anglo-Saxon England written in Latin as part of its solemnity, in its full and fully developed form consists of the following parts (i) the chrismon or cross, (ii) the invocation (In the name of God, or variant), (iii) what has been nicely called the pious preamble, wherein, often at great length and in inflated Latin, the (pious) reasons for the grant are argued (*e.g.* that by good works on earth one may lay up treasures in heaven etc.), (iv) the *verba dispositiva*, whereby the actual grant is recorded, (v) the anathema, *i.e.* the curses called down on anyone who shall infringe the donor's grant, (vi) the date; and finally (vii) the witnesses, in proper order or precedence. In the Anglo-Saxon royal diploma also, the boundaries of the estate are given, in the vernacular, usually after the *verba dispositiva*. These solemn diplomas are, in Galbraith's words,[1] 'astonishing documents. They are in origin nothing more than the written account of a religious ceremony before witnesses' – for it is to be understood that they are no more than a record of the conveyance which was itself an oral and a visual ceremony. Further 'they shout of the Church', for in the beginning they were exclusively ecclesiastical documents, recording donations to churches, until lay magnates were eventually able to take advantage of the privileged tenure of 'book-land', *i.e.* land held by charter. Also, written in the name of theocratic kings, 'they look for their sanction not to legal penalties but to hair-raising comminations that in time become organized as excommunication', *i.e.* like the conveyance they record, they depend upon spiritual rather than secular authority, though contemporaries might not have made the distinction. Bureaucrats and the documents they produce are essentially conservative (thus we still put crosses on our ballot papers). By the mid-eleventh century the world was perhaps changing or about to change, but certainly the ancient and solemn diplomas were for long the product of a society where literacy was closely confined, and 'they record the effort to impress illiterate minds (by minds themselves not much more literate) with superstitious awe and reverence.'

Set the context thus, and the Anglo-Saxon vernacular sealed writ seems at least to presage another world. By comparison crisp, short, sharp and to the point, comparatively cheap and easy to produce, it is almost entirely secular in tone, announcing the king's will with few frills, and above all authenticated by his seal. The Old English royal diploma, by contrast, had no viable means of authentication, unless the names of the witnesses count as such: the crosses against their names (let alone the names themselves) were not autograph, and it bore no seal or other authenticating device like the royal monogram on Carolingian diplomas amongst the Franks. It could be, and in the conventional view normally was, drawn up after the event either by the beneficiary (who wanted the record and was most often a literate cleric), or by some other interested ecclesiastic, or in the equipped scriptorium of a royal religious house, some *eigenkloster*, where the modest amount of the king's secretarial business was done. Certainly the sealed writ, in the form of the writ-charter, will come to displace the ancient diploma as a title deed; in the form of a precept

---

[1] For the following quotations see *Studies in the Public Records*, London, 1948 pp. 31–3. For a full discussion of the Old English diploma and sealed writ, the significance of each, and the vexed question of an Anglo-Saxon royal 'chancery', see P. Chaplais, 'The Origin and Authenticity of the Royal Anglo-Saxon Diploma' and 'The Anglo-Saxon Chancery: from the Diploma to the Writ', respectively in *Journal of the Society of Archivists*, iii, 2, October 1965, and iii, 4, October 1966, both reprinted in *Prisca Munimenta, studies . . . presented to A.E.J. Hollaender*, ed. Felicity Ranger, London, 1973. For a contrary view of diploma and 'Chancery', see Simon Keynes, *The Diplomas of King Aethelred 'the Unready'*, Cambridge, 1980.

or of a notification it will come to articulate the whole structure of an expanding royal government; and it will require an increasingly organized Chancery within the royal household to draft, engross, seal and send it out in increasing number. In England on the eve of the Norman Conquest, however, there is no evidence that any of these developments had gone very far. Only four certainly sealed pre-Conquest writs survive,[2] all four only from the reign of Edward the Confessor. Since it is now realized that the origin of the writ lies in oral messages (hence the vernacular; hence the alliterative jingles easily memorized – sake and soke toll and team, etc.) by an accredited messenger with some royal token to accredit him (e.g. a loose seal), and since the writ itself makes no reference to a seal, loose or affixed, in its text, we cannot and do not know that those apparent writs surviving only as copies in later cartularies, registers and the like, were ever sealed, and the probability may be thought against it. Further, if we put them all together, the few originals with or without clear evidence of sealing and the later copies,[3] the series only begins with two rather doubtful specimens of Ethelred II, the great majority come from the reign of Edward the Confessor, and all are in effect writ-charters announcing grants and kept as title deeds. Even so, the sealed writ has not replaced the diploma, for both record king Edward's grant of Taynton to St. Denis (**157–8**). There is no evidence of the executive writ, sealed and carrying the king's commands in writing to his officials about the land, before the Conquest[4] though there is an increasing amount thereafter (e.g. **177–8**). In short, there is no compelling reason from the evidence of the writs to deduce a developed writing office or scriptorium or 'Chancery' – to which there is no reference until after 1066 – in the household of the last Old English kings. Still less when it is discovered that even the sealed writ could be produced not by royal household clerks but by an interested party (e.g. **158**) and afterwards be sealed. Still less if it is believed that the diplomas were not written by royal household clerks either.[5] Furthermore, the diplomatic evidence of royal *acta* or written deeds does not of itself proclaim an Old English kingdom, on the eve of the Norman Conquest, centralized and unified by a precocious administration far ahead of that of other contemporary states, especially Normandy. Such claims have been made and reiterated by English historians of the last two generations; and these are the issues posed by the diplomatic evidence of records.

On the evidence, the secretarial arrangements of the Norman dukes in the eleventh century seem comparable to those of their royal contemporaries in England, and, if anything, superior. By a crude but significant numerical test, the total number of charters

---

[2] T.A.M. Bishop and P. Chaplais, *Facsimiles of English Royal Writs to AD 1100*, Oxford, 1957, Pls. III, XVIII, XXIII and XXVI. The last three are printed below, Nos. **158–60**. Pl. III is a genuine sealed writ of Edward the Confessor, two-thirds of which has been erased and re-written.

[3] All pre-Conquest writs have been collected, edited and annotated by F.E. Harmer, *Anglo-Saxon Writs*, Manchester, 1952. The total number of royal writs from Aethelred to Harold therein is 112.

[4] The argument that such writs, being ephemeral in import, were not kept, seems weakened by the increasing numbers of such writs surviving from the period after 1066. Similarly, the argument that they were not kept because written in the vernacular, may seem weakened by the number of vernacular writ-charters that survive.

[5] But here *cf*. Simon Keynes, *The Diplomas of King Aethelred 'the Unready'*, cited above.

issued or subscribed by duke William before 1066, and surviving as originals or authentic copies,[6] approximately equals the total number of diplomas and writs in king Edward's name similarly surviving from the same period for the far larger English kingdom. Many of the duke's charters are of the ancient diploma type(**165, 168**), but others, it should be noted, are in the simpler, and to the modern mind more sophisticated, form of the relatively briefer notification(**164, 170**). There are differences between the Norman and Old English royal diplomas which are ultimately to be explained by the fact that, whereas the latter is derived from the late Roman private deed, the former, in what is a Carolingian successor-state, is derived from the late Roman public deed via the diplomas of the Frankish Carolingian kings and emperors. Thus the vernacular boundary clauses of the Old English diploma are absent from the Norman. Other differences point to the superiority of the Norman diploma over its Old English counterpart, at least from the modern point of view which, in the mid-eleventh century, may no longer be entirely anachronistic. As is proper by Carolingian custom, the Norman dukes did sometimes seal their charters(**166**),[7] notwithstanding reiterated denial of the fact by English historians. They also sometimes used other methods of authentication derived from Carolingian practice, like the monogram;[8] and the 'signs' or crosses against the names of witnesses and subscribers are regularly autograph as they never are in England. There are also references to a chancellor in pre-Conquest Normandy[9] though none in the contemporary English kingdom. As to the question of where and how these Norman charters were produced, which has seemed so important to historians in our day, while there is explicit reference to an eleventh century diploma in favour of St Ouen having been written by the beneficiary,[10] and evidence also of the duke's use of the abbey of Fécamp as a writing-office,[11] so also are there references to charters written by the duke's chancellor,[12] or by his chaplain[13] or in his chamber in his household.[14]

For the immediate post-Conquest period in England, almost no work has been done upon the diploma, which continues in use at least until the reign of Stephen and thus had clearly not been overtaken by the writ-charter by 1066. It would be surprising, however, if no change were introduced by the Normans in accordance with their own practice, and that such changes did take place, including the occasional affixation of a seal, is indicated by No. **173** below.[15] Changes which came about in the form and use of the writ at

---

[6] The Norman ducal *acta* for the pre-Conquest period are available in a splendid edition by Marie Fauroux, *Recueil des actes des ducs de Normandie (911–1066)*, Mémoires de la Société des Antiquaires de Normandie XXXVI, Caen, 1961.

[7] Cf. Fauroux, No. 34, p. 125n (Richard II) No. 61, p. 187 and No. 9, p. 235 (both Robert the Magnificent).

[8] Fauroux, Nos. 15–17, 34, 47, 90.

[9] Fauroux, No. 18, p. 102; No. 34, p. 131 (both Richard II).

[10] Fauroux, No. 42, p. 148.

[11] Fauroux, p. 43.

[12] Fauroux, No. 18, p. 102; No. 34, p. 131 (both Richard II).

[13] Fauroux, No. 13, p. 89 (Richard II).

[14] Fauroux, No. 227, p. 437 (William the Conqueror).

[15] It would be interesting to know how many post-Conquest Anglo-Norman diplomas have been

Norman hands, notably the change of language from Anglo-Saxon to Latin in and after *c*.1070,[16] the addition of witness and dating clauses, and the growing number of surviving writs used for executive purposes, are also sufficiently indicated by the examples printed below(**177 – 8**). Finally, the Conquest also brought about changes to the royal seal and the method of its attachment to the document. The first royal official seal, used for making a wax impression upon a document to authenticate it, is that of Edward the Confessor (**197**). It was a two-faced seal showing on each side the king in majesty. Under the Conqueror, and all his medieval successors (and beyond) the royal seal shows only on one side the king in majesty, and, on the other, the king armed and mounted as a knight (**197**). The change may be thought doubly significant. In the first place, the 'equestrian' representation seems symbolic of feudal lordship, and on the Conqueror's seal the legend on that side proclaimed him as duke of the Normans, while that on the 'majesty' side proclaimed him as king of the English. In the second, the change at least implies the existence, before 1066, of a Norman ducal and official seal, now combined, so to speak, with the English royal equivalent.[17] As for the method of attaching the seal (strictly, the wax impression of it) to the deed, all Edward the Confessor's sealed writs have it on a 'tongue' or horizontal strip cut at the foot (a second and thinner strip being the 'tie'). This method continues after 1066, but we now also find alternatives, as when the seal is attached *en placard*, *i.e.* applied to the face of the document in continental and Carolingian fashion[18] (inconvenient with a two-faced seal), or suspended on a 'tag', *i.e.* a parchment strip passed through slits and hanging vertically from the foot of the deed.[19] A variant of the latter is to use silk strings, which appear for the first time on a deed of William Rufus dating from 1095 – 7.[20].

Finally in this section of 'Documentary Evidence', two Old English leases are included, both from Worcester, together with bishop Oswald's celebrated 'Memorandum' to explain those many leases which he issued. There is no mystery about the Old English lease which, like a modern lease, is a means of conveying property for a term only – in the west of England in the pre-Conquest period normally for three lives. No necessarily privileged tenure was involved as with book-land, nor are we dealing with grants in perpetuity: in consequence the granting of leases is no royal monopoly, and the document recording the transaction is less solemn than the diploma, and can be in English as opposed to Latin. As it happens, a great series of leases survives for the pre-Conquest diocese of Worcester, copied into Hemming's Cartulary of the eleventh century, and these, one

dismissed as spurious by English historians simply because they do not conform to what is no longer 'English' practice. Cf. the extraordinary remark of D.C. Douglas, 'An initial suspicion rests on all the solemn diplomas of William the Conqueror' (*English Historical Documents*, ii, London, 1959, p. 601).

[16] Which presumably effectively cut any surviving link between the writ and the verbal message delivered orally.

[17] Cf. Fauroux, p. 47

[18] Bishop and Chaplais, *Facsimiles of English Royal Writs*, Pl. XXIX and note.

[19] *Ibid.*, Pl. XXVIII and **173** below.

[20] Bishop and Chaplais, Pl. XIX.

might almost say, have encouraged an unhealthy concentration by English historians upon that area and the bishop's triple-hundred or liberty of Oswaldslow in particular. In fact, leases and lease-hold (*laen*-land, loan-land) are not confined to the bishopric of Worcester nor to pre-Conquest England. Since Maitland's day the Worcester leases and various ancillary documents which go with them, not least St Oswald's 'Memorandum', have attracted the attention of English historians seeking (without much success, one may add) the origins of English feudalism.[21]

The charters and writs printed in translation in this section have been chosen partly in illustration of the points made above. Yet the historical information this type of document may provide is very much more than of the growth of literacy and the development of government, or the explicit message of the deed itself, that the king or duke has given such and such a property to A, or ordered that B do this and that. So, to take but a few examples from the few specimens given below, No. 155 shows, for once, the interior of an Old English borough. The king's, and no less the duke's, control of his Church is illustrated by Nos. 160 and 165. The 'decisive moment in the history of Norman monasticism'[22] is rung by duke Richard II's appointment of William of Volpiano to Fécamp in the same No. 165, and a flood of light is thrown by No. 169, upon what was to be the most distinguished of all the Norman monasteries. The feudalization of society in Normandy and subsequently in England is illustrated by Nos. 164 and 178; and (directly relevant to the Norman Conquest) the support of the Norman ducal house for the exiled Edward the Confessor is dramatically confirmed by Nos. 167 and 168.

Pre-Conquest England

155 Ealdorman Ethelred and Aethelflaed his wife grant to the cathedral church of St Peter at Worcester rights in the borough of Worcester (c. 884–901)

Though dating from a period earlier than that covered by the present volume, this charter is included here as, in Stenton's words, 'the one surviving document which illustrates the internal condition of a new Alfredian *burh*'.[1] It is not drawn up in regular diploma form, but nor is it strictly royal, being in the names of Ethelred the ealdorman, who ruled Mercia under king Alfred's overlordship, and his wife Aethelflaed who was Alfred's eldest daughter. It survives only in a later copy entered in Hemming's cartulary (eleventh century, BL Cott. Tiber A. xiii, f. 1b).

Source and translation: *English Historical Documents*, i, ed. and trans. D. Whitelock (1955), No. 99.

To Almighty God, the True Unity and the Holy Trinity in heaven, be praise and honour and thanksgiving for all the benefits which he has granted us. For whose love in the first

[21] For all of which see R. Allen Brown, *The Origins of English Feudalism*, London, 1973, pp. 55ff. The best discussion of the English lease, both before and after the Conquest, will be found in R. Lennard, *Rural England, 1066–1135*, Oxford, 1959, Chaps, VI and VII. For Hemming's cartulary, see especially N.R. Ker, in *Studies in History presented to F.M. Powicke*, Oxford, 1948.
[22] David Knowles, *The Monastic Order in England* (2nd. ed., Cambridge, 1963), p. 84.

[1] F.M. Stenton, *Anglo-Saxon England* (2nd. ed.), p. 521.

place, and for that of St Peter and of the church of Worcester, and also at the request of bishop Waerferth their friend, ealdorman Ethelred and Aethelflaed ordered the borough at Worcester to be built for the protection of all the people, and also to exalt the praise of God therein. And they now make known, with the witness of God, in this charter, that they will grant to God and St Peter and to the lord of that church half of all the rights which belong to their lordship, whether in the market or in the street, both within the fortification and outside; that things may be more honourably maintained in that found-ation and also that they may more easily help the community to some extent; and that their memory may be the more firmly observed in that place for ever, as long as obedience to God shall continue in that minster.

And bishop Waerferth and the community have appointed these divine offices before that which is done daily, both during their life and after their death; *i.e.* at every matins and at every vespers and at every tierce, the psalm *De profundis* as long as they live, and after their death *Laudate Dominum*; and every Saturday in St Peter's church 30 psalms and a Mass for them, both of them living and also departed.

And moreover Ethelred and Aethelflaed make known that they will grant this to God and St Peter with willing heart in the witness of king Alfred and of all the councillors who are in the land of the Mercians; except that the wagon-shilling and the load-penny[2] at Droitwich go to the king as they have always done. But otherwise, land-rent, the fine for fighting, or theft, or dishonest trading, and contribution to the borough-wall, and all the (fines for) offences which admit of compensation, are to belong half to the lord of the church, for the sake of God and St Peter, exactly as it has been laid down as regards the market-place and the streets. And outside the market-place, the bishop is to be entitled to his land and all his rights, just as our predecessors established and privileged it.

And Ethelred and Aethelflaed did this in the witness of king Alfred and of all the coun-cillors of the Mercians whose names are written hereafter.[3] And they implore all their suc-cessors in the name of Almighty God that no one may diminish this charitable gift they have given to that church for the love of God and St Peter.

156 Cnut restores to the New Minster at Winchester land in Drayton which he had previously granted to a citizen of Winchester by mistake, 1019

A charter or solemn diploma of king Cnut, accepted as genuine; reproduced in facsimile in W. B. Sanders, *Facsimiles of Anglo-Saxon Manuscripts*, 3 vols., Ordnance Survey, Southampton, 1878–84, ii, Winchester College Charters no. 4; printed in E. Edwards, *Liber Monasterii de Hyda*, Rolls Series, 1866, pp. 324–6.

Source and translation: *English Historical Documents*, i, ed. and trans. D. Whitelock (1955), no. 132.

Christ Jesus our Saviour, true and highest God, three in Unity, one in Trinity, born by an incomprehensible birth of one substance with his co-eternal Father – who, most beautiful of things, bearing with profound mind the beautiful empyrean before the material

---

[2] The payments on a cart-load or pack-load of salt (Dorothy Whitelock).
[3] The witnesses are lacking in the cartulary copy.

formation of heaven, earth and ocean, brought forth by the power of a mere word alone the shining hierarchy of the angles, and the bright clear vessels of the sun, the moon and the fiery stars, and the various decoration and adornment of the four quarters of the universe, and the inconceivable abundance of fish in Neptune's tempestuous element — reigning continually and triumphing and perpetually guiding all things: I, Cnut, ruler and *basileus* of the noble and fair race of the English, have ordered this parchment to be inscribed by the furrowing reed with the forms of letters, on behalf of the minster which is called 'New', situated in the famous and populous city of Winchester, in which the wonderful bodies of the illustrious confessors Judoc and Grimbald to this day are efficacious in miracles; for an estate containing in it the extent of five hides (*cassati*), which the tongue of the natives is accustomed to call Drayton, that this land may be applied for the benefit of the monks dwelling in the aforesaid minster, just as it was a long time before. This land, indeed, a certain inhabitant of the aforesaid city, young, daring and inconstant, acquired for himself from me with cunning and lying, saying that the land was mine and that I could easily give it to him, which also I did. But when I realized the truth, I caused the inheritance of God rather to be restored to worthy heirs, and ordered this to be manifested for testimony and confirmation in the present charter. And since we have discovered that there are in the possession of the afore-mentioned youth letters contrary to this privilege, and acquired by fraudulent investigation, we both condemn those under pain of anathema, and hold as worthless any other such if there are any anywhere; and we endow only this writing with perpetual liberty and confirm it.

Moreover, we desire that Christ will grant blessing and mercy to those consenting to the privilege; and we wish that the everlasting pains of hell will threaten those opposing it, unless they the more quickly come to their senses from the wickedness of their malice and from injustice.

The sides, truly, of the aforesaid estate thus extend their limits for the countrymen:[4] first from the *Humera* east of the boundary of the men of Middleton to Tidbury, from Tidbury to Micheldever, and so long Micheldever to Leofwine's boundary, from Leofwine's boundary to the heathen barrow; and from the heathen barrow back into Drayton.

For indeed the authorative page of this title-deed was drawn up in the year of our Lord's Incarnation 1019, the first week of Easter, in the presence of the king, for the confirmation and testimony of illustrious great men, whose names follow:

+ I, Cnut, king of the English, have granted and strengthened this gift with a willing mind.
+ I, Lifing, archbishop of the Church of Canterbury, have confirmed the stability of the testimony
+ I, Wulfstan, archbishop of York, have consented
+ I, Aelfgifu,[5] consort of the same king, have assisted
+ I, Aelfsige, bishop [of Winchester], have placed [my mark]

---

[4] The boundaries are in the vernacular.
[5] *I.e.* Emma of Normandy.

+ I, Brihtwold, bishop [of Ramsbury], have made it secure
+ I, Aelfmaer, bishop [of Selsey], have put my mark
+ I, Eadnoth, bishop [of Crediton], have impressed [my mark]
+ I, Godwin, bishop [of Rochester], have acquiesced
+ [6]I, Thorkel, earl. + I, Eric, earl. + I, Godwin, ealdorman. + I, Eilaf, earl.
+ I, Leofwine, ealdorman. + I, Regnold, earl. + I, Aethelsige, abbot. + I, Brihtwig, abbot + I, Brihtmaer, abbot. + I, Aelfhere, abbot. + I, Brihtwold, abbot. + I, Sihtric, king's thegn. + I, Hakon, king's thegn. + I, Halden, king's thegn. + I, Thored, king's thegn. + I, Atsere, king's thegn. + I, Aelfgar, king's thegn. + I, Thurkil, king's thegn. + I, Brihtric, king's thegn. + I, Aethelweard, king's thegn. + I, Sigered, king's thegn. + I, Oslac, king's thegn. + I, Leofwine, king's thegn.

Glory and riches and happiness and blessing in the tabernacles of the righteous be granted to all promoting this privilege.

157 Edward the Confessor grants to the abbey of St Denis[7] the vill of Taynton, 1059

This diploma survives at Paris in the Archives Nationales, either as the original or (as Miss Harmer thought) a very early copy. In the latter case, the receipt or note of Baldwin at the end may have been originally an endorsement. The diploma is associated with, and results from, king Edward's writ to the shire court of Oxfordshire announcing his grant (No. 158 below) and ending 'my will is that the bishop[8] draw up a charter concerning it with my full permission.' This, then, is not the product of any royal 'writing-office'. Further, its date, 1059, is at least two years later than the writ, and therefore, presumably, than the grant. Baldwin the monk of St Denis, who was evidently instrumental in obtaining the grant, was king Edward's physician and in 1065 was appointed abbot of Bury St Edmunds by him. For further discussion of both diploma and writ, see Harmer (cited below) pp. 35 *et seq*.,243–4; T.A.M. Bishop and P. Chaplais, *Facsimiles of English Royal Writs to AD 1100*, Pl. xx.

Source: F.E. Harmer, *Anglo-Saxon Writs*, Manchester, 1952, pp. 538–9.

In the name of the supreme living and seeing God. And indeed God is the entity of the Trinity, unchanging in eternity, in truth, in will, without beginning and without end, all ambiguity utterly cast aside, as truly must be believed. Which Trinity of persons, Father, Son and Holy Spirit, of one substance, ineffable, incomprehensible, indescribable and inscrutable to all human and angelic understanding, an impenetrable mystery beyond enquiry, is ever to be proclaimed, praised and exalted with boundless jubilation. Wherefore I Edward king of the English, in the peace and glory of my reign, for the salvation of my soul and of the souls of my forefathers who reigned before me, with the counsel and resolution of my magnates and faithful men, have given to St Denis, who amongst us as with the Franks is named, revered and held in holy memory, a certain vill called Taynton in the territory and shire of the town called Oxford, with all its appurtenances, that is to say lands, woods, pastures, waters, meadows and lands cultivated and

[6] All the remaining witnesses are arranged in two columns.
[7] Then near Paris.
[8] *I.e* Wulfwig of Worcester, to whom with earl Ralph the writ is addressed as joint presidents of the court.

uncultivated. Moreover this land is to be exempt and free from every burden save only military service and the repair of bridge and fortress. If any shall violate this grant let their part, by the decree of God and of me and of all the bishops named here below, be with Judas the traitor, with Dathan and Abiron, in the eternal fire wherein neither shall they die nor the flames be extinguished, unless they shall have redeemed their guilt before God and St Denis. [The boundaries of the estate are then given in the vernacular.]

In the year of the Incarnation of the Lord 1059 this charter was written with the consent of these witnesses whose names are seen to be written below.

+ I Edward king of the whole land of Britain have made this my gift to St. Denis and have given it strengthened with the sign of the Holy Cross.

+ I Edith consort of the same king have willingly declared that this has my consent.

+ I Stigand metropolitan archbishop of Christ Church [Canterbury] and also [bishop] of Winchester have most gladly confirmed the gift of the king with the sign of the Holy Cross.

+ I Cynesige, archbishop of the church of York have supported the aforesaid grant.

+ I Wulfwine bishop of the church of Dorchester have with a most willing hand witnessed this gift of the king.

+ I Dudoc bishop [of Wells] have assented.

+ I Herman bishop [of Ramsbury and Sherborne] have consented.

+ I Ealdred bishop [of Worcester] have offered my consent.

+ I William bishop [of London] have agreed.

+ I Aethelmaer bishop [of Elmham] have corroborated.

+ I earl Harold. + I earl Aelfgar. + I earl Tostig. + I earl Leofwine. + I earl Gyrth. + I Swein thegn. + I Edric thegn. + I Godric thegn. + I Atsor thegn. + I Esgar thegn. + I Ralf thegn. + I Robert thegn. + I Brihtric thegn. + I Ulf thegn.

And I Baldwin, monk of St Denis, under the rule of my abbot Hugh, and at that time physician to Edward king of the English, have received from the hand of the same king without anyone's objection the charter of this gift confirmed by all those whose names are appended, both charter and gift to be held by St Denis forever.

158 King Edward announces that he has granted to St Denis the land of Taynton (1053–7)

This is one of the four genuine and certain sealed writs to have survived as an original, though the seal is now detached. It is of particular interest that the diploma, which was the formal record of the conveyance and for which permission is given in the writ, survives also (writ, seal and diploma are together in the Archives Nationales, Paris). Certain peculiarities in the hand and vocabulary lead Bishop and Chaplais to suggest that the writ was written by the monk Baldwin (*Facsimiles of English Royal Writs*, No. 20). There are facsimiles in Bishop and Chaplais (*op. cit.*, Pl. xviii) and in Harmer (Pl. 2). See also No. **197**.

Source and translation: Harmar, *Anglo-Saxon Writs*, No. 55.

[Vernacular] King Edward sends friendly greetings to bishop Wulfwig and earl Raulf and all my thegns in Oxfordshire. And I inform you that I have granted to Christ and to the holy monastery of St Denis beyond the sea the land of Taynton, and everything lawfully pertaining thereto in woodland and in open country with sake and with soke as fully and as completely as I myself possessed it, during my lifetime and after it, for the salvation of my soul. And let him who shall alienate it from the holy foundation account for it with God. And my will is that the bishop draw up a charter (*boc*) concerning it with my full permission.

159 King Edward announces that he has granted to Westminster Abbey the land of Perton (1062–66; probably c.28 December 1065 for the dedication of the church)

A second genuine sealed writ of Edward the Confessor with the seal still attached. It is, however, thought by Bishop and Chaplais (No. 25) to have been written in the scriptorium of the abbey. Facsimile, Bishop and Chaplais, *op. cit.*, Pl. XXIII (b) and (c).

Source and translation: Harmer, *Anglo-Saxon Writs*, No. 96.

[Vernacular] + King Edward sends friendly greetings to bishop Leofwine and earl Edwin and all my thegns in Staffordshire. And I inform you that I have given to Westminster, to Christ and to St Peter, the land at Perton (Staffs), and everything belonging thereto, in woodland and in open country, with sake and with soke, as fully and as completely as I myself possessed it in all things, for the sustenance of the abbot and the brethren who dwell in the monastery. And I will not permit anyone to alienate there any of the things that belong to that foundation.

160 King Edward announces that he has granted to the monk Wulfstan the bishopric of Worcester (1062, c.8 September)

This writ has lost its seal, though it retains the stump of its tongue and tie, to the first of which it would have been affixed. It is accepted as genuine by Harmer (pp. 407–8, 528) and Bishop and Chaplais (No. 28). Facsimile in Bishop and Chaplais (Pl. XXVI) and E.A. Bond, *Facsimiles of Ancient Charters in the British Museum*, 4 vols., 1873–8, iv, 41.

Source and translation: Harmer, *Anglo-Saxon Writs*, No. 115.

[Vernacular] King Edward sends friendly greetings to earl Harold and earl Aelfgar and all the thegns in Worcestershire and Gloucestershire and Warwickshire. And I inform you that I have granted to the monk Wulfstan the bishopric of Worcester with sake and with soke, toll and team, within borough and without, as fully and as completely in all things as ever any one of his predecessors possessed it. Therefore I will not permit anyone in any matter to do him wrong, or to deprive him of any of the things that he ought lawfully to have for his bishopric.

161 Oswald, archbishop of York and bishop of Worcester, leases land at Bredicot for three lives to Goding the deacon (not later than 985)

Source and translation: A.J. Robertson, *Anglo-Saxon Charters*, Cambridge, 1939, No. lxi, pp. 124–7.

[Vernacular] + I, Oswald, archbishop by the grace of God, with the consent and leave of Ethelred, king of England, and earl Aelfric and the community at Worcester, having freely granted a certain piece of land, namely 3 hides at Bredicot and a yard-land at the place called *Genenofer* [unidentified], to a certain cleric whose name is Goding,[9] with everything pertaining thereto for his lifetime, and after his death to two heirs of his own choice, and after their death to the holy foundation at Worcester for the use of the bishop. And I grant him in addition 7 acres of meadow in the river pasture belonging to Tibberton – $3\frac{1}{2}$ acres in one place and $3\frac{1}{2}$ acres in another, as it may fittingly be divided. We convey to him likewise the message which he has before the gate.

These are the boundaries of the 3 hides at Bredicot. . . . [the boundaries of the estate follow].

This estate, moreover, shall be free from every duty of a secular nature except the repair of bridges and fortifications and military service against enemies. May St Mary and St Michael with St Peter and all the saints of God, have mercy on those who uphold this. If anyone, without due cause, attempts to break it, he shall have to account for it to God on the last day of this life, unless he has set about making amends.

Here are the signatures . . . [The names of 17 witnesses with their crosses follow, beginning with those of archbishop Oswald].

162 Ealdred bishop of Worcester leases land in Ditchford to Wulfgeat (1046–53; probably 1051–2)

Source and translation: Robertson, *Anglo-Saxon Charters*, as above, No. cxi, pp. 208–9.

[Vernacular] + Here it is declared in this document that bishop Ealdred has granted to Wulfgeat a certain piece of land, namely $1\frac{1}{2}$ hides in the manor called Ditchford, to be held and enjoyed for three lives, and after their time the estate shall return once more to the disposal of him who is in control of the bishopric of Worcester at the time. And they shall always be submissive and obedient and acknowledge the lordship of whoever is bishop at the time, and if they are guilty of any defection, they shall forfeit the property.

The witnesses of this are all the community[10] at Worcester and the community[10] at Evesham and the community[10] at Pershore and earl Leofric and earl Odda and Aelfric his brother and Brihtric, Aelfgar's son, and Owine, and Wagen and Aethelric, the bishop's brother, and Ccolmacr and Atser and Esbearn and Ordwig and Aethelstan the Fat and Aelfweard of Longdon and all the leading thegns in Worcestershire, both Danish and English.

And at the king's summons the holder shall discharge the obligations on these $1\frac{1}{2}$ hides at the rate of one, for three lives.

---

[9] Evidently Goding the deacon, who elsewhere in Hemming's cartulary of Worcester (whence this lease and No. 163 are derived) is said to have undertaken to act as scribe for the monastery in return for the lease (*Hemingi Chartularium Ecclesiae Wigornensis*, ed. T. Hearne, Oxford, 1723, i, 265).
[10] *I.e.* of the monastery.

163 Memorandum of Oswald bishop of Worcester[11] concerning his leases (c.963–72).

Source: T. Hearne, *Hemingi Chartularium Ecclesiae Wigornensis*, Oxford, 1723, i. 292–6.

Indiculum of the liberty of Oswaldslow Hundred.[12] – I, Oswald, bishop of the church of Worcester, give thanks before God and man to my most beloved lord, Edgar, king of the English, for all the gifts bestowed upon me by his clemency. . . . Wherefore it pleased both me and those my patrons and counsellors that, with the permission and attestation of my lord the said king, I should set out clearly in detail in the form of a chirograph[13] for my brothers, the bishops who will succeed me, in what manner I have been granting to the faithful men (*fideles*) subject to me the lands which have been committed to my charge, for the term of three lives, that is, of the grantee and two heirs after him . . . I have granted the lands of Holy Church to them to hold under me on these terms, namely that they shall fulfil the whole law of riding as riding men should, and that they shall pay in full all those things which justly belong to the right of the said church, that is to say those which in English are called church-scot, and toll, and *tacc* or *swinesceade*,[14] and the other dues of the church, unless the bishop shall have pardoned anything to anyone, and they shall swear that so long as they hold the said lands they will continue humbly subject to the commands of the bishop with all submission. In addition, they shall hold themselves available to supply all the needs of the bishop, they shall lend horses, they shall ride themselves, and, moreover, be ready to build bridges and do all that is necessary in burning lime for the work of the church. They shall be prepared to make deer-hedges for the bishop's hunting, and they must send their own hunting spears to the chase whenever the lord bishop wishes. Further, to meet the many other wants of the bishop, whether to fulfil the service due to him or that due to the king, they shall always with all humility and submissiveness be subject to the authority and will of that *archiductor*[15] who presides over the bishopric, on account of the benefice (*beneficium*) which is leased (*prestitum*) to them, according to his command and the amount of land which each possesses. When, however, the aforesaid term has run out . . . it shall be entirely at the bishop's discretion, whatever decision he reaches being final, whether he retains those lands to his own use . . . or whether he leases them to someone else for a further term . . . And if there shall be any malicious withholding of any of the aforesaid dues, the default shall be made good in accordance with the right of the bishop, or gift and land shall be confiscated from him who possessed them. And if, which passes belief, there should be any man who at the instigation of the Devil should be tempted through our grant (*beneficium*) to deprive the church of God by fraud or force of her possession and due service, he shall be deprived of

[11] Oswald became archbishop of York in addition in 972. He died in 992.

[12] This is the heading in Hemming's cartulary.

[13] A document, often an agreement, written in duplicate on one piece of parchment, which is then cut into two by a wavy or indented line (hence indenture) through the key word *CHIRO-GRAPHUM*. Thereafter only these two genuine halves will fit together if confirmation is required.

[14] Payment for swine-pasture.

[15] A literal translation would be 'chief leader' or 'commander in chief'.

our blessing and the blessing of God and his saints, unless he make the fullest amends and restore all things as they were before. . . . Now, therefore, in the name of God, and of St Mary in whose name this monastery is dedicated, I declare and command that no one shall dare in anyway to trangress this which . . . shall last for ever. Who soever shall keep it shall be replete with blessing, and whosoever goes against it shall be cursed by God and all the saints. Amen. . . .

Pre-Conquest Normandy

All the surviving *acta* or deeds issued or subscribed by the dukes of Normandy down to 1066 inclusive, whether as originals or copies, to the number of 234, have been collected and edited, with a full *apparatus criticus* of introduction, notes and indexes, by Marie Fauroux, *Receuil des actes des ducs de Normandie (911–1066)*, Mémoires de la Société des Antiquaires de Normandie, t. xxxvi, Caen, 1961. From that edition all the examples which follow are taken.

164   Richard I subscribes the charter of Walter count of Dreux

Richard I subscribes the charter whereby Walter count of Dreux gives his assent to the grant by his vassal Teodfredus of the church of Saint-Georges-Motel to the monastery of Saint-Père (St Peter) of Chartres, 965
This, the earliest known and genuine Norman charter, survives only in cartulary copies. Its form is that of a notification rather than a diploma.

Source: Fauroux No. 2.

Walter count of the *comté* of Dreux by the grace of Christ Our Lord and Saviour. We wish it to be known to all the faithful both present and future of the holy church of God that the noble vassal (*nobilis vassallus*) Teodfredus came into our presence with the request that we would give him our assent concerning a certain church of his benefice (*beneficium*), namely that consecrated in honour of St George, which he was proposing to give to the monastery of St Peter of Chartres where the humble abbot Guibert presided. And indeed the whole monastic community of St Peter desired that the said church be given to them by perpetual gift, in such a manner and by such agreement as was determined between the parties. Attentive therefore to his salutary request, I have most readily given assent to his wish, especially for the salvation of my soul and of the souls of my parents and of my predecessor count Landricus; and in like manner Teodfredus has confirmed that he will make the grant for the remission of his sins and those of his parents. To guard against the possibility, in which we can scarcely believe, of any rival claimants hereafter, we have decreed that they shall pay the sum of three shillings annually at the mass of St Remigius which is celebrated in the kalends of October [1 October]in recognition of our lordship. And if anyone shall be tempted to move against the record of this gift, or at any time ever to bring any claim against it, he shall be damned by ecclesiastical authority, and smitten by the episcopal anathema of excommunication, and also compelled by surety to pay us and our successors five pounds of pure gold in amends. From the monks, however, nothing else shall ever be required to the end of time except the payment which is written above. So that this our known written deed may have a lasting and inviolate validity, we have caused it to be corroborated below by our hand and by the hands of duke Richard, in whose *comté* it is seen to be, and of noble laymen. Done publicly in the *comté* of Evreux. The sign of count Walter, author of this charter. The sign of Teodfredus, knight (*miles*). The sign of duke Richard. This grant was written by Germanus the deacon in the year of the Incarnation of the Lord 965, in the eighth indiction, in the eleventh year of the reign of King Lothar.

165   Richard II to Fécamp, 1006

Richard II, having previously (1001) appointed William (of Volpiano) as abbot of the monastery of Fécamp founded by his father, Richard I, now gives further property to that church. The monks shall also have the liberty of electing an abbot according to the custom of Cluny, and exemption from all external authority except in the necessity of present reform. 1006, 30 May, Fécamp.

This charter is the earliest from Normandy to survive as an original (still at Fécamp). A reduced facsimile is printed by C.H. Haskins, *Norman Institutions*, London and New York, 1918; 1960, Pl. 1. A ducal charter, it is drawn up in full diploma form.

Source: Fauroux No. 9.

In the name of the holy and undivided Trinity Richard by divine grace count and patrician. That place which was hitherto in common parlance called Fécamp (Fiscamnum) the learned nowadays wish to call, by the study of its etymology, some 'established bench' (*fixum scamnum*), others 'established field' (*fixum campum*). Leaving therefore to the disputants the decision as to the meaning of the place name, we know the inspiration to divine service which is felt there, whenever and in whatever manner it may have begun. Just as in all parts of the earth holy mother church rejoices in an increase in the number of her sons, so also she longs to exult in an increase of good works through them. While many are engaged in different pious activities, others dispense alms to the poor and yet others guard the temples of the saints, as if they would make an exchange with Christ and, casting off worldly goods, live more prosperously with them. By whose example, be it known to present and future generations that my father count Richard [I] built from the foundations the church in honour of the holy and undivided Trinity, Father, Son and Holy Spirit of one substance, with the intention that one family of monks, under the rule of St Benedict, should perpetually live in dedication to the praise of God. I, count Richard [II], his son of the same name, undertook to give effect to his desires of which death took the realization from him, and not long afterwards came upon the venerable abbot William [of Volpiano] and by my entreaties installed him as head of this burgeoning religious community. Now under his rule as the number of monks increases I wish to add to the temporal possessions which were granted by my father to that place and confirmed by charter, and to this end I give the following in perpetual right: in the county of Caux, in the same vill of Fécamp, a third part of the tenants who are called *coloni*, with the arable land pertaining thereto, one part of the wood between the public highway and the sea, and half the dues; in Grainville-Ymauville, whatever I am seen to have together with two mills; in the vill of Arques-la-Bataille, a third part of the fishery and two-salt-pans and some arable land with meadow, and the church of Ecretteville-les-Baons with some arable lands; at

Harfleur one measure of land with 60 loads of salt and 4 acres of meadow; in the city of Rouen, one measure of land with a chapel and 30 acres of arable land with 7 acres of meadow; and in the county of the said city, the church of Pîssy-Peville and some arable land with the church of the vill of Barentin; in Vaudreuil, the church of St Mary, the church of St Stephen, the church of St Cecilia, the church of St Saturnin, the church of St Quentin, with the chapels subject to them and whatever arable land and meadow pertains to them; on the banks of the Seine, the vill of Aizier and whatever Tursten held there; Hennequeville on the sea. These I grant to the aforesaid place to have in perpetuity, in such a way that everything pertaining to them or to those possessions given by my father, within or without, shall be at the disposition of the abbot or those subject to him, and no one, great or small, of whatever office or dignity, is to oppose their authority. And not only in the lawful management of their affairs, but in the election of a new abbot, when death has brought about a vacancy, they shall enjoy the liberty justly granted by us, that is to say that in the election and ordination of an abbot they shall in all things observe that custom which has hitherto been followed at Cluny, most illustrious of monasteries, whence the spring of holy monastic religion has by now flowed forth through many places far and wide even unto the gracious God – and may the observance of that holy religion more and more profit my soul together with the souls of my father and mother and of all the faithful. Whereas we have declared that no one of whatever rank, office, power or inheritance shall have the right of authority over that monastery of Fécamp, yet if henceforth it shall be shown to have deviated from the right way, which God forbid, we do not prohibit the means of its revival to those who now seek its reformation. Finally, those who resist, break or go against our decrees in these matters, if they do not make amends, may know that they will not escape the curse of God, but with Satan and Judas the betrayer shall endure the pains of the damned in Hell, where the Serpent never ceases nor is the fire extinguished.

+ I therefore Richard, duke of the Normans, so that thus eternal reward may accrue to me, have confirmed by my hand the testimony of this charter written at my request by Guy the notary, in order that it may be proved by my humble agreement, and have delivered it to these witnesses requesting their support. R.alph. William.

I Guy the notary, at the command of lord Richard the illustrious duke, who because of his zealous devotion to works of mercy is called the almoner, have written this charter, in the year of the Incarnation 1006, in the fourth indiction, on the third day before the kalends of June [30 May] on Thursday the feast of the Ascension. With joy, acclamation and beatitude.[1]

166   Richard II to St Quentin, 1015

Richard II, at the request of Dudo canon of St Quentin[2] and of Ralph count of Ivry the duke's uncle,

---

[1] The words *Gaudio, celeberrima, feliciter* are written at the end of the last line of the document.
[2] Dudo of St Quentin, author of the first Norman history of the command of dukes Richard I and Richard II, *viz* the *De moribus et actis primorum Normanniae ducum*, for which see p. 2 above.

grants to St Quentin property which Richard I granted to Dudo in fee, to take effect after Dudo's death. 1015, 8 September, Rouen.

This charter, drawn up in something less than full diploma form, survives as an original although the bottom has been cut off. The first four lines of the script are written in the hand of Dudo himself. In the eighteenth century the charter bore a pendant seal of Richard II (see Fauroux, p. 100 and n.; Tassin and Toustain, *Nouveau traité de Diplomatique . . .*, Paris, 1750–1765, iv. 224, n.1, and 225).

Source: Fouroux No. 18.

The conduct of worldly affairs and juridical causes perpetually requires that those matters which require lawful definition should be truthfully set down in writing in charters (*chartulis*) so that without any possibility of deceit or trickery the whole and unvarnished truth may be made credibly clear to all. Wherefore let it be known to all present and future men of Normandy and to my successors that Dudo, canon of St Quentin the precious martyr of Christ, and our faithful man (*fidelis idoneus*), came to me who am called Richard, son of the glorious count Richard, and, though unworthy, by the grace of the supreme, divine and undivided Trinity, duke and patrician of the Normans, beseeching through count Ralph my uncle and with many and repeated supplications of his own that I would grant the churches which my abovesaid father gave him in fee (*beneficio*) to the precious martyr of Christ Quentin for the salvation of my father's soul and mine. Approving and assenting to his most humble petitions and sincere requests, I grant to the above-written martyr Quentin those same churches situate in the *comté* of Caux, one, a former abbey called Everard's church, above the Dun stream, and the other by the sea shore in the place which is called Sotteville [sur-Mer] for (the expense of) the table of the brethren living in that place and serving Christ under the protection of His glorious witness St Quentin, so that after the death of Dudo my man (*fidelis*) the canons of St Quentin shall hold, possess, receive the usufruct and freely do whatever they may wish with the property, the heir of Dudo my man (*fidelis*) attending to the service of Quentin the most glorious champion of Christ and, if it shall please the canons, also in my service. And if Dudo shall survive to give anything further to you [*i.e.* the canons] in his lifetime for the renown of my father's soul he shall have our and eternal thanks. If anyone shall go against the tenor of this my command and gift, nay if any of my heirs shall choose to break it, may he first of all incur the wrath of Almighty God, and not appropriate to himself what he has unjustly sought, but withdraw confounded and damned and excommunicated and ana-thematized, and he shall pay to the king of the Franks 20 pounds of gold and to the duke of Normandy a further 20. This precept was given in the city of Rouen in the feast of the Nativity of Mary the Mother of God in the year of the Incarnation of Our Lord Jesus Christ 1015, in the thirteenth Indiction and in the twenty-seventh year of the reign of king Robert [the Pious].

The sign of Richard who commanded this precept to be made. The sign of Gunnor his mother. The sign of Judith his wife. Of Richard son of Richard. The sign of William the count [of Eu]. The sign of Robert the archbishop [of Rouen]. The sign of Malger the count [of Corbeil]. The sign of Ralph the count [of Ivry]. The sign of his sons. The sign of Tursting. The sign of Hugh. The sign of Hugh the bishop [of Bayeux], the son of Ralph, The sign of Hugh [the bishop] of Evreux. The sign of Roger the bishop of

Lisieux. The sign of Hugh the bishop [of Auxerre?]. The sign of Roger. The sign of Gilbert the knight (*miles*). The sign of Turchilamnus. The sign of Ralph the knight (*miles*). The sign of Ralph. The sign of Roger. Dudo[3] the chancellor wrote and subscribed this.

167 Edward the Confessor to Mt St Michel (c. 1033–4)

Edward, king of the English, grants to Mont-St-Michel St Michael's Mount and other property in England. (1027–1035: probably 1033–4).

This charter in reduced-diploma form is entered in the cartulary of Mont St-Michel and is accepted as genuine by Marie Fauroux. It must be dated to the reign of duke Robert the Magnificent who subscribes it, and may be thought more particularly to fit the context of that duke's abortive expedition to invade England on the aethling's behalf (*c*.1033–4), reported by William of Jumièges and which in the event finished at Mont-St-Michel (see Fauroux, p. 217 and cf. **12** above). See also **168** where 'king Edward' appears among the subscriptions.

Source: Fauroux No. 76.

In the name of the holy and undivided Trinity. I, Edward, by the grace of God king of the English, wishing to make some offering for the salvation of my soul or the souls of my progenitors, have with the consent and witness of good men given to St Michael the Archangel, for the use of the brethren serving God in that place, St Michael which is next the sea,[4] with all appurtenances, that is to say vills, fortifications (*castellis*), fields and other things belonging thereto. I have added also all the land of *Vennesire*[5] with towns (*oppidis*), vills, fields, meadows, cultivated and uncultivated lands, and with the revenues of these. I have further added to these grants the port which is called *Ruminella*[6] with all things which pertain to it, that is to say, mills and fisheries and all land cultivated and uncultivated and the revenues thereof. If, moreover, anyone shall try to make a false claim against these grants, he shall incur by anathema the perpetual wrath of God. And in order that the authority of our gift shall be held more truly and enduringly in future times, I have written beneath with my hand in confirmation and many have made their witness.

The sign of king Edward +. The sign of count Robert [of Normandy] +. The sign of Rabel[7] +. The sign of Robert archbishop of Rouen +. The sign of Herbert bishop of Lisieux +. The sign of Robert bishop of Coutances +. The sign of Humphrey +. The sign of Nigel the *vicomte* +. The sign of Anschitell +. The sign of Ralph +. The sign of Choschet +. The sign of Turstin +.

---

[3] The MS has 'Odo' in error.
[4] *I.e.* St Michael's Mount, Cornwall.
[5] Variously identified as Devonshire or, more probably, Wevelshire in Cornwall.
[6] Probably to be read *Riuuiuella*, i.e. Trevalga, Cornwall.
[7] Named by Orderic Vitalis as the commander of duke Robert's fleet.

168   Robert the Magnificent to Fécamp (c.1031–5)

Robert the Magnificent grants to Fécamp properties and rights of various kinds. The subscriptions include that of king Edward (1031/2 – 1035).

This original charter in diploma form survives in three copies, A, B and C, all at Fécamp. Haskins, who did not know of B, printed facsimiles of A and C, *Norman Institutions*, Pls. 4 and 5.

Source: Fauroux No. 85.

In the name of the Father and the Son and the Holy Ghost. I Robert, son of the second Richard, by the will of God duke of the Normans, and myself by God's grace prince and duke of the Normans, wish present and future generations to know of those things which I have bestowed upon the Universal God, that is the holy and undivided Trinity, in the place which is called Fécamp, after the death of my father, for the salvation of my soul and the souls of my progenitors, my brothers also and my sisters. All of which I have wished specifically to be written below as follows, lest they slip from the memory of future ages: Petiville with all things pertaining to it; certain of my men, that is to say knights (*milites*), with all things pertaining to them – they are, Hundal son of Gosman and his grandsons (*nepotes*) the sons of Bloc, also Walter son of Girulf, the sons of Gonfred who are all of Grainville-Ymauville, Torquitil son of Anslec,[8] Justaldus the clerk[9] and Ralph the layman and their brothers the sons of Hugh de Bardeville. I have given also the land which is called Ecretteville-les-Baons with all its appurtenances. Also I have restored the entire half of the vill of Bernay with everything that pertains to that half in entirety. I have given also the vill which is called Eletot. I have restored also all the land which Rainald the *vicomte* was known to hold at Arques [la-Bataille] and in Tourville-la-Chapelle and at Saintigny with the churches and mills and the wood which is called 'Appasilva', with salt-pans, fisheries, meadows, customary tenants (*hospites*), and all other appurtenances, and all the men who were subject to him. I have given also the whole wood called Boclon next to Fécamp. I have given them also in exchange the wood which is called 'between the two waters' and all things which pertain to it; and I have given the land called Ourville-en-Caux which my grandmother assigned to Fécamp for the salvation of the souls of our progenitors and hers, and, in addition, the wine-cellar and vineyard. I have also bestowed other knights (*milites*), namely Osbert son of Gosman, with his allod, and Urse and William his brother, the sons that is to say of Anslec. I have given at Argences the area of jurisdiction (*leuva*) pertaining to the market of that town according to the custom of my duchy. All these things I have given for the salvation of my soul and the souls of my forbears to the one living, true and triple God. If, moreover, which we cannot believe possible, anyone shall attempt to go against or bring a false claim against this charter which is the expression of our will, his lot shall be with Judas the traitor unless he shall make amends. And in order that this charter (*descriptio*) shall remain valid and enduring, I have confirmed it below with my own hand and have commanded my vassals (*fideles*) to confirm it.

I have restored also the tithe of the fairs of Caen. I have given also the fishery, commonly called fishing place (*gordus*) at Oissel. In addition I have given the tithe of

---

[8] MS Adlec.
[9] Perhaps a nickname since he occurs in a list of knights.

meadows in the vill called Couronne. Finally, I have given Ansfred de Sorquainville with all the land he was known to hold wherever it may be.

+ The sign of Robert duke of the Normans. + The sign of William his son. + The sign of the lord Robert the archbishop [of Rouen].

+ The sign of Robert the bishop [of Coutances]. The sign of Junguené the archbishop [of Dol]. + The sign of the lord John the abbot [of Fécamp]. + The sign of William the abbot [of Jumièges]. + The sign of Gradulfus the abbot [of St Wandrille]. The sign of Rainer the abbot.[10] + The sign of Durandus the abbot [of Cerisy-la-Forêt]. + The sign of Isembert the abbot [of la Trinité-du-Mont]. + The sign of king Edward.[11] The sign of Baldwin the count of Flanders. The sign of Euguerran [I] the count [of Ponthieu]. The sign of Gilbert the count [of Brionne]. The sign of Nigel [the *vicomte*]. The sign of Humphrey de Vieilles. The sign of Richard the *vicomte*. The sign of Gocelin the *vicomte* [of Arques-la-Bataille]. The sign of Turstin the *vicomte*. The sign of Aymo the *vicomte*. The sign of Turold the constable.

169 William The Conqueror to Bec-Hellouin, 1041

William the Conqueror confirms to the abbey of Le Bec the grants of various donors including himself, abbot Herluin and his family, and count Gilbert of Brionne (1041, 24 February). Le Bec.

The whole of the following ducal confirmation of various grants relating to the foundation (1034–5) and earliest history of Le Bec is derived ultimately from a lost Bec *pancarte* (a charter bringing together and confirming in one document a series of earlier charters) which survives now only in incomplete, seventeenth-century transcripts (B and C in Fauroux). The ghosts, so to speak, of the several original charters can be detected in the duke's confirmation of them, as they could have been also in the lost *pancarte*. A later Bec *pancarte* of c.1070 or 1077, containing the same material, and more, is printed by A. Porée, *Histoire de l'abbaye du Bec*, 2 vols., Evreux, 1901 (repr. Brussels, 1980), i. 645–9. The confirmation of duke William here printed in translation from Marie Fauroux's edition of the seventeenth-century transcripts states that it was made 'on the day of the dedication of the said monastery', *i.e.* the second (and first masonry) church dedicated on 23 February 1041. For the dedication of the third and final church in 1077, see **64** above.

Source: Fauroux No. 98.

Be it known to all worshippers of the Christian religion that I abbot Herluin,[12] the son of Ansgot, with the support and commendation of my brothers, the ratification of count Gilbert [of Brionne], and the consent of count Robert [of Normandy] and Robert the archbishop [of Rouen], have given to St Mary the third part of the land of Bonneville-Aptot and that which pertains to it, and the third parts of Quevilly and Surcy and that

[10] Fauroux's suggested identification of Rainer as abbot of la Trinité-du-Mont at Rouen poses difficulties since he did not become abbot until 1051 and at this time was only a monk there (he subscribes as such Fauroux No. 84) while abbot Isembert signs below. It is possible that the former's name was added later, and perhaps significant that there is no autograph cross against it.
[11] *I.e.* Edward the Confessor. Cf. No. **167**. Since it is sometimes said that Edward is well down the list of subscribers, it should be noted that his position is both honourable and strictly correct in precedence. The duke and his son come first, followed by the ecclesiastics, followed by the lay magnates headed by the exiled Edward. There the name of Edward alone has an autograph cross against it.
[12] This charter of Herluin was given in 1035.

which pertains to them, together with the land of Cernay and is appurtenances, which lands my father Ansgot held in his lifetime, and also the dower of my mother given to me in entirety at the command of my father; before witnesses, namely Fulbert the priest, the laymen Vitalis and Rainald, and many others.

The aforesaid count Gilbert gave to the same church of Bec the fishery of Pont-Authou, the meadows of Val-Aunay, and the forest and land of Malleville with Norman's mill.

At the time when Baldric gave himself and his son to the monastic order, he gave to the above-written monastery whatever land belonged to him in Servaville, but, because he gave in that grant more than he had there, his kindred, the brothers Ralph, Roger and Baldric, renounced whatever Baldric conceded that they had, in exchange for the fief (*beneficium*) of the castle which is called la Ferté. These witnesses were present, Seifrid the priest, etc.

The same abbot Herluin bought from his brother Odo half the church of Surcy with the tithe and the priest's land for 4 *livres* . . .[13] The sign + of Roger concerning the exchange (or mint) of the territories of Surcy and Bonneville-Aptot for the use of the cellarer of the monastery of Bec for the purchase of the mill 4 *livres*.

+ [13] the sign of Odo brother of the said abbot, who gave to the said monastery the land which he had in Etretat and that part which he had of the church of Bonneville-Aptot and its tithe together with his son; that part which the said Odo had in the church and tithe of Quevilly and Surcy the aforesaid lord abbot bought from him for the estate of the church of St Mary of Bec.[14]

Count Gilbert [of Brionne] gave to the said church of Bec the services and customs which Odo and Roger, the brothers of Herluin the lord abbot, formerly rendered for their allods. This grant after Gilbert's death was confirmed by his successor count Guy.

Drogo son of Ralph sold to abbot Herluin and the church of St Mary the Mother of God at Bec whatever by right he possessed of the paternal allod, and Robert son of Humphrey transferred the service and jurisdiction (*districtus*) of it to that same church.

All these things which we have set out above count William, the son of count Robert, freely confirmed on the day of the dedication of the said monastery,[15] and gave to it the tithe of the issues of the whole dues of Brionne. He added the customs and profits of justice of Servaville which were formerly Baldric's and who is now a professed monk of Bec.

The witnesses who saw and heard, with their signs – The sign + of Mauger the archbishop [of Rouen]. The sign + of W. the count, son of count Robert. The sign + of Hugh the bishop [of Lisieux].[16] The sign + of count William [Busac] brother of the same bishop.

The sign + of Nigel the *vicomte*. The sign + of Geoffrey the *vicomte*. The sign + of Ralph Taison. If anyone shall presume to take away from the said monastery anything

[13] Presumably reference to another charter.

[14] Thus C. B, which Marie Fauroux prints (p. 98) has *ecclesiae Petrariae*.

[15] 23 February 1041. See above.

[16] As Fauroux points out, Hugh did not become bishop of Lisieux until 1049, and his subscription must have been added later.

from any of the above grants let him know beyond doubt that he will find himself cut off and excommunicated from the whole Church.

170   William the Conqueror to St Martin of Marmoutier (c.1050–64)

William the Conqueror grants to the abbey of St Martin at Marmoutier land and a stream at Luot. (c.1050–64).

This ducal charter survived as an original until 1944. Comparatively brief and lacking both Invocation and Pious Preamble, it is not a diploma but is drawn up in the relatively simple form of a notification in the manner of many private charters in post-Conquest England. There were close links of patronage between the Norman duke and Marmoutier (near Tours) from which the Conqueror obtained monks for his foundation at Battle (also dedicated to St Martin) after 1066.

Source: Fauroux No. 16

We wish it to be known to all those who shall hear this in future times that I, William, by the grace of God count of the Normans, for the salvation of my soul and of the souls of my progenitors, especially those of my father and mother, and also of my wife and my heirs, grant in perpetual right to God and St Martin, to the monks, that is to say, who at Marmoutier serve God under abbot Albert, land situated in the place which is called Luot, as quit and free of any claim from anyone else as I hold it and as it was left by my father, grandfather and forefathers. There are 10 manses in that land which is defined by these limits: on the one side is the common way which leads from the city of Avranches into the interior of Normandy, and on the other the stream, which I also give them to make a mill. All the rest of the land of Luot is mine, and of the part concerned I have given 10 manses to them, namely to the monks who are to fight in God's service in the aforesaid monastery, in the presence of those witnesses whose names are written below. Should anyone, moreover, seek to take these my alms from St Martin, let him be excommunicated and his presumption come to nought, that my bequest may remain inviolate and my remembrance live in that house for ever.[17] The sign of count William. The sign of Neal the *vicomte*. The sign of Maino de Fougères. The sign of Richard the son of Turstin. The sign of Roger de Montgommery. The sign of Ralph Taisson. The sign of Gerald the seneschal. The sign of Robert the son of Giroie. The sign of Hugh Brito. The sign of Theobald the son of Berner.

171   William the Conqueror to St Martin of Marmoutier, 1066

William the Conqueror, on the eve of his invasion of England causes his son Robert to confirm to the abbey of Marmoutier all the property which the former had given them or permitted them to hold in his dominions, 1066.

This notice of a confirmation surviving only in seventeenth-century and later transcripts is included here for its echoes of the Norman Conquest and for an early appearance of the Conqueror's eldest son and heir, Robert Curthose (and his tutor).

Source: Fauroux No. 228

[17] The witnesses are arranged in single column.

Be it known to all future inmates of this monastery of St Martin of Marmoutier that when William count of the Normans was about to cross the sea to wage war against the English people he was sought out and requested by one of our brethren called John, the son of Guy de Valle, at the bidding of our lord abbot Bartholomew, that he would cause all those things which he himself had given us, or permitted us to hold in the territory under his power, to be confirmed by the authority of his son Robert, because, that is to say, he [Robert] was now of sufficient age to be able to exercise such authority on his own account. Whereupon the count, so liberal and generous in giving, and no less prudent and zealous in confirming his gifts, sent for his son and asked him to give the confirmation requested, and he, nothing loth, gladly confirmed all that had formerly been given us by his father and all that he had allowed us to hold in all the lands subject to him. Given in the city of Rouen, in the year of the Incarnation 1066, in the third year of the lord abbot Bartholomew's rule over us. Witnessed by John bishop of Avranches, count Robert, Roger de Montgommery, William fitz Osbern, William his son, Roger de Beaumont, Hugh de Grandmesnil, Ilgerius the tutor of the said Robert son of the count, Robert de Gutot, Gerald the cook of the monastery.

172 Roger of Montgommery to La Trinité-du-Mont at Rouen, 1066

Roger de Montgommery, in the presence of William the Conqueror and with the duke's confirmation, quitclaims to la Trinité-du-Mont at Rouen the land of Givervilla, 1066.
   This notice is entered in the cartulary of la Trinité-du-Mont and is included here chiefly for its echoes of the Conquest.

Source: Fauroux No. 233

Be it known to all the faithful of Christ that, in the year of the divine Incarnation 1066, when, that is to say, William duke of the Normans, was about to cross the sea with his fleet made ready, a certain renowned man, by name Roger de Montgommery, totally remitted to the lord abbot Rayner and his monks, in the presence of the aforesaid duke, that which he had claimed in the land of Holy Trinity which is called Givervilla, in such a way that from that time forward that land should never again suffer a claim from him or his heirs, but should remain freely and in peace to Holy Trinity and its monks in perpetuity. This was approved and confirmed by William the illustrious prince of the Normans.

   + the sign of the same [William]. + the sign of Roger de Montgommery. + the sign of William fitz Osbern. + the sign of Gerald the seneschal. + the sign of Ralph the chamberlain. + the sign of Hugh the butler.
   Witnesses, Richard the seneschal. Bernard the cook, Ansfridus son of Athla.

Post-Conquest England

173 William the Conqueror to St Denis, 1069

William the Conqueror grants to St Denis the church of Deerhurst and confirms to that abbey Taynton which king Edward had granted to it. 1069, 13 April, Winchester.

This original charter is written in diploma form in all respects save that a protocol replaces the Invocation. In detail it is hybrid as between Old English and Norman practice. It lacks the Old English vernacular boundary clauses; in Old English fashion the *signa* are not autograph as they were in Norman custom; contrary to Old English practice the diploma bears a seal, suspended on a tag at the bottom.

Source: Bishop and Chaplais, *op. cit.*, Pl. XXVIII (photograph of seal). See also **197**.

William king of the English, count of the Normans and of the men of Maine, to all the faithful of Christ of whatever race. The compassionate and pitiful Lord, enduring and all-merciful, has amongst other precepts of his clemency, since all that a man may have can be said to be less than nothing by comparison with eternal beatitude, commanded us that we do not fail to lay up treasures from those things which we lawfully possess, saying: Lay up for yourselves treasures in heaven, where neither moth nor rust doth corrupt.[1] For love of which inspiring command I and my consort Mathilda with the sagacious counsel of our magnates for the salvation of our souls and those of all our children have given the church of Deerhurst situated in the territory and county of the city of Gloucester, with all its appurtenances, to St Denis for whose apostolic precedence the people of Gaul give thanks, as our illustrious ancestor king Edward gave it for his own proper use to our faithful Baldwin, monk of St Denis, before he received from the same king the abbey of St Edmund over which he now presides and which we afterwards granted him when we had attained the kingdom. And let this church and all its known appurtenances be free from all secular burdens (*ab omni negotio*). We confirm also by this charter (*privilegium*) the grant (**157**) which the aforesaid king [Edward] gave to the same Saint [Denis] to obtain eternal reward, that is to say Taynton with all its appurtenances, establishing it as free as we our-selves have given, so that we and our issue by the prayers of the same saint and his com-panions Rusticus and Eleutherius, may merit success in this present life and the haven of perpetual peace. If moreover anyone of whatever power shall pillage this our gift then by the authority of omnipotent God he shall have the lot of Dathan and Abyron unless he shall make amends and reparation to the Saint and the brethren assigned to that place.

In the year of the Lord's Incarnation 1069 and the third year of the reign of king William, in the second day of Easter (13 April), this charter (*privilegium*) was confirmed in the monastery of St Swithun in the city of Winchester during the celebration of Mass, these witnesses consenting: I William, king, have strengthened this gift and confirmation with the sign of the holy cross + . I Mathilda, queen of the same king, have publicly pro-fessed my consent. I Richard, son of the king, have freely assented to the gift of my father and mother.

+[2] I Stigand, archbishop of the church of Canterbury have confirmed. + I Aldred, archbishop of the church of York have confirmed. + I William, bishop of London. + I Aielric, bishop [of Selsey]. + I Hereman, bishop [of Sherborne]. + I Giso, bishop [of Wells]. + I Leofric, bishop [of Exeter]. + I Odo, bishop, brother of the king have signed

[1] Mat. 6:20

[2] All the subscriptions in the first paragraph are arranged in a column on the left. All those in the second in a column on the right.

145

with the cross. + I Geoffrey, bishop [of Coutances]. + I Baldwin, bishop of Evreux. + I Ernald bishop of Le Mans.

+ I Robert, count [of Mortain], brother of the king, have consented with goodwill. + I William son of Osbern, earl [of Hereford]. + I Robert count of the castle (*castrum*) of Eu. + I Ralph, earl [of Norfolk]. + I Brian. + I Fulk de Alnou. + I Henry de Ferrers. + I Hugh de Montfort. + I Richard, son of count Gilbert [of Brionne]. + I Roger d'Ivry. I Hamo, of the king. I Robert, brother of the same Hamo.

+ [3] The sign of the queen. + The sign of the king. + The sign of Richard his son.

174   Writ of William the Conqueror concerning the city of London (1067)

King William announces that the city of London shall enjoy all the rights which it had in the time of king Edward, including the right of inheritance, and that he will defend its liberties, 1067.

This famous writ still survives among the City records, together with its seal (now detached). Dated by general consent to 1067, it obviously belongs to the early years of the Conquest because it is written in the vernacular and in a good Old English hand. Facsimile, Bishop and Chaplais, *op. cit.*, Pl. XIV.

Source and translation: A.J. Robertson, *The Laws of the Kings of England from Edmund to Henry I*, Cambridge, 1925, pp. 230–1.

[Vernacular] King William sends friendly greetings to William the bishop [of London]and Geoffrey the mayor [portreeve] and all the burgesses in London both French and English. And I declare to you that it is my will that you both[4] shall be entitled to all the rights that you were entitled to in king Edward's day. And it is my will that every child shall be his father's heir after his father's day. And I will not allow any man to offer you any wrong. God keep you.

175   Notification of William the Conqueror transferring the see of Dorchester to Lincoln, 1072

King William announces that he has transferred the seat of the bishopric of Dorchester to the city of Lincoln and has given sufficient land there for the building of the new cathedral. The king also grants to the cathedral church various properties (1072, after Whitsun).

Accepted as genuine, its seal gone but leaving clear traces of its affixation (tie and stump of tongue), this, again, may be regarded as a hybrid document. It begins, so to speak, as a writ or mere notification, with its particular address and announcement that the transfer of the bishopric has taken place: it then grants properties, in the present tense, to the re-established church, and thus may be called a writ-charter. No diploma-type charter recording these grants is known in the extensive Lincoln records. In any case changes have now come upon the formerly Old English but now Anglo-Norman writ: the language is Latin, the hand continental, and there is a witness clause at the end.

Source: Bishop and Chaplais, *Facsimiles of English Royal Writs*, No. 14.[5]

---

[3] These last three *signa* are in line below the columns.
[4] *I.e.* bishop and mayor as representative respectively of ecclesiastical and secular authority in the city.
[5] See also *Registrum Antiquissimum of the Cathedral Church of Lincoln*, i, ed. C.W. Foster (Lincoln Record Society, 27,1931) No. 2 and Pl. IV.

W[illiam] king of the English to T[urald] the sheriff and all the sheriffs of the bishopric of bishop Remigius, greeting. Know that I have transferred the seat of the bishopric of Dorchester to the city of Lincoln with the authority and counsel of Pope Alexander [II] and his legates, and also of archbishop Lanfranc and the other bishops of my kingdom, and have given there sufficient land, quit and free of all customs, for the construction of the mother church of the entire diocese and its subsidiary buildings. Wishing also to make some grant to the same church for the salvation of my soul, I give, first, two manors, namely Welton and Sleaford, with·their appurtenances, and then the churches of three of my manors with lands and tithes, that is to say of Kirton, Caistor and Wellingore. I give also the whole tithe of the entire rent of the aforesaid manors, and two churches in Lincoln, namely St Laurence and St Martin. Furthermore at the prayer and entreaty of bishop Remigius I grant to the same [cathedral] church a certain manor called Leighton which earl Waltheof formerly gave to the same bishop by my hand, and another which is called Wooburn which I formerly gave him with his episcopal staff. I also grant in perpetuity and with my royal authority confirm to the same church, with his leave and consent, the four churches of Bedford, Leighton Buzzard, Buckingham and Aylesbury which I had formerly given him in perpetual possession. Witnessed by archbishop L[anfranc] and E[rnisius] the sheriff.

176 Writ of William the Conqueror concerning Westminster, 1087

King William announces that he grants the manor of Pyrford to Westminster Abbey freed from geld as well as other customs (1087, before 9 September).

A genuine writ of the Conqueror, with the seal still attached (Facsimile, Bishop and Chaplais, Pl. XXIV) in the form of a notification to the shire court. It is to be noted that the sheriff (*vicecomes*) is now the addressee, as opposed to the bishop, earl and thegns of king Edward's day. Added to the witnesses this writ has another new feature of a dating clause, which is itself a reference to the Domesday survey of 1086–7. The exemption from geld is noteworthy, and so is the fact that Pyrford had previously been held by Harold.

Source: Bishop and Chaplais, *Facsimiles of English Royal Writs*. No. 26

William king of the English to Ralph the sheriff and all his officials in Surrey, greeting. Know that for the salvation of my soul I grant to God and St Peter of Westminster and abbot Gilbert[6] 8 hides of the manor of Pyrford which are in my demesne in the forest of Windsor, quit and free henceforth and for ever from scot and all my royal custom and from the monetary tax which in English is called geld. Witnessed by W[illiam] bishop of Durham and I[vo] Tailebois, after the description of all England.

177 Writ of William the Conqueror concerning spiritual pleas (1070–6)

Notification by William the Conqueror that with the counsel of his prelates and magnates he has decided to emend the hitherto unsatisfactory and uncanonical administration of ecclesiastical justice in England, and that henceforth no spiritual pleas shall be heard in the hundred court nor be brought before laymen but in ecclesiastical courts appointed by the bishop for that purpose (1070–6, possibly April 1072).

[6] *I.e.* Gilbert Crispin, author among other works of the *Vita Herluini* for which see above, pp. 41–3.

This writ in the form of a notification was evidently issued bilingually (which argues for an early date within the bracket given above) and in many copies sent out to the appropriate authorities throughout the realm. It survives, however, only in Latin transcripts entered in the registers or cartularies of the two cathedral churches of St Pauls and Lincoln (apart from various later Chancery enrolments) each with a different and appropriate address. It is included here mainly for its historical importance as marking the feudal establishment of separate ecclesiastical courts in England.

Source and translation: A.J. Robertson, *Laws of the Kings of England from Edmund to Henry I*, Cambridge, 1925, pp. 234–7.

William by the grace of God king of the English to R[alph] Bainard and G[eoffrey] de Mandeville and Peter de Valognes and my other faithful men (*fideles*) of Essex and of Hertfordshire and of Middlesex, greeting. Be it known to you all and my other faithful men (*fideles*) in England that I have determined, with the common counsel and advice of the archbishops, bishops, abbots and all the magnates of my kingdom, to emend the episcopal laws, which were neither satisfactory nor in accordance with holy canon law until my time. Wherefore I command and enjoin by my royal authority that no bishop or archdeacon shall henceforth hold a plea of the episcopal laws in the hundred court, nor bring a cause touching the rule of souls before the judgement of laymen, but whoever is summoned according to the episcopal laws concerning whatever cause or offence shall come to that place which has been chosen and named by the bishop for that purpose and there answer concerning his cause or offence and do right to God and his bishop not according to the law of the hundred but according to canon and episcopal law. If, however, anyone, puffed up with pride, shall disdain or refuse to come before the bishop's justice, let him be summoned once, twice, and thrice. But if then he will not come to make amends, he shall be excommunicated; and if it is necessary to enforce this, the power and jurisdiction of the king or sheriff shall be brought to bear. And he who does not come before the bishop's justice when summoned must pay the episcopal fine for each summons. I also forbid and by my authority prohibit any sheriff or reeve or royal official or any layman to interfere with those laws which pertain to the bishop. Nor may any layman bring any man to the ordeal without the bishop's authority. Nor may the ordeal take place anywhere except at the bishop's see or in that place which he has appointed for the purpose.

In this same document the same words are translated *verbatim* in the English language.[6]

178 Writ of William the Conqueror to Aethelwig abbot of Evesham (c.1072)

King William commands Aethelwig abbot of Evesham to summon all the knights under his administration to the king at Clarendon one week after Whitsun and then to be there himself with the five knights owed by him as abbot. (1072?)

This well-known writ in the form of a precept survives only in a copy entered in the Evesham cartulary, and is included here, again, chiefly for its historical importance, which was first publicized by J. H. Round in his seminal essay 'The Introduction of Knight-Service into England'.

Source: J.H. Round, *Feudal England*, London, 1909, p. 304.

[6] This note is added to the text in the register, signifying that the writ was drawn up bilingually.

W. king of the English to Aethelwig abbot of Evesham, greeting. We command you to summon all those who are in your bailiwick and jurisdiction that they have all the knights (*milites*) which they owe me duly equipped before me on the octaves of Whitsun at Clarendon. You also are to come to me on that day and bring with you duly equipped those five knights (*milites*), which you owe me from your abbey. Witnessed by Eudo the dapifer. At Winchester.

Laws, customs and custumals

179 The Laws of Cnut (1020–3)

It was an inherent part of Germanic kingship to declare as well as defend the law. The resulting law codes of kings are less legislative, in the sense of making law, than declaratory – hence Alfred, 'I, then, Alfred, king, gathered these laws together, and commended many of those to be written which our forefathers held, those which to me seemed good. . . . For I dared not write much of my own.' In England the last in the series of such codes is that of Cnut, the belatedly Christian king, whose laws are thought to have been drafted with help from Wulfstan, archbishop of York (1003–23) and bishop of Worcester (1003–16). No laws are extant for Edward the Confessor, though the 'law of king Edward' became something of a shibboleth after the Conquest, and the Norman kings, while certainly not deficient in a legislative function, issued their laws and 'assizes' piecemeal(183–6). Though the Anglo-Saxon law codes are not systematically comprehensive, those of Cnut are very full, and, of course, draw heavily on the laws of his predecessors. Obviously such legal evidence is invaluable for the light it throws upon society, its assumptions, aspirations and organization. It is to be noted that in Germanic society most offences which we should think of as criminal were amendable by monetary payments scaled according to the gravity of the offence and the rank of the offender and injured party. There were two categories of such payment, the *bot* or compensatory payment to the injured party, and the *wite* or penalty payment to the king or his delegate. In effect the highest *bot* is the wergeld or blood-price, payable to the kin of the slain man, if they will accept it (the alternative is the blood-feud).

Source and translation: A.J. Robertson, *Laws of the Kings of England from Edmund to Henry I*, Cambridge, 1925, pp. 154ff. 174ff; D. Whitelock, *English Historical Documents*, i, 1955, No. 50, pp. 419ff.[1]

I Cnut: Ecclesiastical. Prologue and first two clauses only

[Vernacular] This is the ordinance which king Cnut determined with the advice of his councillors, for the praise of God and for his own royal dignity and benefit; and it took place at the holy Christmas season at Winchester.

1. First, namely that above all other things they would ever love and honour one God and steadfastly hold one Christian faith, and love king Cnut with due loyalty.

2. And let us maintain the security and sanctity of the churches of God, and frequently attend them for the salvation of our souls and our own benefit.

[1] The translation of the latter is followed here where possible as likely to be from a text more easily available.

II Cnut: Secular (1020–3) Prologue and select clauses

[Vernacular] This is now the secular ordinance which I, with my councillors (*mid minan witenan*), wish to be observed over all England . . .

12. These are the rights which the king possesses over all men in Wessex, namely *mundbryce*[2] and *hamsocn*,[3] *forstal*[4] and [the fine for] the harbouring of fugitives and the fine for neglecting military service, unless he wishes to honour anyone further.[5]

13. And if anyone commits a deed punishable by outlawry, the king (alone) is to have power to grant him peace.

13.1. And if he has bookland, it is to be forfeited into the king's possession, no matter whose man he be.

14. And in Mercia he possesses just what is written here above, over all men.

15. And in the Danelaw he possesses the fine for fighting and that for neglecting military service, *grith bryce*[6] and *hamsocn* unless he wishes to honour anyone further.

20. And it is our will that every free man who wishes to be entitled to right of exculpation and to a wergild[7] if anyone slays him, be brought, if he is over 12 years old, into a hundred or tithing; otherwise he is not to be entitled to any rights of free men.

20a. Whether he has a home of his own, or is in the following of another, each is to be brought into a hundred and under surety, and the surety is to hold him and bring him to every legal duty.

31. And each lord is to have the men of his household under his own surety.

32. And if a slave is convicted by the ordeal,[8] on the first occasion he is to be branded.

38.1 And ever as a man is mightier or of higher rank, he must atone the deeper for wrongdoing both to God and to men.

57. If anyone plots against the king or his lord, he is to forfeit his life and all that he owns, unless he goes to the three-fold ordeal.

64. House-breaking[9] and arson and obvious theft and manifest murder and betrayal of a lord are beyond compensation[10] according to the secular law.

65. If anyone neglects the repair of fortresses or bridges, or military service,[11] he is to pay 120 shillings compensation to the king in the area under English law, and in the Danelaw as it stood before. . . .

70. And if anyone departs from this life intestate, be it through his heedlessness, or

---

[2] Breach of the king's protection.

[3] Attack on a homestead or forcible entry.

[4] Violent opposition, obstruction, ambush.

[5] *I.e.* unless the king will grant or delegate these rights to some other lord as a liberty or franchise.

[6] Breach of peace or protection. Cf. *mundbryce*.

[7] The blood-price or price put upon a man's life, scaled according to his rank.

[8] The ordeal, of various kinds, was an appeal to the judgement of God to establish innocence or guilt.

[9] As Whitelock observes, this must therefore be a more serious offence than *hamsocn* above, presumably including the destruction of the buildings.

[10] *I.e.* bot-less, bootless.

[11] Here, then, is the so-called *trimoda-necessitas*, the threefold royal right and common obligation seldom if ever lifted.

through sudden death, the lord is then not to make more from his possessions than his legal heriot.

70.1 But by his direction, the property is to be very justly divided among the wife, the children and the close kinsmen, each in the proportion which belongs to him.

71. And heriots are to be so determined as befits rank:-

71a. an earl's as belongs thereto, namely eight horses, four saddled and four unsaddled, and four helmets and four coats of mail and eight spears and as many shields and four swords and 200 mancuses of gold.

71.1. and next, the king's thegns, who are closest to him: four horses, two saddled and two unsaddled, and two swords and four spears and as many shields and a helmet and coat of mail and 50 mancuses of gold;

71.2. and of the lesser thegns: a horse and its trappings, and his weapons or his *healsfang*[12] in Wessex; and two pounds in Mercia and two pounds in East Anglia.

71.3. And the heriot of the king's thegn among the Danes, who has right of jurisdiction; four pounds.

71.4. And if he has a more intimate relation with the king: two horses, one saddled and one unsaddled, and a sword and two spears and two shields and 50 mancuses of gold.

71.5. And he who is of lower position: two pounds.

77. And the man, who in his cowardice deserts his lord or his comrades, whether it is on an expedition by sea or on one on land, is to forfeit all that he owns and his own life; and the lord is to succeed to his possessions and to the land which he previously gave him.

78. And the heriot is to be remitted for the man who falls before his lord in a campaign, whether it is within the land or outside the land; and the heirs are to succeed to the land and to the possessions and divide it very justly.

83. And he who violates these laws which the king has now given to all men, whether he be Danish or English, is to forfeit his wergild to the king.

83.1. And if he violates it again, he is to pay his wergild twice.

83.2. And if he then is so presumptuous that he violates it a third time, he is to forfeit all that he owns.

180 'Of People's Ranks and Laws'. (c. 1002–23). Extracts only

This compilation on status is generally attributed to the same Wulfstan (I) archbishop of York. It is a private, not an official, compilation and has an evident element of wistful looking back to the good old days (which may never have quite been).

Source and translation: Whitelock, *English Historical Documents*, i (1955), No. 52, pp. 431ff.

[Vernacular] *Concerning wergilds and dignities*

1. Once it used to be that people and rights went by dignities, and councillors of the people were then entitled to honour, each according to his rank, noble and peasant, retainer and lord (*eorl* and *ceorl*, *thegen* and *theoden*).

[12] Evidently the tenth-part of the wergild and in Wessex rendered as the heriot. Cf. the money-payments of Mercia and East Anglia in this same clause and in 71.3.

2. And if a peasant (*ceorl*) prospered so that he possessed fully five hides of his own, church and kitchen,[13] a bell and a burgh-gate (*burhgeat*), a seat and special office in the king's hall, thenceforth he was entitled to the rights of a thegn.

3. And if a thegn prospered so that he served the king and rode in his household and on his missions, if he himself had a thegn who served him, possessing five hides on which he discharged the king's dues, and attended his lord in the king's hall and thrice went on his errand to the king, thenceforth he was allowed to represent his lord with his preliminary oath, and legally obtain his [right to pursue a] charge, wherever he needed.

6. And if a merchant prospered so that he thrice crossed the open sea at his own expense, thenceforth he was entitled to the rights of a thegn.

181 The Rectitudines Singularum Personarum or 'The Rights and Ranks of People' (First half of the eleventh century)

Presented by D.C. Douglas as 'a description of agrarian conditions in the time of Edward the Confessor, made by one familiar with the management of a great estate.' Its principal interest is the evidence it provides for the development of the manor in pre-Conquest England, but only the section dealing with the thegn is printed in translation here.

Source and translation: D.C. Douglas, *English Historical Documents*, ii. (1959) No. 172, pp. 813ff.

[Vernacular] *Thegn's Law*. The rights and obligations of a thegn are, that he be entitled to his book-right[14] and that he shall contribute three things in respect of his land: armed service, and the repairing of fortresses (*burhbotam*) and work upon bridges.[15] Also in respect of many estates further services arise on the king's order, such as service connected with the deer fence at the king's residence (*ham*), and equipping a guard ship, and guarding the coast, and guarding the lord, and military watch, alms-giving and church dues, and many other divers things.

182 The Consuetudines et Justicie or 'The Customs and Rights of the Duke of Normandy' (1091)

This retrospective document, surviving only in later copies, sets down the rights exercised in Normandy by duke William the Conqueror during his reign. Only the prologue and the clauses relating to the control of fortification including castles, and to hostages, are given here. Others refer to the expanding concepts of the duke's peace and pleas, the maintenance of law and order, and the ducal monopoly of the coinage through the mints of Rouen and Bayeux.

Source: C.H. Haskins, *Norman Institutions*, New York and London, 1913, 1960, pp. 281ff.

Here are the rights which King William who acquired the kingdom of England had in Normandy, and they are written here as Robert count of Normandy and William king of England, the sons and heirs of the aforesaid king, with the counsel of the bishops and

---

[13] 'church and kitchen' omitted in some texts.

[14] *I.e.* the privileges arising from the possession of 'book-land', land held by charter or land-book (if he has any).

[15] *I.e.* the *trimoda-necessitas* again.

barons, caused them to be written at Caen on 18 July [1091].

c.4. No one in Normandy might dig a fosse in the open country(*in planam terram*) of more than one shovel's throw in depth, nor set there more than one line of palisading, and that without battlements or alures.[16] And no one might make a fortification (*fortitudinem*) on rock or in island, and no one might raise a castle (*castellum*) in Normandy, and no one in Normandy might withhold the possession of his castle (*castellum*) from the lord of Normandy if he wished to take it into his hand.

c.5. And if the lord of Normandy required the son or brother or grandson (*nepos*) of one of his barons (*baro*) who was not a knight (*miles*) as a hostage for good faith no one might refuse him.

183   The Ten Articles of William I

This unofficial compilation of laws attributed to the Conqueror, the earliest copies of which are found in early twelfth-century manuscripts (e.g. the *Textus Roffensis* or register of the cathedral priory of Rochester), is generally agreed to contain some genuine enactments of the king. Particular interest attaches to the origin of the *murdrum* fine in c.3, as echoing the reality of the Norman settlement which was sociologically the imposition of a new and alien ruling class upon a potentially hostile indigenous population including former Old English lords. Normans and other French lords already in England before 1066 find a place in c.4, and those who came after 1066 in c.3. The Norman judicial procedure of trial by battle (another form of the ordeal) gets an early mention in c.6, and the Norman frankpledge system (an efficient combination of the Old English surety group and tithing or police group) in c.8.

Source and translation: Robertson, *Laws of the Kings of England*, pp. 238–43.

Intimation is hereby given of the enactments made by William king of England and his magnates (*principes*) after he had obtained possession of England.

1. In the first place he desires above all that one God should be honoured throughout the whole of his kingdom, and that one Christian faith should be kept inviolate, and that peace and security should be maintained among the English and Normans.

3. I desire likewise that all the men whom I brought with me or who have come after me shall enjoy the benefit of my protection.

　(i) And if any one of them is slain, his lord shall arrest the slayer within five days if he can. If not, however, he shall begin to pay me 46 marks of silver[17] from the property of that lord as long as it lasts out.

　(ii) When, however, the property of the lord fails, the whole hundred in which the murder is committed shall pay in common what remains.[18]

4. But every Frenchman who, in the time of king Edward, my kinsman, was admitted to the status of an Englishman[19] . . . shall be paid for according to English law.

---

[16] *I.e.* the timber equivalent of wall-walks about the summit.
[17] The mark was 13s. 4d., *i.e.* 160 pence. The coinage was, of course, the silver penny.
[18] Later the whole fine from the outset was laid upon the hundred.
[19] *Lit.* 'was a sharer of English customs'.

This decree was enacted at Gloucester.[20]

6. It has likewise been decreed that, if a Frenchman summon an Englishman for perjury or murder, theft, homicide or *ran*, by which the English mean open robbery which cannot be denied, the Englishman shall defend himself by whichever method he prefers, either the ordeal of iron or trial by combat. . . .

8. Everyone who desires to keep the status of a freeman shall be in frankpledge, so that the frankpledge may bring him to justice, if he has committed an offence. . . .

. . . The hundred and county courts shall be attended in accordance with the decrees of our predecessors.

184   Reported ecclesiastical legislation of William the Conqueror

There is no reason not to accept the following extract from the early twelfth-century *Historia Novorum in Anglia* ('The History of Modern Times in England') of Eadmer, the Canterbury monk, historian and biographer of St Anselm, as giving the substance of certain ecclesiastical enactments of the Conqueror's reign, designed to perpetuate that control over the Church which his predecessors had enjoyed in England and he himself in Normandy. In William's day, the time-honoured royal position *vis-à-vis* the Church needed defence against the ideas of the Gregorian reformers.

Source: Eadmer, *Historia Novorum in Anglia*, ed. M. Rule, Rolls Series, London, 1884, i, 9; W. Stubbs, *Select Charters* . . ., 9th ed., Oxford, 1946, p. 96.

I will set down certain of those new rules which he [William] established to be observed throughout England . . .

1. He would not allow anyone in all his realm without his authority to recognize as Pope any bishop elected to the Roman see,[21] or to receive in any way his letters if they had not been first shown to him.

2. Also he did not permit the primate of his kingdom, whether the archbishop of Canterbury or of York, when presiding over an assembled general synod of bishops, to establish or prohibit anything unless in accordance with his will.

3. He did not allow his bishops without his permission publicly to implead any of his barons (*barones*) or ministers charged with incest or adultery or other mortal sin, or to excommunicate or bind them by any ecclesiastical penalties.

185   The primacy of Canterbury, 1072

The following extract is taken from a formal document recording the case and judgement, subscribed by William the Conqueror and many others after the manner of a solemn diploma, and itself transcribed in the lengthy Memorandum on the whole proceedings of the assertion of the supremacy of Canterbury over York included in the Lanfranc's Letters.

Source and translation: Margaret Gibson, *The Letters of Lanfranc Archbishop of Canterbury*, Oxford Medieval Texts, 1979, No. 3 (iv). pp. 44–9.

---

[20] The Conqueror is known to have been at Gloucester in 1072, 1081, 1082, 1085 and 1086. One would expect the *murdrum* fine to be imposed early in the reign.

[21] *I.e.* in the case of a disputed election.

In the year of Our Lord Jesus Christ 1072, the eleventh year of the pontificate of the lord Pope Alexander [II] and the sixth of the reign of William, glorious king of the English and duke of the Normans, at the command of the same Pope Alexander and with the consent of the aforesaid king, in the presence of the king himself and the bishops and abbots, there was a formal examination of the case for the primacy, which archbishop Lanfranc of Canterbury was advancing as a right of his church over the church of York, and of the case for ordaining certain bishops, where it was not at all clear to whose jurisdication they belonged. Finally it was established and demonstrated by written proofs of various kinds that the church of York should be subject to Canterbury and should obey the directions of its archbishop, as primate of the whole of Britain, in all matters relating to the Christian religion. . . . This constitution has received the assent of the aforesaid king and archbishops, Lanfranc of Canterbury and Thomas of York, and of Hubert, subdeacon of the holy Roman Church and legate of the aforesaid Pope Alexander, and of the other bishops and abbots who were present.

This case was examined first in the city of Westminster at the festival of Easter, in the royal chapel which is in the castle (*in castello*), and then on the royal estate called Windsor, where it was settled in the presence of the king, the bishops, abbots and the men of various ranks who had assembled there at court at the feast of Whitsun.

186 The ecclesiastical synod at London, 1075

This is the only one of Lanfranc's great councils of which a formal record exists, entered in his Collected Letters. It too was evidently a formal document, subscribed by all the prelates present.

Source and translation: Gibson, *Letters of Lanfranc*, as above No. 11, pp. 72–9.

In the year of Our Lord 1075, in the ninth year of the reign of William, glorious king of the English, a council of the whole land of England was assembled in the church of St Paul the Apostle in London, namely of bishops, abbots and many ecclesiastics. The council was summoned and presided over by Lanfranc, archbishop of the holy church of Canterbury and primate of the whole island of Britain . . .

[The list of those present then given includes] Geoffrey of Coutances, who though an overseas bishop was sitting with the others in the council because he had a great deal of property in England. . . .

Because the custom of holding councils had been in abeyance in the realm of England for many years, some legislation which is already defined in ancient law was renewed.

(i) A clause on the proper precedence of the archbishops of Canterbury and York and the bishops of London and Winchester then follows.

(iii) Following the decrees of Popes Damasus and Leo and also the councils of Sardis and Laodicaea, which prohibit the existence of episcopal sees in small townships, by the generosity of the king and the authority of the synod permission was granted to three of the bishops mentioned above to move from townships to cities: Hermann from Sherborne to Salisbury, Stigand from Selsey to Chichester, and Peter from Lichfield to Chester. The case of certain others who remained in townships or villages was deferred until the king, who was at that time fighting overseas, could hear it in person.

(vii) No one shall buy or sell holy orders nor any position in the Church which carries pastoral responsibility. This crime was originally condemned in Simon Magus by the Apostle Peter; later on it was forbidden and outlawed by the holy Fathers.

(ix) Following the council of Elvira and the eleventh council of Toledo, no bishop or abbot nor any of the clergy shall sentence a man to be killed or mutilated; nor shall he lend the support of his authority to those who are passing sentence.

187   The Penitential Ordinance of Bishop Ermenfrid of Sion after the Battle of Hastings (c.1070)

This penitential ordinance to be imposed on those who had fought at Hastings and taken part in the subsequent campaign was drawn up by the Norman bishops in Normandy and confirmed by papal authority exercised by the legate Ermenfrid, bishop of Sion. It survives in several early episcopal copies in England, and, in the words of one of its most recent editors 'may be accepted with confidence as an authentic document'.[22]

Source: H.E.J. Cowdrey, *Journal of Ecclesiastical History*, xx, 1969, pp. 241–2; C. Morton, *Latomus*, 34, 1975, pp. 381–2.[23]

This is the institution of penance according to the decrees of the bishops of the Normans, confirmed by the authority of the supreme pontiff by his legate Ermenfrid bishop of Sion, to be imposed upon those whom W[illiam] duke of the Normans by his command[24] . . . and who before this decree were his men and owed him military service as their duty.

1. Whoever knows that he has killed in the great battle is to do one year's penance for each man slain.

2. Whoever struck another but does not know if that man was thereby slain, is to do 40 days penance for each case, if he can remember the number, either continuously or at intervals.

3. Whoever does not know the number of those he struck or killed shall, at the discretion of his bishop, do penance for one day a week for the rest of his life, or, if he is able, make amends either by building a church or by giving perpetual alms to one.

4. Those who struck no one yet wished to do so are to do penance for three days.

5. Clerks who fought, or were armed for the purpose of fighting, because they are forbidden to fight are to do penance according to the institutions of canon law as if they had sinned in their own country. The penance of monks is to be determined according to their rule and the judgement of their abbot.

6. Those who fought motivated only by gain are to know that they owe penance as for homicide; but because they fought in public war the bishops out of mercy have assigned them three years' penance.

[22] H.E.J. Cowdrey, 'Bishop Ermenfrid of Sion and the Penitential Ordinance following the Battle of Hastings', *Journal of Ecclesiastical History*, XX, 1969, p. 240.
[23] The translation offered below in general follows the improved text printed by C. Morton. This in turn results in a slightly different arrangement of numbered sections from those printed by Cowdrey. The division of the text into numbered sections, is, of course, itself a modern editorial device.
[24] A lacuna in all copies of the text follows.

7. Archers who do not know how many they killed or wounded without killing are to do penance for three Lents.

8. That battle aside, whoever before the consecration of the king killed anyone offering resistance as he moved through the kingdom in search of supplies, is to do one year's penance for each person so slain. Anyone, however, who killed not in search of supplies but in looting, is to do three years' penance for each person so slain.

9. Whoever killed a man after the king's consecration is to do penance as for wilful homicide, with this exception, that if the person killed or struck was in arms against the king the penance shall be as above.

10. Those who committed adulteries or rapes or fornications shall do penance as though they had thus sinned in their own countries.

11. Similarly concerning the violation of churches. Things taken from a church are to be restored to the church from which they were taken if possible. If this is not possible they are to be given to some other church. If such restoration is refused, the bishops have decreed that no one is to sell or buy the property.

Surveys

188   The Burghal Hidage (c.911–919)

This famous survey, surviving only in later copies of the eleventh to the fourteenth century, was evidently drawn up in the time of Edward the Elder, Aldred's successor. It is included here for its information about the early organization of the boroughs which presumably remained the basis of the Old English defensive system down to 1066. It is to be compared, therefore, with No. 155 above. Its information requires supplementing wherever possible by archaeological evidence, for which see C.A. Ralegh Radford, 'The later pre-Conquest boroughs and their defences'. *Medieval Archaeology*, xiv, 1970.

Source and translation: A.J. Robertson, *Anglo-Saxon Charters*, pp. 246–9; amendments from N.P. Brooks and David Hill, respectively in *Medieval Archaeology*, viii, 1964, pp. 74–90, and xiii, 1969, pp. 84–92. See also Simon Keynes and Michael Lapidge, *Alfred the Great*, Harmondsworth, 1983, pp. 193–4 and notes.

[Vernacular] To *Eorpeburnam* (*unidentified*[1]) belong 324 hides, to Hastings belong 500 hides, and to Lewes belong 1200[2] hides, and to Burpham belong 720 hides, to Chichester belong 1500 hides. Then to Portchester belong 500[3] hides, and 150[4] hides belong to Southampton, and to Winchester belong 2400 hides, and to Wilton belong 1400 hides,

[1] Hill suggests the possibility of Castle Toll, Newenden, Kent.
[2] Or 1300.
[3] Possibly a variant reading of 650 is to be preferred. See Robertson, *Anglo-Saxon Charters*, p. 495, note.
[4] This figure seems insufficient. See Robertson as above.

and to Chisbury belong 500[5] hides (and to Shaftesbury likewise[6]), and to Twyneham belong 500 hides less 30 hides, and to Wareham belong 1600 hides, and to Bridport [or Bredy][7] belong 800 hides less 40 hides, and to Exeter belong 734 hides, and to Halwell belong 300 hides, and to Lidford belong 150 hides less 10 hides,[8] and to Pilton (that is Barnstaple[9]) belong 400 hides less 40 hides, and to Watchet belong 513 hides, and to Axbridge belong 400 hides, and to Lyng belong 100 hides,[8] and to Langport belong 600 hides, and to Bath belong 1000 hides, and 1200 hides belong to Malmesbury, and to Cricklade belong 1400 hides, and 1500 hides to Oxford, and to Wallingford belong 2400 hides, and 1600 hides belong to Buckingham, and to Sashes[10] belong 1000 hides, and 600 hides to Eashing, and to Southwark belong 1800 hides.

[11]For the maintenance and defence of an acre's breadth of wall 16 hides are required. If every hide is represented by 1 man, then every pole [$5\frac{1}{2}$ yards] of wall can be manned by 4 men. Then for the maintenance of 20 poles of wall 80 hides are required, and for a furlong 160 hides are required by the same reckoning as I have stated above. For 2 furlongs 320 hides are required; for 3 furlongs 480 hides. Then for 4 furlongs 640 hides are required. For 6 furlongs 960 hides are required; for 7 furlongs 1120 hides; for the maintenance of a circuit of 8 furlongs 1280 hides; for 9 furlongs 1440 hides; for 10 furlongs 1600 hides are required; for 11 furlongs 1760 hides are required. For the maintenance of a circuit of 12 furlongs of wall 1920 hides are required. If the circuit is greater, the additional amount can easily be deduced from this account, for 160 men are always required for 1 furlong, then every pole is manned by 4 men.

189 Domesday Book, 1087

The great 'Domesday' survey of the Conqueror's last years was, we know, decided upon at the Christmas court of 1085 and finished in the form which we have, *i.e.* Domesday Book, at the king's death in 1087. What we have is, in fact, two volumes, the first of which is far the larger and contains surveys of all the counties of England south of the Tees and the Westmorland fells, except Norfolk, Suffolk and Essex. Those three eastern counties comprise volume two, 'Little Domesday', which is not only smaller (in all dimensions) but differs in other ways which include more detail in its entries. The explanation of this discrepancy is that Little Domesday is in fact the circuit return of the commissioners for those three counties, sent in to Winchester where Domesday was finally written up, but never entered and abbreviated like the rest in the main volume because of the death of the king in September 1087. The Domesday Survey was thus never entirely completed, and the fact is a dramatic example of the implications of personal monarchy. In it own way, it is no less a monument to William the Conqueror than the Tower of London or St Stephen's at Caen. In the words of

---

[5] Or 700.

[6] Words in parenthesis an addition in some texts.

[7] MS *Brydian*: possibly Bredy (8 miles west of Dorchester) rather than Bridport.

[8] See Robertson, p. 495.

[9] Words in parenthesis an addition in some texts.

[10] An island in the Thames at Cookham, Berkshire. See Brooks, *op. cit.*, pp. 79–81.

[11] Some texts lack what follows and have an alternative ending which reads:- 'That is all 27,000 hides and 70 which belong to it; and 30 burghs belong to the West Saxons. And to Worcester 1200 hides. To Warwick 2400 hides.'

Stenton,[12] 'as an administrative achievement it has no parallel in medieval history' – and, one may add, in England at least, no parallel before the nineteenth century.

From a world so local as that of the late eleventh century a survey so vast as Domesday scarcely lends itself to brief anthologizing. It also bristles with technical terms, some still only half understood. Of the extracts which follow, the first is the list of the tenants-in-chief for Suffolk, such as heads each county survey in either of the Domesday volumes. A glance at any of them shows, as here, that overwhelming preponderance of Norman and French lords which is the Norman settlement, rendered even more absolute when it is recalled that in the English Church also only one English bishop and two abbots of any importance remained by 1087. Such lists also stand witness to feudalism, and Domesday Book has been described as 'the formal written record of the introduction of feudal tenure, and therefore of feudal law into England'.[13] In any given county, if the holdings of the king and the tenants-in-chief are entered, then all the land is covered, for the principle and the practice are *nulle terre sans seigneur*. The next extract, or pair of extracts, relating to Eye and Hoxne, are also from Suffolk, and therefore from Little Domesday, to show the detail of the Great Survey itself which is even greater than the comparatively abbreviated entries of the proper Domesday volume, *i.e.* Volume I ('not one ox, nor one cow, nor one pig which was there left out and not put down in his record'[14]). It may also be thought illustrative of the golden rule that no record should be used without understanding of its original function. Whatever the purpose of Domesday Book, its function is to record land, its tenure, and its value mainly in terms of agricultural assets. Anything else is incidental, including, for example, churches and castles. At Eye the church of St Peter is recorded, but its castle raised by William Malet soon after 1066 is not. For that we have only an incidental reference in another place, at Hoxne where the bishop's market had suffered from the competition of the new market at the neighbouring castle of Eye. The third extract is taken from Volume I, from the customs of Berkshire, and is a well known passage which provides incidental information about the Old English military system.

Both Great and Little Domesday are printed in the so-called 'Record Commission' edition of 1783, which faithfully follows the foliation of the original – *viz. Domesday Book seu liber censualis* . . . ed. A. Farley, 2 vols. Translations (only) of the Domesday text for most counties are found in the relevant volumes of the Victoria County Histories.

Note. In the following Domesday extracts, being translations, some proper names have been rationalized or modernized to make them more easily recognizable, and place names have been identified where possible. Certain standard abbreviations employed by the Domesday clerks themselves have been retained, notably 'T.R.E.', *i.e. tempore Regis Edwardi*, 'in the time of king Edward.'

Suffolk: the holders of lands

Source: *DB* ii f 281.

I	William, king of the English
II	[Robert] count of Mortain[15]
III	Count Alan [of Brittany]
IV	Earl Hugh [of Chester]
V	Count Eustace [of Boulogne]

[12] F.M. Stenton, *Anglo-Saxon England* (2nd ed., 1947), p. 610.
[13] V.H. Galbraith, *The Making of Domesday Book*, Oxford, 1961, p. 160.
[14] *Anglo-Saxon Chronicle*, No. 110 above.
[15] The king's half-brother.

VI	Robert Malet
VII	Roger Bigot
VIII	Roger of Poitou
IX	William de Scoies[16]
X	Hermer de Ferrers[17]
XI	Ralph de Belfou.
XII	Frodo, the abbot's brother[18]
XIII	Godric the steward (*dapifer*)
XIV	The abbot of St Edmunds.
XV	Archbishop Lanfranc
XVI	[Odo] bishop of Bayeux
XVII	The abbot of Ramsey
XVIII	The bishop of Thetford[19]
XIX	The fee of the same bishop
XX	The bishop of Rochester
XXI	The abbot of Ely
XXII	The bishop of Evreux
XXIII	The abbot of Bernay
XXIV	The abbot of Chatteris
XXV	Richard[20] son of count Gilbert[21]
XXVI	William de Warenne[22]
XXVII	Swein of Essex[23]
XXVIII	Eudo the steward (*dapifer*)[24]
XXIX	Roger de Otburvil[25]
XXX	William his brother
XXXI	Hugh de Montfort[26]
XXXII	Geoffrey de Mandeville[27]
XXXIII	Ralph Baignard
XXXIV	Ranulph Peverel
XXXV	Aubrey de Vere[28]
XXXVI	Robert Grenon

[16] Ecouis.
[17] Ferrières.
[18] *I.e.* of Baldwin, abbot of Bury.
[19] Soon to be Norwich.
[20] *I.e.* de Clare.
[21] *I.e.* of Brionne.
[22] Varenne.
[23] The son of Robert fitz Wimarch, for whom see above Nos. **49, 123.**
[24] Son-in-law of Richard son of count Gilbert.
[25] Auberville-sur-Yère.
[26] Montfort-sur-Risle.
[27] Manneville.
[28] Ver.

XXXVII	Peter de Valoines
XXXVIII	Roger de Ramis[29]
XXXIX	Ralph, brother of Ilger
XL	Robert son of Corbutio
XLI	Walter the deacon
XLII	Tihel de Herion[30]
XLIII	Ralph de Limesey[31]
XLIV	Robert de Toeni
XLV	Walter Giffard
XLVI	The countess of Aumale
XLVII	William de Arcis[32]
XLVIII	Drogo de Beureria[33]
XLIX	Hugh de Grentemesnil[34]
L	Ralph de Felgeris[35]
LI	Walter de St Valery
LII	Humphrey the chamberlain
LIII	Eudo son of Spiruic
LIV	Walter de Watevil
LV	John son of Waleram
LVI	Humphrey son of Aubrey
LVII	Hubert de Monchensey
LVIII	Gondwin
LIX	Saisselin
LX	Robert de Verli
LXI	Ralph Pinel
LXII	Isaac
LXIII	Norman
LXIV	Juhicell the priest
LXV	Gerald the marshal
LXVI	Robert Blund
LXVII	Hervey de Bourges
LXVIII	Gilbert the crossbowman
LXIX	Ralph the crossbowman
LXX	Rainold the Breton
LXXI	Robert de Stratford
LXXII	Stannard [son of Alwi]

[29] Rames.
[30] Helléan, in Brittany.
[31] Limésy.
[32] Arques-la-Bataille.
[33] Beuvrières.
[34] Le Grand-Mesnil.
[35] Feugères.

LXXIII   Ulmar
LXXIV   The Vavassors
LXXV   The king's free men
LXXVI   Encroachments on the king

Suffolk: VI Lands of Robert Malet in Suffolk: Hundred of Hartismere: Eye.

Source: DB, ii, ff. 319b–320; translation VCH *Suffolk*, i. 459

[At] Eye Edric[36] held 12 carucates of land T.R.E. Now Robert holds them in demesne; and his mother holds 100 acres and 1 villein and 3 bordars and 9 sokemen with 16 acres, then 2 ploughs, now 1, worth 20s. Then 39 villeins, now 20. Then and afterwards 9 bordars, now 16. Then 12 serfs, now none. Then and afterwards 8 ploughs on the demesne, now 5. Then and afterwards 15 ploughs belonging to the men, now 6. And the other ploughs might be made up again. And [there are] 50 acres of meadow. Then wood [land] for 120 swine, now for 60. Then as now a mill. And a fishery. Then 7 rounceys, now 1. Then 24 beasts, now none. Then 50 swine, now 17. Then 80 sheep, now 90. And now 1 market.[37] And a park. And in the market 25 burgesses have their dwellings. To this manor belong 48 sokemen with 121 acres of land. Of these sokemen 37 [are] on the demesne; and Herbert holds 9 with 20 acres; and Walter 1 with 5 acres; and Walter the crossbowman (*arbalistarius*) 1 with 16 acres. The whole is worth 9s. Then 4 ploughs, now 3. And 1 acre of meadow. Then worth 15 li., now 21 li. Edric had soke and sac of the bishopric which the bishop ought to have. To this manor also belong 9 freemen with 110 acres of land [who were] in Edric's soke and commendation T.R.E. Then $4\frac{1}{2}$ ploughs, now 4. And 3 acres of meadow. Then wood [land] for 16 swine, now for 6. Worth 20s. These nine were called Alestan, Uluric, Godwin, Lewin, Edric, Alfsi, Aluric, Godric, Dynechaie.

In the same [vill] a freeman Uluric under commendation to Edric [held] 30 acres as a manor T.R.E. Now Walter de Caen holds of Robert. Then as now 2 bordars. Then 1 plough, now half a plough. Worth 20s.

In the same [vill is] a church, Saint Peter's, to which belong 2 carucates of free land and 7 bordars. Then 1 plough on the demesne, now 3. Then 1 plough belonging to the men. And 3 acres of meadow. And a mill. Worth 40s.

In the same [vill] a freeman Suartric under Harold's commendation and in his soke held 120 acres as a manor T.R.E. Now Robert holds in demesne. Then as now 4 bordars. And 1 plough on the demesne. And 4 acres of meadow. Wood [land] for 3 swine. Worth 20s. It is $2\frac{1}{2}$ leagues long, and $1\frac{1}{2}$ leagues broad. And [pays] 2s. in geld.

Suffolk: XVIII Lands of William bishop of Thetford: Bishop's Hundred: Hoxne

Source: DB, ii, f. 379; translation VCH *Suffolk*, i, 515

---

[36] *I.e.* Edric of Laxfield, the pre-Conquest predecessor (*antecessor*) of Robert Malet (and William Malet his father) in the land.
[37] For this market see below.

[At] Hoxne bishop Ailmar held T.R.E. as a manor 9 carucates of land . . ., In this manor there used to be a market T.R.E. and [it went on] after king William came hither; and it was held on Saturdays. And William Malet made his castle at Eye, and on the same day as the market used to be held on the bishop's manor William Malet made another market in his castle and thereby the bishop's market has been so far spoilt that it is of little worth; and now it is held on Fridays. But the market at Eye is held on the Saturday.

Berkshire, customs of

Source: DB, i, f. 56b.

If the king sent an army anywhere, only one warrior (*miles*) went from 5 hides and 4 shillings were given to him from each hide for his maintenance and wages for two months. This money, however, was not sent to the king but was given to the warriors (*militibus*). If anyone summoned on an expedition did not go, he forfeited all his land to the king. And if anyone having a reason for staying behind promised to send another in his place, and that substitute then failed to go, his lord was quit by the payment of 50 shillings.

III   Letters

Of the letters or extracts from letters printed below, the two papal missives (**190–1**) refer directly and respectively to the pre-Conquest relations between England and Normandy and the Norman Conquest itself, and the letter of William I to Pope Gregory VII (**192**) is a famous document in the context of the relationship between William's monarchy and the Gregorian papacy. The four letters of Lanfranc as archbishop of Canterbury (**193–6** show) as nothing else can the reactions and activity in time of crisis of a highly intelligent monk and scholar involved against his wishes in the Norman settlement of England.

Falling somewhere between the two, early medieval letters are generally so formal as to come closer to documentary or record evidence than to literary sources. Nevertheless the selected letters of Lanfranc, though included in the quasi-official collection made after his death, contain a marked personal element and even some of that freely expressed emotion characteristic of the Bec fraternity. They thus bring us closer to a very great man as well as to some of the events of his time.

190   Pope John XV to all the faithful, 991

Pope John XV to all the faithful concerning the peace between Ethelred, king of the West Saxons and Richard I marquis of Normandy (991, March 1)
This letter surviving in an early eleventh-century copy (and others later), cannot be authentic in its present form, but is accepted as genuine in substance.[1]

Source: Fauroux, *Receuil des actes des ducs de Normandie*, p. 22, n. 15; William of Malmesbury, *Gesta Regum*, Rolls Series, ed. W. Stubbs, i, 191–3; and elsewhere. Translation D. Whitelock, *English Historical Documents*, i, (1955) No. 230, pp. 823–4.

John the fifteenth, pope of the holy Roman Church, to all the faithful, greeting.

All faithful members of holy Mother Church, and our sons of either order[2] spread throughout the regions of the world, should know how we have been informed by many of the enmity between Ethelred [II], king of the West Saxons, and Richard the marquis.[3] Greatly saddened by this, seeing that it concerns our spiritual sons, I at length took wholesome counsel and summoned a certain legate of ours, namely Leo, bishop of the holy church of Trèves, and sent him thither with our letters of exhortation, that they should repent this folly. Traversing the great intervening space of land, he at length crossed the

---

[1] See Stenton, *Anglo-Saxon England* (2nd. ed., 1947), p. 370, n. 2.
[2] *I.e.* clerical and lay.
[3] *I.e.* Richard I of Normandy. 'Marquis' is one of several titles used by those whom we invariably call 'dukes' of Normandy.

boundaries of the sea, and arrived in the presence of the aforesaid king on the day of Our Lord's Nativity; and after greeting him on our behalf, gave the letter which we had sent to him. The king summoned all the loyal men of his kingdom and the councillors of both orders, and for the love and fear of Almighty God, and also of St Peter, Prince of the Apostles, and through our paternal admonition he granted a most firm peace, with all his sons and daughters, present and future, and with all his loyal people, without deceit. Therefore he sent Aethelsige, bishop of the holy church of Sherborne, and Leofstan son of Aelfwold, and Aethelnoth son of Wigstan, and they crossed the boundaries of the sea and came to Richard the aforesaid marquis. After peacefully receiving our warning and at the same time hearing the decision of the above-mentioned king, he confirmed the same peace with a willing heart, along with his sons and daughters, present and future, and with all his faithful people, on the following terms: that if any of their people, or they themselves, were to commit any wrong against the other, it should be atoned for with a fitting compensation; and the peace should remain for ever unshaken, and confirmed by the mark of the oaths of both parties, namely on the part of king Ethelred, Aethelsige, bishop of the holy church of Sherborne, and Leofstan son of Aethelwold, and Aethelnoth son of Wigstan; on the part of Richard, bishop Roger [of Lisieux], Ralph son of Hugh, Thurstan son of Turgeis.

Done at Rouen on 1 March in the year of Our Lord's Incarnation 991, the fourth indiction. And Richard is to receive none of the king's men, or of his enemies, nor the king of any of his [Richard's], without their seal (*sine sigillo eorum*).

191 Pope Gregory VII to William the Conqueror, 1080

Pope Gregory VII to William the Conqueror, reminding him of past favours and seeking his support and obedience (1080 April 24)

Source: P. Jaffé, *Monumenta Gregoriana* (*Bibliotheca Rerum Germanicorum*, ii, Berlin, 1865), pp. 414–16.

Gregory the bishop, servant of the servants of God, to William, king of the English, greeting and apostolic benediction. It is known to you, I believe, most eminent son, how great is the love I have always borne you, even before I rose to the supreme height of the papacy, what effective concern I have shown in your affairs and, moreover, with what zeal I laboured that you might rise to the dignity of kingship. For which reason one may say that I suffered great infamy through the mutterings of certain brethren that by my exertions on your behalf I encouraged so great a slaughter. But in fact I know that, as God was my witness, I did this in good faith, trusting in the grace of God and, not vainly, in the virtues which were in you, whereby the higher you rise the better disposed you show yourself towards God and Holy Church, even as now you have cause to give thanks to Him . . . [The letter goes on to request William's support and obedience in general terms] . . . Given at Rome, 24 April, in the third Indiction (1080).[4]

---

[4] For an unusual interpretation of this letter, see C. Morton in *Latomus*, xxxiv, 1975, pp. 362ff.

192 William the Conqueror to Pope Gregory VII, 1080

William the Conqueror to Pope Gregory VII refusing fealty and promising the arrears of Peter's Pence (1080, summer)

The appearance of this famous letter in Lanfranc's collected correspondence presumably indicates that he at least drafted it. A covering letter in Lanfranc's name (No. 38 in M. Gibson's *Letters of Lanfranc*, cited below) went with it, ending 'I presented the text of your message and your above-mentioned legate with what skill I could to my lord the king; I commended it to him but without success. Why he has not complied with your wishes in all respects the legate himself is explaining to you both orally and in a letter.' Gregory VII's demand for fealty has not survived and was probably made orally by his legate, Hubert.

Source and translation: Margaret Gibson, *The Letters of Lanfranc Archbishop of Canterbury*, Oxford Medieval Texts, 1979, No. 39.

To Gregory, most exalted pastor of Holy Church, William, by the grace of God king of the English and duke of the Normans, sends greetings and the assurance of friendship.

Your legate Hubert, who came to me, holy father, has on your behalf directed me to do fealty to you and your successors and to reconsider the money payment which my predecessors used to send to the Roman Church. The one proposition I have accepted; the other I have not. I have never desired to do fealty, nor do I desire it now; for I neither promised on my own behalf nor can I discover that my predecessors ever performed it to yours. As to the money, for almost three years it has been collected without due care, while I was engaged in France. But now that by God's mercy I have returned to my kingdom, the sum already collected is being sent to you by the above-named legate and the balance will be conveyed, when the opportunity arises, by the legates of our faithful servant archbishop Lanfranc.

Pray for us and for the welfare of our kingdom, for we held your predecessors in great regard, and it is our desire to show to you above all men unfeigned respect and obedient attention.

193 Lanfranc to Pope Alexander II, (1072/3)

Lanfranc to Pope Alexander II begging to be released from the office of archbishop (1072, December 25–1073, April 21)

Source and translation: M. Gibson, *The Letters of Lanfranc*, as above, No. 1.

To Pope Alexander, the highest pastor of the holy Church, Lanfranc, an unworthy bishop, offers canonical obedience.

I do not know to whom I may more appropriately unfold my misfortunes than to you, father, who have brought these misfortunes upon me. When William duke of the Normans had removed me from the community at Bec, where I took the religious habit, and I was in charge of the monastery at Caen, I was unequal to ruling a few monks; so I cannot conceive by what judgement of almight God I have at your insistence been made the overseer of many and numberless peoples. Although that duke, now king of the English, endeavoured in many different ways to bring this about, his labours were in vain. He could not win his point from me until finally your own legates came to Normandy,

Ermenfrid, bishop of Sion, and Hubert, cardinal of the holy Roman Church; they assembled the bishops, abbots and magnates of that country and in their presence commanded me by the authority of the apostolic see to assume the government of the church of Canterbury. I pleaded failing strength and personal unworthiness, but to no purpose; the excuse that the language was unknown and the native races barbarous weighed nothing with them either. In a word: I assented, I came, I took office. Now I endure daily so many troubles and vexations and such spiritual starvation of nearly anything that is good; I am continually hearing, seeing and experiencing so much unrest among different people, such distress and injuries, such hardness of heart, greed and dishonesty, such a decline in holy Church, that I am weary of my life and grieve exceedingly to have lived into times like these. . . . I implore you for God's sake and your own soul's, as you bound me by your authority that could not lawfully be disputed, to free me from bondage, using that same authority to break the shackle of this duty and giving me leave to return to the monastic life, which I love more than anything else. I do not deserve to have a petition rejected which I implore you to grant me so devoutly, so urgently and for such excellent reasons. . . . On another point, when I was in Rome and by God's grace had the privilege to see and talk with you in person, you asked me to visit you the following year about Christmas and stay in the palace (*palatium*) at your expense for three months or longer. But I could not have done this without great inconvenience, both physical and financial; God and his angels are my witness. There were many different factors preventing me, more than can be included in the brief compass of a letter. But if the King above grant me life and health with sufficient means, I do long to visit the holy apostles and both you and the holy Roman Church. If this is to come about, I urge you to entreat God mercifully to grant long life to my lord the king of the English, to establish him in security from all his enemies and to stir up his heart to love Him and His holy Church with all godly devotion. While the king lives we have peace of a kind, but after his death we expect to have neither peace nor any other benefit.

194   Lanfranc to Roger earl of Hereford (1075)

Earl Roger was the son and heir of William fitz Osbern, the Conqueror's closest friend (d. 1071). In the following three letters Lanfranc is acting in his quasi-secular capacity as not only a principal councillor of the king but a principal minister in his absence overseas. The changing tone of the letters echoes the political facts as the young Roger takes part in the so-called 'Rebellion of the Earls'.

Source and translation: Gibson, *Letters of Lanfranc*, No. 31.

Lanfranc, by the grace of God archbishop, greets his dearest son and friend earl R[oger] and sends him his blessing.

Our lord the king of the English greets you and all of us as his faithful subjects (*fideles*) in whom he places great trust, commanding us to do all in our power to prevent his castles (*castella sua*) from being handed over to his enemies: may God avert such a disaster. I urge you then, as I must urge the dearest of my sons — whom God knows I love wholeheartedly and long to serve, whose father too I loved like my own soul — to be so scrupulous in this matter and in all your duty as a vassal of our lord the king (*et de omni fidelitate domini nostri regis*) that you may have praise of God and the king and all good men. Never forget your father's distinguished career: the faithful service he gave his lord, his zeal in winning great possessions and how honourably he held what he had won.

On another point, the king has ordered his sheriffs not to hold any courts within your lands until he himself returns to England and can hear personally the matters in dispute between you and those sheriffs.

I wish that I could speak to you in person. If that is your desire too, let me know where we can meet and discuss both your affairs and the interests of the king. For my part I am ready to meet you at whatever place you may name.

You are asked to see that Beringer, who brings you this letter, has a just settlement with those men whom he accuses of having stolen his horse.

The Lord almighty bless you and direct your whole life in righteousness.

195   Lanfranc to the same (1075)

Source and translation: Gibson, as above, No. 32.

Lanfranc by the grace of God archbishop, greets his dearest son and friend, earl R[oger] and sends him his blessing.

I grieve more than I can say at the unwelcome news I hear of you. It would not be right that a son of earl William – a man whose sagacity and loyalty to his lord and all his friends is renowned in many lands – should be called faithless and be exposed to the slur of perjury or any kind of deceit. On the contrary, the son of such a great man should follow his father's example, and be for others a pattern of integrity and loyalty (*fidelitatis*) in all respects. I therefore beg you, as a son whom I cherish and the dearest of friends, for the sake of God and your own good name, if you are guilty of such conduct to return to your senses; and if you are not, to demonstrate this by the clearest possible evidence. In either case, come and see me: you have an unqualified assurance that you will not be hindered in any way by me or by the king's men either in making the journey or in returning home.

The Lord almighty bless you.

196   Lanfranc to the same (1075)

Source and translation: Gibson, as above, No. 33A.

Lanfranc, by the grace of God archbishop, to his one-time dearest son and friend earl Roger: may he have sound judgement and some concern for his soul's welfare.

I grieve for you inexpressably, for God knows I loved you and desired with all my heart to love and serve you. But because the Devil's prompting and the advice of evil men have led you into an enterprise which under no circumstances should you have attempted, necessity has forced me to change my attitude and turn my affection not so much into hate as bitterness and the severity of justice. I have sent messengers, I have sent letters not once but a second time inviting you to come to me: to receive counsel for your soul from me your father in God and true friend, and on better advice to abandon the foolish undertaking which you had planned. You would not do so. Therefore I have cursed and excommunicated you and all your adherents by my authority as archbishop; I have cut you off from the holy precincts of the Church and the assembly of the faithful, and by my pastoral authority I have commanded this to take effect throughout the whole land of England. I can free you from this bond of anathema only if you seek my lord the king's mercy and if you render satisfaction to him and the other men whose property you have unjustly seized.

IV Artistic Sources

In early periods artistic evidence, including architectural, is of double importance. Not only do surviving objects give direct and physical contact with the past, but also in an age whose traditions at least are illiterate the message will often be conveyed by visual means, and symbol and ceremony play a part which they have almost lost in the modern world.

Unfortunately, considerations of cost prohibit more than a very few illustrations in this volume, but we are able to do two things. One is to reproduce impressions of the seals of Edward the Confessor and William the Conqueror (197), whereon the message of regality, and also in the latter case (i.e. on the 'equestrian' side), feudal lordship, is formally conveyed at the highest level of iconography. The other is to reproduce at least some scenes from the Bayeux Tapestry, one of the artistic wonders of its age, whereby the whole story of the Norman Conquest of England from 1064–1066 was told in continuous series of embroideries for public display.

197 Royal seals

Seals of (i) Edward the Confessor (A, obverse or front, and B, reverse) and (ii) William the Conqueror, after 1066 (C, obverse, and D, reverse).

Source: Collections Archives Nationales de France, Paris, respectively K 19 no. 6 and K 20 no. 5.

(i) is thought originally to have been attached to No. 158 above, and (ii) is attached to No. 173 above. The legend or inscription on Edward's seal reads, on both sides, + SIGILLVM EADVVARDI ANGLORUM BASILEI.

The legend or inscription on William's seal reads, on the obverse and equestrian side + HOC NORMANNORVM WILLELMVM NOSCE PATRONVM SI, and on the reverse + HOC ANGLIS REGEM SIGNO FATEARIS EVNDEM.

(i) A obverse
Seal of Edward the Confessor

(i) B reverse

(ii) C obverse
Seal of William the Conqueror

(ii) D reverse

The Bayeux Tapestry

Still on public display in its museum at Bayeux in Normandy, where it has recently been inspected and rehung, the Bayeux Tapestry is unique in its survival, though other pictorial and narrative hangings are known to have been produced and used in this period. Traditionally referred to as the 'Tapestry' it is in fact an embroidery in coloured wools on a linen base, 230 feet and 20 inches long by 20 inches wide (70.34 metres by 50 centimetres). Still more traditionally and popularly known in France as 'la Tapisserie de la Reine Mathilde', it is now in fact very generally attributed to Odo, bishop of Bayeux, in terms of commission and patronage, and to English workmanship as an exercise in the famed *opus Anglicanum*, made in Kent (of which Odo was earl), more specifically at Canterbury, and probably more specifically still at the abbey of St Augustine's there. In the conventional view it was produced for bishop Odo's new cathedral of Bayeux, dedicated in 1077, and the fact that it is entirely secular in spirit in no way rules out this accepted hypothesis.[1] The first reference we have to the Tapestry occurs in an inventory of the treasures and furnishings of the cathedral of Notre-Dame at Bayeux drawn up in 1476, when it was certainly hung round the nave of the church at the Feast of the Relics and throughout the Octave (week following), as evidently continued to be the case down to the Revolution. If, however, the dedication of the cathedral in 1077 were to be rejected as a *terminus ad quem*, we would still be left with Odo's political fall and imprisonment in 1083, or his death in 1097 at the outside, as dates before which the creation of the Tapestry was well in hand. There is little doubt that Odo was the patron, the evidence for this including the prominence given to him and his tenants in the narrative; and in any case there is an immediacy about the Tapestry's version of events which requires an early date after 1066.

In short, the Bayeux Tapestry may be regarded as a contemporary record, commissioned by one who was at the very centre of affairs and present beside duke William at Hastings. Moreover, it was made for public display before those who had taken part in or lived through the Norman Conquest. It can thus claim a formidable authority. Of course it presents a narrative, from Harold's departure for Normandy (at a date which must be 1064) to his death at Hastings two years later, from the Norman point of view. It would be surprising if it did not, and in so doing it agrees closely with the versions of events and their interpretation found in William of Poitiers and William of Jumièges. But the Tapestry's testimony is largely silent, pictorial, each scene being captioned with a brief Latin inscription or legend only. Its artistic theme, binding the whole together, is the fate which necessarily overtakes a man who breaks his oath taken on the relics of Bayeux. The great oath-taking scene (No. **199** below) thus occupies a central position, and , it is to be noted, the central figure of Harold, the hero we may almost say, is treated with appropriate respect throughout.

The scenes reproduced below represent the salient events in the story which is

[1] Cf. C.R. Dodwell, 'The Bayeux Tapestry and the French Secular Epic.' *Burlington Magazine*, civ, 1966.

concerned with the rights and wrongs of the disputed succession to the English throne eventually fought out in 1066 – Harold's departure for Normandy; his public oath to duke William; the death of Edward the Confessor; the Battle of Hastings; and the death of Harold.

Source: Musée de la Tapisserie de Bayeux, avec autorisation spécial de la Ville de Bayeux. The best edition of the Tapestry is that of F.M. Stenton (2nd edition, London, 1965) because of the quality of the plates plus the *apparatus criticus* of notes and commentary. See also for commentary N.P. Brooks and H.E. Walker, 'The authority and interpretation of the Bayeux Tapestry', *Battle*, i, 1978.

198 Bayeux Tapestry, King Edward sends earl Harold to Normandy (1064)
Legend: 'King Edward'.

199 Bayeux Tapestry. Harold swears his oath to William at Bayeux (1064) Legend: 'Where Harold made an oath to duke William.'

200 Bayeux Tapestry. The death of Edward the Confessor (1066).
Legend: 'Here king Edward in bed addresses his faithful friends; and here he is dead'.

201 Bayeux Tapestry. Hastings, the first assault of Norman knights against the English shield-wall (1066).

177

202 Bayeux Tapestry.
The death of Harold
(1066).
Legend: 'Here king
Harold is slain'.

Select Bibliography

A short Select List of basic reading

Barlow, F., *William I and the Norman Conquest*, London, 1965
  Edward the Confessor, London, 1970.
Barraclough, G., *The Medieval Papacy*, London, 1968.
Bates, D., *Normandy before 1066*, Harlow, 1982.
de Bouard, Michel, *Guillaume le Conquérant*, Paris, 1958
Brown, R. Allen, *The Origins of Modern Europe*, London, 1972.
  The Normans and the Norman Conquest, London, 1969.
  The Origins of English Feudalism, London, 1973.
  English Castles, London, 1976.
  'The Battle of Hastings', *Anglo-Norman Studies, Proceedings of the Battle Conference*, iii, 1980.
Conant, K.J., *Carolingian and Romanesque Architecture*, Harmondsworth, 1973
Darlington, R.R., *The Norman Conquest*, London, 1963.
Davis, R.H.C., *A History of Medieval Europe*, London, 1957.
  The Normans and their Myth, London, 1976.
Douglas, D.C., *The Norman Conquest and British Historians*, Glasgow, 1946
  William the Conqueror, London, 1964.
  The Norman Achievement, London 1969.
Guides Bleus, *Normandie*, Paris, 1961.
Knowles, David, *Christian Monasticism*, London, 1969.
  The Monastic Order in England, Cambridge, 2nd ed. 1963
Le Patourel, J., *The Norman Empire*, Oxford, 1976.
Loyn, H.R., *The Norman Conquest*, London, 1983
Musset, L., *Normandie Romane*, 2 vols., Zodiaque, 1967, 1974.
Stenton, F.M., *Anglo-Saxon England*, Oxford, 1947.
Southern, R.W., *The Making of the Middle Ages*, London, 1953
  Western Society and the Church in the Middle Ages, Harmondsworth, 1970
Sumption, J., *Pilgrimage: An Image of Medieval Religion*, London, 1975
Williams, A., 'Some notes and considerations on problems connected with the English royal succession, 860–1066', *Anglo-Norman Studies, Proceedings of the Battle Conference*, i, 1978.

Select Bibliography

A list of Sources drawn upon for this volume

Literary and Narrative Sources

Guillaume de Jumièges, Gesta Normannorum Ducum, ed. J. Marx, Société de l'histoire de Normandie, Rouen-Paris, 1914.

Guillaume de Poitiers, Histoire de Guillaume le Conquérant, ed. and trans. Raymonde Foreville (Classiques de l'histoire de France) Paris, 1962.

J. Armitage Robinson, *Gilbert Crispin, Abbot of Westminster*, Cambridge, 1911.

C. Plummer, *Two of the Saxon Chronicles Parallel*, 2 vols., Oxford, 1892, 1952.

The Anglo-Saxon Chronicle. A Revised Translation, ed. and trans. D. Whitelock, D.C. Douglas, S.I. Tucker, London, 1961.

Florentii Wigornensis Monachi Chronicon ex Chronicis, ed. B. Thorpe, London, 1848–9.

The Life of King Edward who rests at Westminster, ed. and trans. Frank Barlow, Nelson's Medieval Texts, London, 1962.

English Historical Documents, i, ed. and trans. D. Whitelock, London, 1955.

The Ecclesiastical History of Orderic Vitalis, ed. and trans. Marjorie Chibnall, Oxford Medieval Texts, Oxford, 1969–80.

Willelmi Malmesbiriensis Monachi De Gestis Regum Anglorum, ed. W. Stubbs, 2 vols., Rolls Series, London, 1887–9.

Willelmi Malmesbiriensis Monachi De Gestis Pontificium Anglorum, ed. N.E.S.A. Hamilton, Rolls Series, London, 1870.

Chronicon Monasterii de Abingdon, ed. J. Stevenson, 2 vols., Rolls Series, London, 1858.

Liber Eliensis, ed. E.O. Blake, Royal Historical Society, Camden 3rd series, xcii, London, 1962.

Hugh the Chantor: The History of the Church of York 1066–1127, ed. and trans. C. Johnson, Nelson's Medieval Texts, London, 1961.

The Chronicle of Battle Abbey, ed. and trans. Eleanor Searle, Oxford Medieval Texts, Oxford, 1980.

Documentary Sources (including Letters)

English Historical Documents, i, ed. and trans. Dorothy Whitelock, London, 1955.

English Historical Documents, ii, ed. and trans. D.C. Douglas, London, 1959.

Facsimiles of Anglo-Saxon Manuscripts, 3 vols., ed. W.B. Sanders, Ordnance Survey, Southampton, 1878–84.

Liber Monasterii de Hyda, ed. E. Edwards, Rolls Series, London, 1866.

T.A.M. Bishop and P. Chaplais, *Facsimiles of English Royal Writs to AD 1100*, Oxford, 1957.

F.E. Harmer, *Anglo-Saxon Writs*, Manchester, 1952.

Facsimiles of Ancient Charters in the British Museum, ed. E.A. Bond, 4 vols., London, 1973–8.

A.J. Robertson, ed. and trans., *Anglo-Saxon Charters*, Cambridge, 1939.

Hemingi Chartularium Ecclesiae Wigornensis, ed. T. Hearne, Oxford, 1723.

Marie Fauroux, ed. *Receuil des actes des ducs de Normandie* (911–1066), Mémoires de la Société des Antiquaires de Normandie, Caen, 1961.

A.J. Robertson, ed. and trans., *The Laws of the Kings of England from Edmund to Henry I*, Cambridge, 1925.

Eadmer, *Historia Novorum in Anglia*, ed. M. Rule, Rolls Series, London, 1884.

W. Stubbs, ed., *Select Charters and other Illustrations of English Constitutional History . . .* 9th ed., Oxford, 1946.

The Letters of Lanfranc Archbishop of Canterbury, ed. and trans. Margaret Gibson, Oxford Medieval Texts, Oxford, 1979.

Domesday Book seu liber censualis . . . ed. A. Farley, 2 vols., Record Commission, 1783 (translations for most counties appear in the relevant volumes of the Victoria County Histories).

Monumenta Gregoriana, Bibliotheca Rerum Germanicorum, ii, Berlin, 1865.

Artistic Sources

Musée de la Tapisserie de Bayeux, Bayeux.

The Bayeux Tapestry, ed. F.M. Stenton, 2nd. ed., London, 1965.